Ethnic Historians and the Mainstream

Ethnic Historians
and the Mainstream

Shaping the Nation's Immigration Story

To My Rabbi, Danny Zemel, With deep appreciation for your love of Jewish history, your warmth and, most of all, your friendship! Best always Alan Kraut

EDITED BY ALAN M. KRAUT
AND DAVID A. GERBER

RUTGERS UNIVERSITY PRESS

NEW BRUNSWICK, NEW JERSEY, AND LONDON

LIBRARY OF CONGRESS CATALOGING-IN-PUBLICATION DATA

Ethnic historians and the mainstream : shaping the nation's immigration story / edited by Alan M. Kraut and David A. Gerber.

    pages cm
    Includes bibliographical references.
    ISBN 978–0–8135–6225–4 (hardcover : alkaline paper) — ISBN 978–0–8135–6224–7 (paperback : alkaline paper) — ISBN 978–0–8135–6226–1 (e-book)
    1. United States —Ethnic relations—Historiography. 2. United States—Race relations—Historiography. 3. Immigrants—United States—Historiography. 4. United States—Emigration and immigration—Historiography. 5. Historiography—United States. I. Kraut, Alan M. II. Gerber, David A., 1944–
    E184.A1E833 2013
    305.800973—dc23   2013000423

A British Cataloging-in-Publication record for this book is available
from the British Library.

Visit our website: http://rutgerspress.rutgers.edu

Manufactured in the United States of America

Dedication from Alan M. Kraut:
In memory of Lorman A. Ratner, teacher, scholar, and dear friend

Dedication from David A. Gerber:
In memory of August Meier, meticulous scholar,
patient editor, and insistent voice for racial justice

CONTENTS

ACKNOWLEDGMENTS

We would like to thank Jane Morris, a skillful and dedicated editor, who has assisted one or both of us on several projects.

We also wish to thank our editor at Rutgers University Press, Marlie Wasserman, for her support of our project and all her kindness, patience, and cooperation as we brought it to fruition.

Finally, we offer our warm thanks and deep appreciation to Marilyn Campbell, Director of the Prepress Department at Rutgers, and to our copyeditor, John Raymond, for the editorial care and attentiveness they brought to our manuscript in the last stages of the publication process.

Ethnic Historians and the Mainstream

1

Introduction

DAVID A. GERBER

The eleven essays in this book are offered to readers with two principal frameworks in mind. The essays provide examples of how some historians come by their creativity as scholars in a field that readily captures the personal stories of millions of ordinary people, intimately caught up in the processes of history. Through the stories these historians tell about how they found their subject matter and the struggle to gain legitimacy for it in the eyes of their discipline, the essays also serve to demonstrate the ways in which the academic mainstream came to be widened to include new voices, ideas, and subjects. The editors have divided the labor of contextualizing these essays. I discuss these two themes in this general introduction, with an emphasis on processes of general societal assimilation and the diversification of academic disciplines. Alan Kraut's coda offers his autobiographical remarks as a narrative of his entrance into the field of history and as a point of departure for reviewing the ways in which the individual authors have imaginatively organized their experiences within the understandings of immigration and ethnic history.

The stories offered in this collection provide a window into understanding the enormous changes in the nature of thinking about what is and who is American that have arisen in the last five decades in the United States. During those decades, the nation evolved from a society in which the formal standard of belonging was more or less an insistent homogeneity to a society in which cultural diversity and identificational diversity have become valorized. Through their writings and careers, historians such as our essayists have played a significant but not widely understood role in the evolution of this new standard of American belonging.

This has not only been true in regard to race and ethnicity but also most evidently displayed in the majority of our essays, to gender. The widening of the academic mainstream reflected in this collection is as much about the gender revolution in the composition of faculties and the subject matter of the disciplines as it is about where people come from in national and cultural terms. Indeed, the most visible transformation of academia in the last half century has been the profound movement of faculties and of research to encompass women across a wide swath of disciplines and discourses. A number of our senior contributors, who began to forge academic careers in the late 1960s and early 1970s, were foot soldiers in this revolution, fighting frequently lonely battles for inclusion of both themselves and women's historical experience of the sort documented in Barbara Posadas's essay.

Before delving more deeply into our two frameworks for contextualizing the essays, it is necessary to make a point about the criteria for inclusion in this collection. The editors did not seek authors primarily because they fit neatly into molds that might document these frameworks. Above all else, we sought those whom we knew, partly from personal acquaintance, but more often from their published work, to be gifted storytellers. We wanted individuals who were both imaginative and analytical, and who might well have a talent for writing a memoir that evoked a crucial part of their autobiographies. It is not that the published work of any of these historians up to this moment has necessarily ever made an explicitly autobiographical statement explaining how and why they became historians, or any other facet of their own lives for that matter. Instead, in conversations with each other the editors came to conclusions about which historians gave evidence just below the surface of their published work of seeming to be moved by an unusual degree of empathy or inspired by identity with their historical subjects. These judgments were ultimately intuitive. They were informed by frequent reading of the authors' works, sometimes in the context of assigning a work for teaching over the course of many semesters.

Yet, however manifest to a sensitive reader, those qualities did not necessarily seem immediately pertinent to our authors' own sense of the foundations of their creativity as scholars. History is the most empirical of the humanities disciplines. It has strong positivist and empiricist traditions, which date from the Enlightenment but have been deepened by the influence of behavioral science in the twentieth century: these traditions insist on emotional distancing of its practitioners from their subject matter and from the human subjects they study. It is true that the boundaries of the personal, the disciplinary and professional, are not nearly as strongly patrolled by teachers, mentors, colleagues, manuscript referees, and book reviewers as they once were. But that is to miss an important, abiding point: the boundaries lie as much within historians as they do outside them in the imposed mechanisms of graduate education and professionalization.

For purposes of filling their assignments, our essayists needed to dig deeper within themselves than their formal research and writing has required. This was not necessarily an easy authorial process for them. It led them to recall difficult times (graduate school bulked large in this particular recollection), and their anxious efforts to find the creative voice manifest in the projects that earned them professional standing. It might involve, too, painful memories of child-hood or of loss and grief in adulthood. The sense of being cultural outsiders—whether as newcomers to America or to academia itself, as racially distinctive, as women in the masculine world of the mid-twentieth-century academic disci-plines, or as working class and without family traditions of, or opportunities for, intellectual cultivation—frequently manifests itself, though the effort to over-come marginality ultimately becomes a source of strength.

In the final analysis, the essays neither register a standing complaint nor celebrate triumph against the odds. Our authors more often record the encour-agement they received from family, friends, teachers, and peers. Moreover, his-torians are inner-directed people, and take their cues mostly from what they feel compelled to do—study and convey what they have learned. Uniting the essays is pride in the ultimate product of scholarly labor in history—the big books by which the historian's progress in the discipline is charted. It is in that spirit that the editors decided eventually not to resist overly strenuously the desire of most of the essayists to devote a portion of their papers to *bio-bibliography*. Among other sources of identity, whether race, gender, class, recent arrival in America, ethnicity, religion, or diasporic consciousness, these individuals define them-selves strongly by their creativity.

How do historians come by their calling as scholars and decide on the projects that eventuate in the books by which they become known? For many, the answer may lie strictly in engagement with the logic of professional dis-courses, whether these discourses involve theory or historiography, the record of the literature of history. Professional logic frequently involves filling a gap in our collective knowledge. For others, however, there is a type of time traveling that manifests itself in fascination with a period in the past, or with events, or processes, or personalities, perhaps because of the drama they involve or the romance connected with them. Still others may be said to have developed their calling through personal history, the narrative of their own lives in the midst of the tides of historical change. By this is meant that whatever role books, men-tors, and disciplinary socialization have played in the origins and development of their calling, these historians live with the understanding that history hap-pened to them, and that they are a product of a transhistorical progression that fits their lives into a narrative of large social forces and processes, more epic than standard family genealogy. The impact of the past on the present for them is not distantly observed or theoretical, but palpable, connected, and existen-tial. Their work then has been the complex task of fusing the making of knowl-edge with their own subject positioning. Such is the case with all of the authors represented in this collection. It is the tie that binds our authors, across the various decades and contrasting circumstances in which they became historians.

The situation is by no means unique to immigration and ethnic historians. But it is certainly overdetermined among many of them. In their background is the living, intimate memory of a family history. It is a history of emigration, resettlement, ethnicization, transnational consciousness, and integration into a new society, which offers opportunity and safety, but also the challenge, often painful and always demanding, of learning new habits necessary to fulfilling basic material and emotional needs. As Virginia Yans suggests in her evocative essay, a common situation of our authors has been the presence of the representational frameworks of a childhood in which were evident, if hardly understood, inexplicable tensions formed by the passage from immigrant generations to Americanizing ones. As in Yans's case, those representational frames, capturing imperfectly the class, generational, ethnic, and racial differences present in the town in which she was raised, provided the nagging questions that ultimately led to writing immigration and ethnic history.

History, with its ability to make sense of change over time that generations come to embody, seems to be ideally poised to make sense of a world informed by those abiding representational frames that follow us from inquisitive children to analytically minded adults. Evidence of history's attraction from this perspective is offered by a survey done in the late 1990s by the immigration sociologist Reuben Rumbaut. He discovered that 55 percent of the academic immigration and ethnic scholars in history were, in fact, "insiders" writing about the same groups to which they described themselves as belonging. No other discipline for which he collected data—sociology, political science/economics, and anthropology—came close to history in the number of insiders within immigration and ethnic studies doing work on their own groups.[1]

Yet the data hardly comprehend the full extent of the existential foundations of work in this field. Many other historians, who do not work on the people among whom they declare themselves to be a part, nonetheless bring questions formed through working outward from their personal stories. They simply chose another place from which to interrogate the past, inspired by the same types of memories and questions. One gets an intimation of this intellectual transference in the essays of our older cohort of historians, most of whom began their careers when African American history was being "discovered" in the popular culture and in academic scholarship in the 1960s and 1970s. This cohort, none of whom are African Americans, records its intense interest in African American history before it went on eventually to write the history of immigration and resettlement experiences. What its members found in the African American past was what they would eventually seek in the history of their own families and peoples: the story of ordinary people, with aspirations to dignity and autonomy, who plotted a course to get out from under the control of what limited them in becoming active agents in their own behalf. As Yans says, quoting the mantra of her mentor, the influential social historian Herbert Gutman— who was himself paraphrasing Jean-Paul Sartre—African American history was guided at the time by an understanding that the subject of the research was not what was done to African Americans, but rather what they did with what was done to them.[2] This understanding became the basis of an innovative history of ordinary people and daily life, the New Social History, which ultimately worked its way outward to encompass novel ways of conceiving of women, immigrants, Native Americans, and industrial workers.

History filled this same cultural and psychological need once decades before. In the early twentieth century, the first generation of social historians of American immigration and ethnicity were men of midwestern German and Scandinavian ethnic family backgrounds, with memories of, or the living presence of, migration, resettlement, and tightly webbed bonds of ethnic networks and institutions in their recent pasts. Active from the 1920s into the 1950s, historians such as George Stephenson, Theodore Blegen, Karl Wittke, and, perhaps the most eminent of them, Marcus Lee Hansen, sought to make a place for the mid-nineteenth-century European immigrant common men and women, for both of the ethnic groups into which they were born, and others, too, within American history.[3] These historians attempted to move the subject of immigration away from anti- or pro-immigrant polemics that accompanied persistent debates about immigration restriction. They argued that immigrants were not simply the problem many Americans believe them to be, and that there was indeed a retrievable, multidimensional immigration history, filled with active, aspiring, thoughtful people, who reached out to create an expanded world for themselves. Long before the term existed, these historians were transnationalist in their vision. They argued that the immigrants' histories did not begin in the United States, but rather in their homelands, which were increasingly linked to America through commerce and the exchange of information, and that, after emigrating, the immigrants continued to be connected with those now distant places through the exchange of personal letters. Although American popular opinion often had it that there was no need to seek to understand why the immigrants came to America, because it was self-evident that America was the best of all possible worlds, these historians did research in archives in Europe to understand the contexts of decisions to leave homelands, and came up with more complicated formulations of immigrant motivations. In Hansen's case, he went beyond retrieving an immigrant past. He endeavored to fit the immigrants into the thesis of his mentor, Frederick Jackson Turner, who argued that the key to the American past was the progressive settlement of frontiers from the Atlantic coast westward that eventuated in distinctively non-European patterns of culture, politics, land use, and agriculture. In folding the immigrants into Western settlement patterns, Hansen made them parties to the peopling of the continent, and hence more American.[4]

That it was important to Hansen to situate the immigrants within not simply the international migration and immigrant resettlement narrative, but also within the narrative of the settlement of the continent, suggests the longings that tie him firmly to the authors in this collection. Born in Wisconsin in 1892 of immigrant parents, his father, a Baptist minister, from Norway and his mother from Denmark, Hansen was profoundly conscious of the forces of change that had transformed his parents' lives, and were directing him away from the patterns of those lives, in his case toward becoming a historian with a doctorate earned at Harvard and an appointment at the University of Illinois.[5] One of his late projects was trying to understand the imaginative engagement with the past of those who, as immigrants or, like him, the descendants of immigrants, were caught up in and trying to make sense of themselves within the great forces of history.

In "The Problem of the Third Generation Immigrant," a still frequently cited 1938 address given before the Swedish American Augustana Historical Society, he laid out a generational template for understanding what there was in the experience and consciousness of Northern and Western European immigrants, their children, and their grandchildren that led each generation to distinctive patterns of thinking about the immigrant past, and in particular in that connection about family biography as history. His immediate concern was the founding of ethnic historical societies (among various Scandinavian peoples and the Scots-Irish) similar to the one he was then addressing. At birth, these were not scholarly organizations as such, but rather popular endeavors by men wishing to preserve a past rapidly slipping away because of assimilation.

Hansen argued that the immigrants' past was their existential reality and not a matter for intellectual contemplation, and that their American-born children denied the past because being foreign was so painful, but that the third generation by virtue of distance and comfort in its American identity was free to roam through history without embarrassment. Hansen smoothed over the rough corners of experience. His generational template, as he himself recognized, was somewhat rigid. His argument, in fact, was contradicted by his own second-generation experience in becoming an immigration and ethnic historian. But he did not seek to interrogate directly the experience of academic historians, only more popular historical endeavors. Yet, for our purposes, what stands out is that, like our authors, Hansen at some level made a reflexive engagement with his own consciousness the basis of an intellectual project about memory and history.[6]

After Hansen's untimely death that same year, this significant line of inquiry on the roots of the historical consciousness of the immigrants and their descendents went dormant.[7] Indeed, the lines of historical analysis of these social historians of immigration and ethnicity proved weak beyond the matters that engaged them. In restricting their analysis to the mid-nineteenth-century Northern and Western European immigrants, who settled in rural areas and small towns of the Middle West, they had nothing to say about the much larger mass wave of immigrants from Southern, Central, and Eastern Europe streaming into and resettling in the country's industrial cities and mining communities during the years in which they mapped out the terrain of their own historical inquiries. Nor did they address the non-European, non-White immigrants from Asia, Mexico, the Caribbean, and elsewhere who had been arriving in the United States, and whose ethnic cultures formed in resettlement were disrupted, in contrast to the immigrants they did study, by repressive laws and forms of economic and social discrimination motivated by racist ideologies.

In consequence, these early historians missed substantial opportunities to address comparatively many interpretive issues underlying the histories of immigrant and ethnic peoples, and to raise questions about the openness of America to newcomers. Perhaps this failure is ultimately testimony to the restriction of their imaginations to questions that eventuated from personal experiences and needs. Thus we find, in effect, the historians of these previously neglected cohorts of immigrants represented in this book—John Bodnar, Deborah Dash Moore, Timothy Meagher, Dominic Pacyga, Barbara Posadas, Eileen Tamura, Virginia Yans, and Judy Yung—delving into the questions Hansen raised in his 1938 address, but from the standpoint of the history of peoples whom earlier historians were not prepared to address.

The failure of Hansen's generation of social historians to make a place for the so-called New Immigrants, who arrived from Eastern, Central, and Southern Europe in the late nineteenth and early twentieth centuries, and for all non-European immigrants of color in the conceptualization of immigration and ethnic history and American history is a context in which to understand the struggles for inclusion of the historians represented in this collection. Hansen and his contemporaries helped to broaden the conception of what the American mainstream is and where it can be located, but they failed to take this challenge beyond reckoning with their own heritage and identity.

Just as Hansen and his contemporaries sought to find a place for themselves within American academia and for the subjects with which they identified within the written American historical narrative, those entering graduate schools in the mid- and late-twentieth century would struggle for and ultimately achieve inclusion. That process would begin in earnest with the coming of age of the baby boom generation in the 1960s and the rise around its restive presence of a number of political and cultural insurgencies that both questioned narrow constructions of American identity and challenged social and political inequities. In the last five decades, a broad-scale transformation of consciousness has taken place in the United States about the culturally diverse character of Americans and an awareness has grown about the necessity of respecting diversity and creating forms of inclusion that respected difference, while working for proactive forms of unity. The transformation of the literature of American history and American departments of history and of American learning in general has been a part of that development, but this transformation has reached down deeply into all American institutions and throughout popular consciousness, and led to a questioning of assumptions once completely taken for granted.

The editors of this book are old enough to remember a public school curriculum in which was embedded notions that American history, American literature, and American folklore all had roots exclusively in Anglo-American life and thought.[8] David Gerber recalls that, of the students in Chicago high schools in the 1950s, tens of thousands were, like him, the children and grandchildren of European immigrants, and many others were descendants of African American migrants from the Deep South. They all lived in tight ethnic and racial working-class enclaves, and yet were taught, among other things, to locate their identities in American narratives completely outside their experience. For example, there was the story of that mythical lumberjack of the northern forests Paul Bunyan and his giant blue ox, Babe. Bunyan, with his capacity for massive, bluff exaggeration, was said in our textbooks to symbolize a typically American, limitless sense of possibility. Such a sense of possibility was completely outside the experience and culture of these mid-twentieth-century, Chicago young people.

Within three decades, however, a new, plural understanding of America had captured the imagination. This complex transformation can best be appreciated for our purposes if we step back from the narrative of why it happened and seek to conceive the relationship between the growth of American society and culture, especially in regard to understandings of American identity and the processes of inclusion of groups, old and new alike, into the American mainstream.[9] A useful starting point is to examine the work of a thoughtful author who ultimately views American development differently and for whom the new pluralism is a source of anxiety rather than celebration. Samuel P. Huntington's widely commented on *Who Are We?* (2004), contends that American history is a narrative of peoples assimilating into an abiding Anglo-American (Huntington prefers "Anglo-Protestant") core culture, which was historically fashioned by British Enlightenment philosophy and by British folk traditions, political and civic history, and Protestantism. For Huntington, this core came to define what is distinctly *American*.[10] Such explanatory schemes, with their essentialist, germ theories of identity and culture, were the same ones that guided the assumptions of the educationists who urged the descendants of Polish or Lithuanian or Italian or Greek or Jewish immigrants and of African Americans from the Mississippi Delta to find their true selves in Paul Bunyan.

The measure of the success of the American experiment for Huntington is both the development of viable and resilient forms of society, politics, and governance arising out of that Anglo-Protestant core and the capacity of the institutions and practices thus fashioned to assimilate groups, especially groups of foreign newcomers. Although certainly ethnocentric, Huntington's narrative of American progress explicitly rejects racialist explanations of America's success. For Huntington, what America has needed for its progress has not been Anglo-Protestants, but rather effective processes and institutions for assimilating, however unevenly over time, all the peoples within its borders into the patterns of thought that constitute a secularized Anglo-Protestantism. It was a source of despair for Huntington toward the end of his long, productive career that he had come to believe that Americans had experienced a failure of will in regard to assimilating newcomers and to preserving this venerable Anglo-Protestant culture. He projected the Hispanization of America based on the failure to stem what he saw as the resistance to assimilation of the massive tide of Mexican immigrants; and he worried about the eventual physical breakup of the country along ethnic, racial, and linguistic lines.

Although the essays in this book are not intended to be a response to Huntington, they certainly pose another possibility for understanding America's past and projecting its future. They suggest a ramifying process by which the mainstream continuously widens in response to the desire of new peoples to be a part of it. As they come to fit into it, they transform it, so that it is not only more inclusive but it is also changed as a consequence of its expanded inclusiveness. It is not so much that society, politics, and culture come to bear the mark of any one group in particular, though here and there are certainly traces of ethnic and minority cultures in language, food, oral tradition, the built environment, and civic commemorations. It is instead that, however unevenly over long historical time, and no matter how contested, inclusiveness itself and the habits that sustain it are constitutive of American society. Inclusiveness is defined and sustained by both societal processes of assimilation and the expanding cultural understanding of the circle of *We* representing the identity of the American people.

From this perspective, Huntington's explanation of America is revealed to be a failure of historical imagination that advances a static view of the nation's past. It skates over American society's ability to embrace and absorb the varied sources of change, whether demographic, economic, technological, or cultural, that have been part of its history. This is only to say that America is not, nor could it possibly be, the same nation that was created by Thomas Jefferson and James Madison and the other founders, however key to its development the political institutions created by the founders have been in enabling Americans to govern themselves effectively. The nation has preserved those foundations, but has also reformulated and enlarged them as it has risen to meet new challenges from early in its existence that the founders of the republic could never have practically anticipated: continental supremacy, massive interregional population exchanges, mass immigration from every corner of the planet, industrialization, urbanization, and global war and superpower status.

Among other changes in our thinking about how to compose aspects of the American narrative, recognition of that dynamism demands a historical model for understanding America's capacity for absorbing newcomers, while being changed by their presence.[11] Without such a model, the temptation is great to look at assimilation, which has happened throughout American history and is happening now, as nothing more than a sinister imposition by elites bent on ethnocentric homogeneity and oppressive stability in order to preserve their own class and cultural privileges. Many native Anglo-Americans in the past and established Americans, in all their distant diversity of origin, in the present have demanded instant assimilation, and have been willing to impose cultural homogeneity on immigrants and minorities. But this abiding nativistic thread in American politics and culture hardly tells the story of assimilation, a process that occurs at many levels of society, including ones less visible to the naked eye and ear than public demonstrations or inflammatory speeches about unwanted outsiders.

In recent American history, too much of the popular discourse about assimilation, past and present, has been composed of people arguing about the necessity of resisting or imposing what is happening inevitably and dynamically around us on its own terms. For as newcomers reach out for opportunity to improve themselves and fulfill their own aspirations, they inevitably learn new habits and adopt new patterns of living that place them closer to the boundaries of society's mainstream at various class levels and in a variety of institutional settings. Their children and grandchildren then move beyond them, as they reach out to grasp their own opportunities. Never necessarily losing the memories and oral traditions that make a part of them at some level culturally distinctive, and thus possessed of complex identities, they nonetheless ultimately come to insert themselves into American institutions and, by doing so, change them.

This has not been a natural process, simply pushed along inevitably by the logic of the free market, though the market was hardly irrelevant in academia, as will soon become clear. It has required struggle and, where racism formed an impediment, social protest movements, proactive state intervention, and changes in law.

The story of the integration of the discipline of history is a suggestive example of this process of the widening of the institutional mainstream. That story remains to be told. But it is nonetheless clear, impressionistically and anecdotally, from a variety of studies of institutional higher education and of the discipline and from the memoirs of the historians who came of age both before, and in the decade just after, World War II, that a battle between meritocratic principle and abiding racial and ethnic prejudices was present in the discipline. This was especially the case at the highest levels of the American academy, the Ivy League and comparably prestigious institutions. (That battle was not nearly as intense in the more democratic but less prestigious public universities.)

The testimonies of Jewish historians, who appear to have been pioneers in opening the profession to non-White Anglo-Saxon Protestants, speak of the intense antisemitic prejudices they encountered in graduate school and in the search for academic employment. Indeed, young Jews were discouraged from going to graduate school in history. They were told that the behavioral sciences were much more welcoming, while history was "for Anglo-Saxons." At work here were perceptions on the part of the discipline's elite that, as a humanities discipline, history passed on values and identities, forming undergraduates into ideal citizens. This socialization project was deepened, of course, in the case of American history, in which those ideal citizens were to be cast in the mold of the founding fathers and mothers.

Only the male heirs to that heritage, and those of earlier Northern and Western European immigrations like Hansen and his contemporaries who were conceived retrospectively to have been easily and successfully acculturated, were thought to be equal to the task. Yet meritocratic principles were present even in the midst of these intense prejudices, so that Jews such as Oscar Handlin, Richard Leopold, and John Morton Blum were admitted to the doctoral program at Harvard in spite of misgivings about the cultural backgrounds they were said to take to their work in American history. The demand for democratization and meritocratic principle grew more intense after World War II, because of the idealism prompted by the stated principles behind the war effort and the national introspection prompted by the Cold War and the civil rights movement. Ultimately, the need for the expansion of higher education was so acute after 1945, because of the massive growth of the American economy and of the overwhelming tide of enrollments from the baby boom generation, that it was difficult to continue to resist the logic of meritocracy (and hence of inclusiveness). By the 1970s this growing inclusiveness had practically laid waste to a broad variety of prejudices in the historical profession and to the authority of those who had long sought to impose them on the discipline. Pressure, thereafter, in the form of federally mandated, institutional affirmative action quotas and targets regarding race and gender further secured diversity.[12]

That is the larger story that is implied in this collection. But more often our authors write narratives about the broadening of their own individual cultural and social locations, and, in doing so collectively, they write about the convergence of the paths of each of them that lead to joining the others in American history departments, in professional organizations, and in the work of writing history.

To be sure, the process suggested in the essays is more complicated than a simple ethnic assimilation narrative. This is the case in at least two distinct ways. First, our essays tell the story not only of an ethnic, religious, and racial widening of the mainstream after the mid-twentieth century but also of a profoundly gendered transformation of that mainstream. Large numbers of women for the first time found their way into academia, and transformed it from the men's club that it still was when the editors entered graduate school in the 1960s. The process by which ethnic and immigration studies within the disciplines were placed squarely within the framework of academia was often accomplished by young women historians who were also newcomers not only by gender but also often by race and ethnicity. Rumbaut found that among the relatively few scholars in the field receiving doctorates before 1965, only about 8 percent were women, but the percentage grew steadily with each decade, reaching more than 50 percent between 1985 and 1994 and 62 percent after 1995. In total, at the time of the publication of his essay in 1999, 47 percent of researchers in immigration and ethnic studies in history and other disciplines were women.[13]

Although the percentage was somewhat lower in history than in sociology, political science/economics, and anthropology, the impact of women on historical scholarship in the field nonetheless cannot be exaggerated. The generation of pioneering women historians represented in our book by Yans, Moore, Posadas, Yung, and Tamura assisted greatly in moving historical analysis beyond policy, law, politics, and population studies to an increasing interest in ordinary people and daily life that brought family, gender roles, women's lives, and domestic economy into prominence. Hence, the field was transformed into an accessible, popular, and multiperspectival social history. Each of these five historians began their careers with work in various aspects of the social history of immigrant woman and immigrant families.[14]

Second, we note a significant difference in identification and identity between those of our authors born in the mid-twentieth-century baby boom, who generally entered academia between the late 1960s and the 1980s, and our younger authors (María Christina García, Violet Showers Johnson, and Theresa Alfaro-Velcamp), whose self-understandings speak to an increasingly global and transnational consciousness, which enters their research and serves to define them as individuals. The narrative of our baby boom authors, across the lines of race and ethnicity, is one of identity with an ethnic group and a sense of participation in the group's progressive assimilation in an increasingly inclusive society. This accounts for the general comparability across the divide of race between the narratives of our European American authors and those of Yung and Tamura.

It is certainly not that the histories are the same, for racism disrupts Chinese American and Japanese American histories in a way it does not do, for example, in the case of Pacyga's Chicago Poles or Bodnar's Slovaks in northeastern

Pennsylvania. Instead, the trajectory of the histories, the organization of daily individual and group life, and the aspirations of the various peoples are more similar than different. Our younger authors, García, Alfaro-Velcamp, and Johnson possess a more complex understanding of themselves. Although they certainly share in the ethnic group experience within the United States and in finding homes in American academia and the American community, they also conceive of themselves as a part of transnational diasporas that unite them in sustaining relationships with others of their ancestral groups across multiple international borders.

This identity self-consciously enters their work and their self-understandings.[15] Johnson informs us that she is offering "an Africana transnational perspective" on race in the United States as complex as the African, West Indian, European, and American connections traced in her work and her life. García explains a personal and scholarly evolution through which she has come to understand the Spanish usage *Americana* as at one and the same time being about both United States and hemispheric citizenship. Alfaro-Velcamp, primarily a historian of Mexico, is conscious of the fluidity of the southern border in her scholarship as in her life at the same time that she is conscious of the Middle East–North American connections at the heart of her research. Relative to the narratives of our older cohort, including that of a well-traveled Eileen Tamura, these three stories are decentered, and seem to present the world, or at least a larger world, as their home. In this understanding, they reflect an increasingly globalized world, characterized by the astonishing globe-shrinking technologies, such as smartphones and Skype, which create instantaneous and intimate electronic communication, and provide opportunities for hypermobility through jet transportation. The demands for exclusive citizenship and exclusive loyalties, like the isolation of peoples and regions, are increasingly a relic of the past. Nation-states are by no means disappearing, but their hold on individuals now must compete increasingly with a new consciousness that is more and more comfortable making the world its home.[16]

Like Marcus Lee Hansen, our authors have attempted to go beyond documenting the experiences represented by their genealogy. They have also variously found a place for themselves within American history, and by doing so they have made American history (and other histories, too) their own. This is a more complicated process than it appears at first, and one seldom addressed in thinking about the meanings of history, whether as memory, or as a composed, interpreted formal record. Under what circumstances do cultural outsiders come to reach the conclusion that their identities lie as much or more in a new place as in an older one, where their ancestors were rooted for many centuries? When and how does Abraham Lincoln or John Wilkes Booth come to captivate the imagination and seem more relevant to self-understanding than the heroes or villains of the place from which one's parents and grandparents, and ancestors centuries before them, came? How and when do people come to have new memories? Our essays suggest answers to these neglected questions. Clearly seeking answers to them is an assignment of importance for anyone interested in making sense of the role that written history plays in a society in which the cycle of cultural outsiders moving toward becoming insiders is an abiding feature of the past, the present, and in all likelihood the future.

Notes

1. Ruben G. Rumbaut, "Immigration Research in the United States: Social Origins and Future Orientations," *American Behavioral Scientist* 42 (June–July 1999): 1285–1301, at 1293. Rumbaut organizes the data for political science and economics into one category, because these disciplines often share a common department in colleges and in some universities. He also presents an "All Other Disciplines" category, which I omit here, because it is not readily comparable to the identifiable disciplinary categories.

2. The exact quote from Sartre is often rendered, "Freedom is what you do with what's been done to you." Though the quote is commonly cited, no textual reference is made to identify it within a specific Sartrean text or even a remembered conversation. In a vast compendium of Sartre quotations, for example, it is listed as "unsourced;" http:// en.wikiquote.org/wiki/Jean-PaulSartre. It is possible that it was a conversational remark that was written down and passed on to posterity by someone now forgotten. That being said, the idea embodied in the aphorism is accurate in so far as it reflects Sartre's existentialist thought; and is evident, for example, in his biographies of both Flaubert and Baudelaire, in which the character and the life's work of both authors are conceived as creative adaptations to the parenting each was given.

   A comprehensive effort to analyze the inclination of various generations of White historians toward African American history is found, among other themes, in August Meier and Elliott Rudwick, *Black History and the Historical Profession, 1915–1980* (Urbana: University of Illinois Press, 1986).

3. On the early ethnic social historians, see Jon Gjerde, "New Growth on Old Vines: The State of the Field: The Social History of Immigration to and Ethnicity in the United States," *Journal of American Ethnic History* 18 (Summer 1999): 40–65; Donna R. Gabaccia, "The Minnesota School of Immigration and Refugee Studies," http://www.ihrc .umn.edu/publications/pdf/MinnesotaSchool-1.pdf; Rudolph J. Vecoli, "'Over the Years I Have Encountered the Hazards and Rewards That Await the Historian of Immigration': George Malcolm Stephenson and the Swedish American Community," *Swedish American Historical Quarterly* 51 (April 2000): 130–149.

4. Gjerde, "New Growth on Old Vines"; Allan H. Spear, "Marcus Lee Hansen and the Historiography of Immigration," *Wisconsin Magazine of History* 44 (Summer 1961): 258–268; Carleton C. Qualey, "Marcus Lee Hansen," *Midcontinent American Studies Journal* 8 (Fall 1967): 18–25; Moses Rischin, "Marcus Lee Hansen: America's First Transethnic Historian," in *Uprooted Americans: Essays to Honor Oscar Handlin*, ed. Richard Bushman, Neil Harris, David Rothman, Barbara Miller Solomon, and Stephen Thernstrom (Boston: Little, Brown, 1979), 319–347.

5. C. Frederick Hansen, "Marcus Lee Hansen—Historian of Immigration," *Common Ground* (June 1942): 87–94; Oscar Handlin, "Introduction to the Torchbook Edition," Marcus Lee Hansen, *The Atlantic Migration, 1607–1860* (New York: Harper and Row, 1961), x–xvii.

6. Marcus Lee Hansen, *The Problem of the Third Generation Immigrant* (Rock Island, Ill.: Augustana Historical Society, 1938).

7. The outstanding exception to the dearth of effort to pick up the thread of Hansen's argument is Vladimir C. Nahirny and Joshua Fishman, "American Immigrant Groups: Ethnic Identification and the Problem of Generations," *Sociological Review*, n.s., 13 (November 1965): 311–365, which disagrees with the consciousness of the past that Hansen ascribes to the various generations.

   To commemorate the fiftieth anniversary of Hansen's lecture a conference was held at Augustana College in 1987, out of which came a book of papers on Hansen's three-generation hypothesis; Peter Kivisto and Dag Blanck, eds., *American Immigrants and Their Generations: Studies and Commentaries on the Hansen Thesis after Fifty Years* (Urbana: University of Illinois Press, 1990). Only a few of the papers follow Hansen's lead in social-psychological theorizing at a more abstract, generational level.

8. On the valorization of multiculturalism and diversity, from critical as well as supportive perspectives, see Charles Taylor, with commentary by Amy Gutmann, editor, Steven C. Rockefeller, Michael Walzer, and Susan Wolf, *Multiculturalism and "The Politics of Recognition"* (Princeton: Princeton University Press, 1992); David Hollinger, *Postethnic America* (New York: Basic Books, 1995); Nathan Glazer, *We Are All Multiculturalists Now* (Cambridge, Mass: Harvard University Press, 1997); Tariq Modood, *Multiculturalism* (London: Polity Press, 2007). For arguments on behalf of the social and specifically organizational efficacy of diversity, which have proven significant in the success of the new pluralism, see Richard D. Bucher, *Diversity Consciousness: Opening Our Minds to Peoples, Cultures, and Opportunities*, 3rd ed. (Upper Saddle River, N.J.: Prentice-Hall, 2009); Scott E. Page, *The Difference: How the Power of Diversity Creates Better Groups, Firms, Schools, and Societies* (Princeton: Princeton University Press, 2008). Two attempts to write reinterpretations of the entire American past from the perspective of an expanded conception of plural groups, especially racialized groups, are the syntheses by Ronald Takaki, *A Different Mirror: A History of Multicultural America* (Boston: Back Bay Books, 1994), and Paul Spickard, *Almost All Aliens: Immigration, Race, and Colonialism in American History and Identity* (New York: Routledge, 2007).

9. "Mainstream" is a concept that is frequently referenced, both in academic and in popular literature, but rarely defined. My own understanding of *mainstream* becomes clearer later in this introduction. For now, it is useful to establish that my understanding is based on the definition found in Richard Alba and Victor Nee, *Remaking the American Mainstream: Assimilation and Contemporary Immigration* (Cambridge, Mass.: Harvard University Press, 2003), 12. The authors state, "A useful way of defining the mainstream is as that part of the society *within* which ethnic and racial origins have at most minor impacts on life chances and opportunities." The authors do not posit in their discussion of mainstream that race and ethnic origins disappear as selection criteria, nor do they claim that class differences cease to exist. Their conception of mainstream instead suggests that mainstreams exist in a great variety of institutional and social locations throughout the class and opportunity structures. There are middle-class and working-class mainstreams. Nor do Alba and Nee suggest that individuals seeking inclusion in the mainstream necessarily shed their ethnic and racial identities and memories or singular cultural practices. The cost of inclusion, in their conception, is not the abolition of difference, though that may take place naturally and logically in the circumstances of pursuing opportunity.

10. Samuel P. Huntington, *Who Are We? The Challenges to American National Identity* (New York: Simon and Schuster, 2005).

11. Highly recommended and influential in the casting of the argument presented here is the reformulation of *assimilation* found in Alba and Nee, *Remaking the American Mainstream*. Among the many virtues of this work is its analytical precision, particularly in its appropriation of the *new institutionalism* literature, and its respect for the complexities of the historical past.

12. Peter Novick, *That Noble Dream: The "Objectivity Question" and the American Historical Profession* (New York: Cambridge University Press, 1988), 15, 172–174 (Handlin), 339–340, 365–366; Steven J. Harper, *Straddling Worlds: The Jewish-American Journey of Professor Richard W. Leopold* (Evanston, Ill.: Northwestern University Press, 2007); John Morton Blum, *A Life with History* (Lawrence: University of Kansas Press, 2004). Richard Hofstadter, a towering presence in American history in the mid-twentieth century, was "half-Jewish" on his father's side, and had an ambivalent relationship with his Jewish identity. But he, too, claimed to have experienced antisemitism in the course of making his academic career. See David S. Brown, *Richard Hofstadter: An Intellectual Biography* (Chicago: University of Chicago Press, 2006), 20–21, 35, 38, 53. Of these four historians, only Handlin can be said to have identified with and participated in American Jewish communal life.

13. Rumbaut, "Immigration Research in the United States," 1291.

14. A book parallel to this collection uses the memoirs of women historians to chart the rise of women in the discipline of history, and it succeeds in bringing together multiple narratives in the service of understanding individual lives, second-wave feminist politics and ideology, and the transformation of the discipline and, with it, of knowledge itself; see Eileen Boris and Napur Chaudhuri, eds., *Voices of Women Historians: The Personal, the Political, the Professional* (Bloomington: Indiana University Press, 1999). See, also, the essays by Joan Wallach Scott, Linda Gordon, Maureen Murphy Nutting, and Temma Kaplan in James M. Banner and John R. Gillis, eds., *Becoming Historians* (Chicago: University of Chicago Press, 2009).

15. Although not acknowledging a change in her self-understanding in line with those of our younger contributors, Barbara Posadas nonetheless writes in her essay for this book that recently she has come to be more conscious in her work of the global and diasporic connections and contexts of Filipino migration.

16. From the now voluminous literature on transnational practices and global consciousness, see Arjun Appadurai, *Modernity at Large: Cultural Dimensions of Globalization* (Delhi: Oxford University Press, 1997); Thomas Faist, *The Volume and Dynamics of International Migration and Transnational Social Spaces* (Oxford: Oxford University Press, 2000); Thomas L. Friedman, *The World Is Flat, 3.0: A Brief History of the Twenty-First Century* (New York: Picador, 2007); Luis Eduardo Guarnizo and Michael Peter Smith, eds., *Transnationalism from Below* (New Brunswick, N.J.: Transaction Publishers, 1997); Christian Joerges, Inger-Johanne Sand, and Gunther Teubner, eds., *Transnational Governance and Constitutionalism* (Oxford: Hart Publishing, 2004); Christian Joppke, *Citizenship and Immigration* (Cambridge: Polity Press, 2010); Aihwa Ong, *Flexible Citizenship: The Cultural Logic of Transnationality* (Durham, N.C.: Duke University Press, 1999); Saskia Sassen, *Globalization and Its Discontents: Essays on the New Mobility of People and Money* (New York: New Press, 1998), and Sassen, *The Global City: New York, London, and Tokyo*, updated 2nd ed. (Princeton: Princeton University Press, 2001); Sidney Tarrow, *The New Transnational Activism* (New York: Cambridge University Press, 2005); John Tomlinson, *Globalization and Culture* (Chicago: University of Chicago Press, 1999).

2

Worlds Apart and Together

From Italian American Girlhood
to Historian of Immigration

VIRGINIA YANS

I came of age during the 1950s in the small town of Mamaroneck, New York. Holding Mother's or Father's hand, when I turned left on our street up the hill and a long stretch away for my little legs, we would arrive at our Sunday destination: the sparkling, open waters of a peaceful harbor extending far away into the saltwater sound. Blue sky and skipping clouds sheltered the moored, bobbing yachts and varnished, sleek sailboats. Rich people owned those boats. Rich people also owned the big houses lining one side of the harbor's edge, an assertion of their claim to its striking natural beauty.

If I turned right on my street, usually holding Grandma's hand, one block away we encountered imposing elevated railroad tracks. We walked under a sooty trestle overhanging a dark, acrid cavern to the other side. Grandma had things to do there. When we emerged from this tunnel, an animated landscape of busy markets, small stores, pungent smells, rooftop and backyard gardens, and people, Black and White, welcomed us—an exhilarating world to a wide eyed, curious child between the ages of six and twelve.

I lived between these two places; I learned to understand and to move back and forth between them.

Our Town

On one side of the railroad tracks—the *other* side—Italian immigrants, mostly Sicilians and Calabrians, and a small group of African Americans, some them descendants of freedmen, lived. A river winding its way toward Long Island Sound sometimes flooded this low lying area, or flats, the town's least desirable real estate—a patchwork of small lots, detached one-family wood-frame homes, and inexpensive apartments. The poorest Italians and Blacks rented whatever ramshackle homes and rooms they could afford, while the more prosperous among them bought or built their own homes. The flats had its own Italian church, butcher, vegetable markets, bakeries, pizzeria, restaurants, and a public school for Italian and Black kids. The flats also had its own sounds and smells. One could walk the saw-dusted floors of the live chicken market, choose evening dinner from a cage, and see the decapitated dead creature feathered and quartered before you, its legs amputated and rolled in waxy paper for tomorrow's soup. I heard Italian and English spoken in the flats. I saw the junkman and the ragman pushing their carts through the streets, heard their singsong shouts and the banging pots and pans that announced their arrival.

Despite the neighborhood's appealing sounds, smells, and noises, I was never to cross the tracks unless Grandma or Mother wanted my company on some excursion to buy special sausages, a clucking chicken, or for visits to an Italian church feast where sweet cookies were the main attraction. Sometimes at home in the mornings a few blocks away, I could hear the junkman's cry in the distance: I knew from his cry, from those visits to the church and the markets and from the Italian spoken there, that I was connected to the Italian people in the flats. Since I did not live there, I was not sure how or why.

I grew up in a better neighborhood, in a better part of town, on the better side of the tracks. Just two blocks away from the flats, it was a world apart. Fate, a bit of luck, and some shrewd calculation took my paternal grandparents to higher ground, to a place, Grandma told Grandpa, where floodwaters would not delay his morning departure for work. Nearby, within this marginal, mixed neighborhood, a smaller group of Italians, White working-class ethnics, and one or two Black families made their homes in modest single-family and multifamily dwellings shared with relatives. Truth be told, although I did not understand the concept then, the flats was a segregated district. My nearby neighborhood, though marginal and close to the commercial center, was not. The railroad tracks made that distinction clear.

Our town's main street ran parallel to my street. By the age of eight or nine, I was allowed to go around the corner to the main street on my own to run errands, join playmates, or to buy an ice cream cone from Gene, the soda fountain guy. I visited Khan's Jewish delicatessen (where my uncle worked), Mr. Oprandy's grocery store, the Margoles brothers' men's clothing emporium, a Jewish family's stationery store, the Italian butcher and shoemaker (who was Grandma's cousin Luigi), a Chinese laundry and restaurant, an A&P supermarket, two banks, and a movie theater (staffed by three of my cousins). There were friendly shopkeepers and relatives, family guardians standing by, to mediate my jaunts into town, my visits to the library up on a nearby hill, and my walks to the Catholic school and church a few blocks beyond. I attended Catholic grammar school with White middle-class kids, Irish, Italian, and German working-class kids, and two Black children. Much farther away from the tracks and home there were three or four wealthy suburban enclaves. Former summer residences lining the town's marshy shoreline, they were now home to upper-middle-class and rich Americans, several of them successful Jews. When I was old enough, my father took me to those places for visits.

These spaces were the bounded outside perimeters of my childhood: neighborhoods, church, school, library, and even Main Street—a puzzling jumble of class, ethnic, and racial differences whose existence was, nonetheless, made real to me by their physically marked and unmovable geographies.

Home

I inhabited another world, smaller and intimate, but no less puzzling to a child: the house I shared with my grandparents, parents, siblings, aunts, uncles, and cousins. Here too, there were boundaries and differences to be understood, negotiated, and crossed.

Grandma and Grandpa (before his untimely death) lived in the downstairs apartment with their bachelor son; I, along with my parents, my brother, and my sister, lived on the top floor; my father's brothers, sister, their spouses, and their children lived in the two remaining apartments. When I went to see Grandma (and her resident bachelor son, Uncle Joe), I entered a different country, a different time. Here Grandma's *staccato* Calabrian dialect was spoken. There was a special sacred corner set aside for her daily prayers, a place with candles, statues of the Blessed Mother, black bead rosaries, and holy pictures on the wall. Sometimes, there were strings of pasta drying on Grandma's great, bulky mattress, and there were dried red peppers hanging from a rafter. In the kitchen white ovals of damp dough rose at Grandma's command. There were toothsome, steaming soups, their preparation initiated, much to my distress witnessing it, by Grandma's occasional execution with an ax of a backyard chicken. Just outside Grandma's back porch, near the vegetable garden and grapevines, stood fig trees put to rest under burlap when cold weather arrived. Two or three times daily, even on days when she went to services at Saint Vito's Church, Grandma would kneel at her altar, praying, and beating her chest rhythmically with the same practiced rhythm she used to knead her bread. Occasionally, Grandma welcomed me into her spirit world, anointing my forehead with pungent olive oil in the sign of the cross, chanting a prayer as she did so. Young girls "with gypsy eyes" had to be protected, Grandma said.

Grandpa, a gardener in mild weather, took odd jobs off-season shoveling snow off rich people's driveways and coal into their furnaces so he could support his wife and seven children. He preferred this outside work to the Pennsylvania coal mining jobs he had taken during his first trips to America. Grandpa hated

FIGURE 1. A typical extended family interaction in Mamaroneck, New York, showing, from left to right, cousin Anthony, Uncle Mike recently returned from military service in Iran, sister Marilyn, and the author, circa 1946. From the personal collection of Michael Yans.

the coal mines, vowed never to return there and never did. One day, he mistook a bottle of poison for a bottle of alcohol; he died a painful death. Grandma found herself a widow surrounded by four of her seven children. Undaunted by her husband's sudden passing and accepting God's will, she continued her job running the entire house and controlling her adoring resident children with an iron hand. She felt it her unquestionable right to incorporate Grandpa's patriarchy: she and Grandpa literally saved nickels, dimes, and dollars to buy the house and their adult children paid only $45 a month rent each to live there. She had once taken boarders in to pay the bills. It was not simply a matter of money. This was the way things should be—according to Grandma. One did not question Grandma. For one thing, she would laugh, run her hands down her black widow's dress followed with a dismissive head shake at anyone questioning her authority and leaving her opponent, sometimes my mother, defenseless. There was no reasonable way out.

Grandma was the past in the present. Her New World children and consequently their children accepted the order of things, the Old Order of things. The older generation rightfully ruled the younger. That meant my parents ruled me. And that meant I could not go away to summer camp. I was forever too young to wear lipstick. It took years for me to get permission to go out on a date. And then I had a curfew. Going away to college, or leaving home, I learned from my older siblings' transgressions, was somehow disloyal. The struggle with authority, with power, with control could be suffocating to me, the youngest female actor in this family enclave.

Something puzzled me, though, about Grandma. That puzzle manifested itself daily in the physical presence of my grandmother, her hair wrapped in braids around her head, her long black widow's dress, her home altar, her refusal to speak English, but most of all: How, I wondered, did she get to America?

Grandma had a secret, and she left it in Italy. People whispered about it including, sometimes, Grandma. When she made tea for me afternoons after school, the warm sunlight breaking through her starchy checked curtains onto the kitchen table, I would ask her, dipping one of her *biscotti* into my milk: "Why did you come to America, Grandma?" Then Grandma told me a story. She began with her shame at being an illegitimate child. What that meant, I was not certain, but it was, to be sure, not good. Her mother, a seamstress, was a beautiful woman and mistress to a wealthy landholder, allegedly a man of noble blood. He fathered Grandma and two of her sisters, but, as I later discovered on their birth records, he refused to acknowledge paternity. In a small southern Italian village, this was an extraordinary disgrace. The villagers knew who my great-grandmother's lover was. I suspect that his stature and perhaps his financial assistance insulated my great-grandmother from the quotidian slights and shame commonly meted out to a disgraced woman. But Grandma told me she wanted to escape indignity, so she accepted Grandpa's marriage proposal, left her life behind, and came to America. This was, she warned, how fate controlled those who broke rules.

Grandma's secret life was my first introduction to the shadowy, obscure past, a real past with princely men, disgraced village beauties, and shamed exiled children. My curiosity intensely aroused, I wanted to know more about this mysterious place, where powerful events expelled people across the ocean far from home, never to return. A thoughtful child, I noticed certain contradictions in Grandma's regime of unquestioned authority: "How come," I asked my mother, "was it OK for Grandma to travel thousands of miles from Italy and never return home, when I cannot even go to summer camp?" The question remained unanswered, relegated to that substantial pile of things as they just are and must be, things I must not question.

Enduring the cheap rent reign of her strong-willed Calabrian mother-in-law with her children's future education at stake, my fair skinned, blue-eyed northern Italian mother, who called herself "the outlaw," somehow managed to fashion her own domain. Mother's northern Italian family was more educated and skilled than Father's Calabrian side. She made her superior origins clear, a history evident in her immaculate, inexpensive, but elegant way of dressing herself and her daughters and her cultural refinements. Mother transmitted a sense of culture and education to us: there was a "good Italian" language, fine Italian food, and a high Italian culture, all of them emanating from the northern part of the peninsula, certainly not from Calabria or Sicily. Her cooking reflected those distinctions: she favored *risotto* over *pasta*, a nuanced "light" red pasta sauce to a "heavy red gravy" and cranberry beans in her soups. Mother narrated the librettos and described the grand operas she attended while working in the city. When we visited her widowed father in the Bronx, to my rapt delight and attention Poppa, playing majestically to his audience of three grandchildren, would roam about his apartment dressed in undershirt and old slacks, suspenders hanging, gesturing and robustly singing Italian opera as loud as he pleased, and "Damn the neighbors, Isabella" he would shout to my harried mother. Following this sonorous performance, he rewarded us with his prize-winning *grissini* (breadsticks) and shiny quarters pulled from behind his back.

Mother encouraged reading and took me to the library. She made some trade-offs: cheap rent and living as an "outlaw" in this southern Italian outpost enabled certain essential advantages. She determined that all of her children would be well educated, have careers, and that they would "never work with their hands." Father, who had to drop out of school by the fourth grade to help support his six siblings, went along though he was somewhat reluctant about the wisdom of educating marriageable daughters. My mother's belief that women should be self-supporting "just in case" made a strong impression; it was the beginning of my feminist consciousness already taking seed with daily evidence of Grandma's strong will, Mother's varying compliance and resistance to it, and the departure of two of my aunts who happily escaped from the authoritarian maternal regime. One of them defied Grandma's authority, changed her first name from Angelica to Jane, embarked upon a glamorous executive secretary career in Miami, and was obviously having more fun than the rest of her siblings.

Next door lived my father's sister with her son and a husband who spoke and cooked Sicilian. Never-ending streams of Sicilian cousins from a clan, which, it was said, was large enough to elect the town mayor (and eventually did), came to visit them. My father's youngest brother occupied the fourth apartment with his Polish and German American wife, the only non-Italian in the house. Without children for many years my uncle and his wife lived the life of a young couple hosting frequent visits from relatives, who looked very different from any of us.

Each of these households was a bounded, yet permeable territory offering different foods, dialects, and cultures, all of them arranged into a hierarchy of related humans over which Grandma presided. Mother often sent me, the youngest family member, between these places to do some chore, play with cousin Richard, or participate in a kind of never-ending New Guinea– style ceremonial *kula* ring of gifts exchanged between each of the households with her own well-appreciated preparations commanding highest value. Food offerings and the purchase of special ingredients not available at home always manifested in our Sunday visits to Mother's relatives as well, a symbolic cementing of more distant family bonds. Meals shared with them and their fluid Italian, so different from Grandma's dialect, offered still another proof of difference.

Mother looked for some way to earn extra income with a job whose hours would allow her to be at home when we returned from school. She renounced her experience and training as an assistant dress designer (which would have required a commute to New York City), adopting instead her blood relatives' talents in the food trades. She found a position as the cafeteria manager in the public school across the tracks that was attended by Black and Italian children. She took it as her mission to make sure that the kids, many of whom came from poor families, had "at least one balanced meal a day." When I walked down the main street holding her hand or accompanied her to the local supermarket, I basked in her local celebrity. Almost every Italian and Black kid in our town and every one of their mothers who saw us stopped to say, "Hello, how are you?" Here was another lesson in boundaries crossed and differences overcome.

Mother was a great cook. She also understood the power of food to please, and to create bonds of respect and friendship. Food also brought me into contact with the Chinese family proprietors of the local Chinese restaurant, the only restaurant other than the pizzeria that my family frequented. For reasons I do not understand, but I think it had something to do with respect for the older generation, my mother held Chinese and Japanese people in high respect regardless of what others thought of them. She made it clear that theirs were ancient civilizations, and, of course, old was good. One of her greatest pleasures was speaking "good Italian" to a wealthy Chinese gentleman who knew something of the language. I stood by in amazement, witnessing this palpable, happy, uncommon small-town cultural exchange.

Journeys with my father highlighted a different set of boundaries and differences. On Saturdays, he sometimes took me along as he made his rounds of what then seemed to me huge mansions in the wealthy suburban sections of our town that he tended and cared for as a carpenter, general fix-it-up person, and small contractor. Most of his customers were wealthy, well-educated Jews. They were warm and welcoming to us, but I sensed my father's discomfort and learned from it, painfully, that we were somehow not their equals. His uneasiness was palpable. My father was a carpenter and worked with his hands. He was short of stature, but I remember his huge fingers surrounded with thick bands of flesh, a body armor evolved to protect from repeated hammer blows, small accidents, pushing and pulling, and the weight-bearing activities of his trade. My father's hands identified his class and his status as a laborer. His hands spoke to others and to himself of where he belonged and where he had come from, the firstborn child of an immigrant coal miner and landscaper. He could not have hidden these hands from others, nor would he have wanted to. These hands did not belong in the social company of rich and educated people. Neither, I guessed, did I.

All around me, in my extended family enclave and within my mother's more distant family as well, people worked with their hands. My maternal grandfather who lived in the Bronx was a baker; I saw and tasted what he created. Behind our house Grandpa, a gardener, had a small grape orchard and vegetable garden where I saw him turn the earth, tend his vegetables, and cultivate his grapes for wine with gusto. Grandma kept her backyard chicken coop, made food and bread, turned flower sacks into sheets, and scrubbed her laundry by hand—all with seeming satisfaction. My Sicilian uncle, a plasterer, returned home covered with white dust, his hands blistering from the lime and chemicals he regularly touched—a malady that he cursed daily as he gazed, resigned, upon his fingers. Mother cooked and sewed with flair and professional competence, producing results—food and clothing—that everyone could enjoy. Because I observed my father and my uncle producing beauty from raw materials—hand-hewn cabinetry and charming plaster archways around our modest home—I understood the value and the magic of their skills. Since everyone around me did manual labor and had tangible results to show for it, my father's shame was puzzling to me. Mother's determination that her children "will not work with their hands" also perplexed me, but her resolve to prepare her children for something better offered an antidote, a way to remove us from the dark and troubling discomfort that gripped my father. This, of course, was a child's experience of class, another bewildering, seemingly fixed hierarchy of difference that imprinted itself on my consciousness.

I learned about social inequality in another unlikely place: at the Catholic grammar school where I was taught by the Sisters of Charity, none of them of Italian heritage, most of them Irish Americans who favored their own kind. I vividly recall my annual humiliation when the principal, Sister Mary Theresa, would visit each classroom to wish us a happy Saint Patrick's Day. When our classroom teacher inevitably asked all the Irish kids to stand up so Sister Theresa could identify them, I slid back into my seat hoping my head would disappear like a turtle's underneath my desk top. Years earlier, in the 1910s and 1920s, the Sisters of Charity—who also educated my father and his six siblings during a period of immigration restriction and xenophobia—changed their last name to Yans from Iannuzzi because, the sisters said, "that name is too hard for Americans to say." My father's report cards and those of his siblings were delivered to children by the name of Yans. When I heard Father explain the origin of this name to curious inquirers, I always felt some visceral disturbance about the casual reconstruction of my family name. What was wrong with it? I sensed the Sisters' disrespect for my family identity—an insult without remedy because Grandma did not speak English and Grandpa would not have entertained the absurdity of shortening his workday to reprimand nuns.

Ethnic, class, race, and gender hierarchies arranged and ordered my world, sometimes offering security, sometimes uncertainty, and occasionally pain. These hierarchies and differences seemed for the most part fixed but sometimes mutable. Grandma, for example, ran the family, easily passing into chief of operations after Grandpa's death. At the same time, she was totally dependent upon all of us. The racial and ethnic hierarchies were not entirely consistent either. Mother let it be known that northern Italians were somehow better than the Calabrians and Sicilians in my own family. She could easily have applied such distinctions to Whites and Blacks, but I do not remember her ever doing so. Her actions spoke to me. As a public school employee, she tended to the needs and nutrition of Black and olive-skinned southern Italian kids—and took great pleasure in doing so. My association with African Americans was limited to one playmate who lived nearby. My parents expressed concern about her precocious physical development and her single mother (with boyfriends), whose long, painted fingernails and makeup fascinated me, but I remained part of the group of Italian kids who played with the only Black child our age in the neighborhood. Nonetheless, there was a sense that our family was better than the people, Italian and Black, who lived on the other side of the tracks.

It was not clear to me just where my family and I belonged. Looking back, it is not difficult to understand why. My father worked for wealthy Jews who, he considered, were better than we were. People who worked with their hands, my people, were not as good as well-educated people. And the Italian children attending my grammar school soon learned that we were not fully American, at least not as American as the Irish. Asian people were to be highly regarded, despite what others thought of them. And, one half of me (my northern Italian half) was better than the other.

I had found my place and proper deportment in this peaceable kingdom of race, gender, and ethnicity, strangely ordered and segregated and unpredictably mutable though it was. I smelled it, lived it, and acted it. I learned to parse, interpret, test, and negotiate those boundaries, to feel comfortable living between, inside, and, ultimately, outside of them. And I continued to wonder about them.

This archaeology of compressed memories, a layered visual, spatial, and emotional imprint of hurts and loyalties, of race and gender hierarchies, of my struggles and strategies for lending coherence and control to an otherwise incomprehensible child's world, framed the consciousness I carried with me into adulthood; there, I sought resolution of some kind in my adult efforts to observe, study, understand, and control the world through disciplined knowledge and academic training. In phenomenological terms, the representational world of my childhood became my adult intellectual work.[1] That child's world pulled me toward the study of immigration and women's history, cultural, racial, and gender differences.

Libraries and Texts: My Secret Life with Twins and Heroines

Sometime between the ages of five and eleven, at our small town library, I discovered aspects of my childhood experience represented in books. Through reading, I grew comfortable in the position of distant observer, a standpoint later formalized in my professional role as a historian. I vividly remember completing every one of Lucy Fitch Perkins's (1865–1937) children's series about twins, a boy and a girl in each book. After a visit to Ellis Island, which had "impressed" her "deeply," Perkins developed her book series on children in foreign countries to show "the best qualities which" foreign youngsters brought to American shores.[2] Perkins's childhood adventures, dispersed over history and geography, introduced me to cultures around the world and to their different gender practices. Her books highlighted the limited expectations of girls . Recently browsing through one, a quote from a little Japanese girl twin named Take stunned me: "There's only one thing I can grow up to be. . . . If I am very, very good, maybe I'll grow to be a mother-in-law sometime."[3] My own family background allowed me to appreciate Take's recognition of the power some females acquired within their families but my library search took me unflinchingly in another direction.

Breaking the rules, I made my way stealthily up the library stairs to the forbidden "adult section." There, I found books to assist me in understanding my identity as an Italian Catholic girl. I combed the rows of books, one by one, looking for works by and about women, particularly those with the word "sex" in the title. Snaring one, I sat hunched over on the floor, attempting to hide my age and trespass as I read the prohibited books. I read Simone de Beauvoir's *The Second Sex* (1952), Margaret Mead's *Sex and Temperament in Three Primitive Societies* (1935), and Ruth Benedict's *Patterns of Culture* (1934). Pearl Buck's epic novel *The Good Earth* (1931) quenched my curiosity about China, Chinese women, and a people so different from my own. I hadn't the slightest idea who Simone de Beauvoir was, nor did I fully understand existentialism and her brilliant application of phenomenology to women's bodies and experience, but de Beauvoir's questioning introduction, her use of myth, history, insect and animal behavior, her articulation of the "otherness" I had come to know—and most of all her passion—were comprehensible to me.[4] Little did I know at age eleven that de Beauvoir's powerful categorization of woman as the "other" would be a foundational text for the women's movement and for the women's history movement that engaged me fifteen years later. A PBS documentary I would later write and produce about Mead found its genesis in my library visits. Some colleagues saw this film as a departure from my study of immigration, but my engagement with Mead (whose master's thesis was on Italian immigrants and whose mother, a sociologist, studied Italians) directly connected to the gender, cultural, and racial differences that had occupied me since childhood.

Intellectual Epiphanies: College and Graduate School

My first years away from home in the 1960s at Skidmore, a woman's college in upstate New York, offered much-needed time to navigate my independence. Even as I became physically distant from them, college gave me the tools to think about my family within the expansive historical changes that brought millions like them to North America. Allen Kifer, my senior thesis advisor, a specialist in African American history, demonstrated that academic historians took the studies of marginalized people seriously. Among my professors were inspiring women with PhDs, women who wrote books, and loved teaching and research. Louise Dalby, a Europeanist who studied French, English, and American women in World War I, was a pioneer in women's history (yes, I learned in the 1960s that women had a history); Marcia Colish, now a distinguished medievalist, shepherded me into a medieval world governed by realities and perceptions completely different from my own. The small college environment encouraged crossing disciplinary boundaries. I found great pleasure engaging with professors and students in the arts. This boundary crossing, a familiar kind of encounter for me, was excellent practice for my future interdisciplinary work as a historian of immigration, women, and anthropology, and for my interpretive work as a public historian and documentary filmmaker.

In graduate school, I constructed a minor in the philosophy of social science, sharpening my comprehension of epistemology and phenomenology and my interest in first-person subjective sources, such as oral histories and autobiographies. In 1965, Professor Herbert Gutman invited me to join his history research seminar. He was, one of my colleagues observed, representative "of a . . . generation of non-theistic deeply Jewish characters who inhabited the academy and made . . . important contributions to labor, African-American, immigration, and women's history."[5] And I was one of a coterie of students who heard the call from Gutman and others of his generation to rewrite the conventional "big White man" narrative, redirecting chronologies and narratives away from war and constitution making and toward stories of working-class culture, slavery, immigration, women, sexuality, family, and popular culture. This subversive agenda appealed to students of the 1960s and 1970s, who participated in the civil rights, women's, and anti–Vietnam War movements. These were passionate times and we, young scholars and our mentors, passionately affirmed the relevance of the historical discipline to public life and culture.

Herb, as everyone called him, arrived in class, his beat-up leather briefcase bulging with documents, any of which he might extract at a moment's notice: a Paterson, New Jersey, manuscript census page showing Black households, a newspaper report on Jewish women's kosher meat riots, a quote from E. P. Thompson's *The Making of the English Working Class* (1963), an excerpt from anthropologist Sidney Mintz's *A Worker in the Cane* (1960). He read these aloud with spirit, reverence, and conviction, canonizing each as a sacred text vital for some point under discussion. Initially, I was uncertain how my interests would mesh with those of a labor historian. I soon found out. Herb, who had no truck with French philosophers, later used a quote from Jean-Paul Sartre to summarize his own philosophy: "The essential is not what 'one' has done to another man, but what man does with what 'one' has done to him."[6] With this unmovable respect for human dignity as his credo, Herb was a liberal rabbi to his students, opening spaces for our interpretation and study.

Meeting Herb at this stage of my intellectual development was something like shouting into a cave and hearing an echo back, my own voice returning enriched by his years of thought, and beckoning me to follow a new, important quest. The questions I was asking about the past, many of them framed by the representational world of my childhood, were the kinds of questions Herb, himself the son of Jewish immigrants, was asking. To put it another way, without my realizing it at the time, our representational frames matched. So did our phenomenologies. Both of us were interested in culture, in consciousness, in the injustices done to and, more important, responses created by those who bore the burden of class, race, ethnic, and gender difference. Both of us knew that "our people" could speak, and had spoken. It was our job to make their voices heard. Joking about how destiny brought me to his classroom, we understood our meeting as a later iteration of our immigrant forbearers' encounters in garment shops and Lower East Side streets. Herb's impact was immediate, profound, and enduring. I was on my way to becoming a historian, a particular kind of historian.

I learned to corral and discipline my childhood representations in the service of historical analysis. I learned from Herb (and his good friend E. P. Thompson, whom he brought to our classroom) that culture and class and even gender were neither fixed nor transhistorical but historical processes that happened over time. People—workers, slaves, free men and women—made their own history. This could be observed, I learned, by examining what happened to the values, culture, and behavior of ordinary people when they encountered developing capitalism or when, as I would later argue, Italian immigrant women drew upon traditional values and practices to support family needs.

In the 1960s and 1970s these ideas challenged the reigning paradigms in immigration history that emphasized victimization, "disorganization," and "breakdown" for the poor and for immigrants. I, along with Rudolph Vecoli—the pioneering historian of Italian American immigration—knew, for example, that Oscar Handlin's narrative did not match our personal experiences.[7] But my personal experiences were anecdote, not history. I developed a counternarrative, one that would make women and the family central actors in the immigration story: so my dissertation and, later, my first book were born. The book was one of the first works by a young generation of scholars to document the history of ethnic working-class women. My reading of anthropological studies led me to posit a dynamic model for family change; proposing neither disorganization nor simple retention of family values and traditions, I argued that the encounter between the Old and the New Worlds could be understood as a dialectical process. I understood Old World culture as a flexible tradition, a position radically different from Handlin's *gemeinschaft/gessellschaft* model. I portrayed Italian immigrants, women and men, as active agents sometimes drawing upon past practices and values, sometimes adapting to their new circumstances in novel ways. My insertion of women into the immigration narrative was a feminist initiative. I felt, nonetheless, that women of the past should be understood in terms of their own perceptions and values, their own phenomenology, not mine. The Italian women I studied chose not to work outside the home unless their children accompanied them to work; they were not radical labor leaders (though they did join strike protests). But to characterize these women as submissive or even passive (as some mistakenly thought I had done) would be to impose modern feminist, individualistic values upon them. As I learned from my own family background, women's power takes many complex forms whether women worked within or outside the home, whether they were radicals or not, whether they put their families before themselves.[8]

It was a short step to proclaiming that not only written history but also history embodied in films, exhibits, and public history could encourage ordinary men and women to recognize themselves as masters of their own destinies. In the 1970s I worked with Herb Gutman, the distinguished oral historian Ronald Grele, and a group of graduate students and faculty at City University New York Graduate Center to collect workers' oral histories. We asked a broad spectrum of workers of different ethnicities and races to document their memories and perceptions of their past lives.

This 1970s project laid the foundation for what later became the American Social History Project, an innovative and prolific producer of texts and videos aiming to integrate the history of ordinary people into the history of the United States. As the daughter of laborers and craftspeople who produced concrete, material manifestations of their labor, I felt uncommon satisfaction in the production of material and visual culture such as exhibits, interpretation of historic places, and films done in collaboration with others. Since 1983, I have collaborated with museum professionals, historic preservationists, architects, and the National Park Service staff on the rehabilitation and accompanying exhibits for the Statue of Liberty Ellis Island National Monument, one of the nation's most heavily visited museum and tourist sites. This ongoing project situates immigration at the center of the American and, more recently, global history. I feel privileged to have played a role in this ongoing project and to have created a film biography of Margaret Mead. Both of these are once-in-a-lifetime projects for any historian; both of them affirm my belief that democratic popular culture forms can successfully translate and affirm the importance of history to public life and to a broad public.

Last, but certainly not least, there is my teaching. Indeed, I purposefully chose to write this coming-of-age essay instead of a full report of my academic career. I hope my peers will find my biography of historiographical interest. But I write especially for future and aspiring young historians, particularly those from working-class and immigrant families, who may feel uncertain of their place in the academy or other history professions. I write also for my graduate students, past, present, and future. Among these students, "Ginny's rainbow children," as one of my colleagues calls them,[9] are descendants of European immigrants (including four Italian Americans), two African Americans, an Argentinean, a Hungarian-Filipino, a Lebanese-Cuban, an Irish-Puerto Rican, and students who call Canada, Japan, and Korea home. Not all of these "rainbow children" studied immigration, ethnicity, women, or culture, but I speculate that all of them chose me, consciously or not, as I chose my mentor: they found echoes of their own representational worlds, their own phenomenology, their own passions in my thinking and acting. I affectionately salute my "rainbow children" even as I salute my mentors and collaborators for our mutual engagement in the process of becoming historians.

Notes

1. Robert D. Stolorow and George E. Atwood, *Faces in a Cloud: Subjectivity in Personality-Theory* (New York: Jason Aronson, 1979), documents subjectivity in psychoanalysts' work biographies.
2. http://www.mainlesson.com/displayauthor.php?author=perkins.
3. Elizabeth Perkins, *The Japanese Twins*, 178, http://www.mainlesson.com/display.php?author=perkins&book=japanese&story=taro.
4. See Sara Heinamaa, "Simone de Beauvoir's Phenomenology of Sexual Difference," *Hypatia* 14, no. 4 (Fall 1999): 114–132.
5. E-mail letter from Nancy Sinkoff, February 14, 2012.
6. Herbert Gutman, "Labor History and the 'Sartre Question,'" *Humanities* 1 (September–October 1980), in Herbert Gutman, *Power and Culture: Essays on the American Working Class*, ed. Ira Berlin (New York: Pantheon Books, 1987), 326; see also 346, in the same

book, from "Interview with Herbert Gutman," reprinted from *MARHO, the Radical Historians Organization, Visions of History*, ed. H. Abelove, B. Blackmar, P. Dimock, and J. Schneer (New York: Pantheon Books, 1983), 185–216. Although translated differently, David Gerber also uses this widely circulated Sartre quote in his introduction to this book. Neither of us could determine its source, but the quote is widely accepted as an accurate description of Sartre's philosophy.

7. Rudolph. J. Vecoli, "'Contadini' in Chicago: A Critique of *The Uprooted*," *Journal of American History* 51 (December 1964): 404–417, originally deconstructed the Handlin paradigm.

8. Virginia Yans-McLaughlin, *Family and Community: Italian Immigrants in Buffalo, 1880– 1930* (Ithaca, N.Y.: Cornell University Press, 1977), paperback edition (Urbana: University of Illinois Press, 1982). I refer here to some critics who, I believe, imposed feminist and political agendas upon Italian immigrant women.

9. This is my Rutgers University colleague Susan Shrepfer's description.

3

Sidewalk Histories

DEBORAH DASH MOORE

In third grade, our class took a memorable field trip to do stone rubbings. I attended Downtown Community School (DCS), a parent-teacher cooperative. A progressive and integrated elementary school, DCS typically linked art projects with social studies, in this case, the required local history curriculum on New York City. However, instead of taking our gear across the street into the cemetery of St. Marks on the Bowery, where we might have done classic rubbings of early American gravestones, we walked around the school neighborhood staring at the sidewalks. When we found a manhole cover, we stopped, pulled out the paper and charcoal, and made a rubbing. How many different metal covers adorned the streets of lower Manhattan! While I don't recall the exact number, I think we rubbed well over a dozen patterns. Each one, we learned, had been placed by a corporation and represented some type of utility underneath the city's streets. Gas, electric, water, sewage, and telephone were most popular, but we also found old covers from defunct companies—an education in nineteenth-century history.[1]

Manhole covers and their lessons stuck with me. Even as I acquired a steadfast commitment to studying the city, I remain fascinated with their often-elegant designs. The covers also hint at some of the characteristics of ethnic history, especially the ease of overlooking what is in plain sight and the rewards of careful excavation of mundane historical features. I learned secrets of New York City in third grade just by examining manhole covers. So, too, did I come to realize that Jewish ethnicity required a similar sensitivity to pleasant and appealing facades that blended nicely within their milieu. Such is the power of acculturation. It naturalizes ethnic distinctiveness, seeming to reduce it to symbolic dimensions that appear on occasion as the calendar and life cycle demand.[2] Yet the reality is far more complex with visible clues suggesting, just like manhole covers, that all that is needed is curiosity and a willingness to look.

I didn't start examining Jews with any measure of historical consciousness until I attended high school, but I did regularly see the city, taking its measure as I traveled its streets. These observations implicitly linked the Jewish world of my family and childhood with New York's urban milieu. As my passion for history blossomed, so did my love for my rather Jewish city.

My New York City meant Manhattan; my Manhattan meant Greenwich Village. In the 1950s, *the city* referred only to New York, the biggest and baddest city of all, the one I grew up in, the one my parents had grown up in, the one three of my grandparents had known as children (my other grandmother grew up in New Haven). I called my neighborhood The Village even though I lived on the corner of Sixteenth Street and Seventh Avenue, two blocks north of Greenwich Village's boundary. (Chelsea had no cachet then.) It was a treeless world of concrete sidewalks where we played games, rode our bikes, roller-skated, jumped rope, and bounced balls. Its urbanism also manifested itself in its mixed class and ethnic character. I lived in one of three middle-class twenty-story apartment buildings that dominated the corners; lower middle-class six-story apartments lined my block of Sixteenth Street, along with a small French church next to the Hebrew Arts School; across Seventh Avenue on Sixteenth Street, working-class six-story tenements housed a Catholic mix of Irish, Puerto Ricans, and Italians. In addition, the neighborhood contained a fairly standard urban combination of industry and commerce along the avenue: factories, offices and bars, as well as candy stores, drugstores, newsstands, and a grocery.

My points on the compass also measured my father and grandfather's place of work. The family printing business initially stood on Greene Street in a dark building with creaking wooden stairs, then across Seventh Avenue in a modern factory building on Seventeenth Street with an elevator, later on Nineteenth Street and Sixth Avenue in what had been an elegant department store before World War I. Much later, after I had graduated from college, a final move took the firm to the corner of Varick and Houston Streets. Growing up, we could gaze out our eleventh-floor living-room window into my grandfather's Seventeenth Street office. Subsequently, I learned that the Jewish builder who constructed our buildings in 1928–1929—and subsequently lost his shirt in the Depression—intended the apartments for people working nearby. The printing industry, one of the city's largest, stretched along Seventh Avenue, from Canal Street up to Twenty-third Street. My parents could not have found a more convenient apartment.

In elementary school, the spine of my urban knowledge stretched along Fourteenth Street, which I traveled daily to get to school. A major crosstown artery, Fourteenth Street contained many clothing, fabric, and hardware stores, Salvation Army headquarters and union locals, an occasional restaurant (Luchow's near Union Square), a huge Con Edison building (across from Luchow's), and pawnshops. These features I noticed; others passed me by. I regularly walked along Second Avenue across from the Café Royale, a popular Yiddish theater hangout, and ignored it, only later realizing that it was once a landmark of the Yiddish intelligentsia. Aside from the kosher dairy restaurant Ratner's (which did not serve meat but did offer delicious onion rolls at every table) further south on Second Avenue, I remained oblivious of much of the area's character as the Yiddish theater center. Instead I gravitated to Washington Square Park, initially for its playgrounds and later for its folk music, fountain, and coffeehouses south of the square.

If I paid no particular attention to the remaining Yiddish theater scene, I did recognize Jewish religious and ethnic culture, both as it existed in my neighborhood and as it flourished on the Upper West Side. I understood from my brief attendance at Hebrew school in a small, Orthodox congregation on Charles Street in the Village and classes in dance and music at the Hebrew Arts School up the block that Jews were part of the city's religious and ethnic environment. As were Catholics: Saint Francis Xavier Church and parochial school dominated a section of Sixteenth Street east of Sixth Avenue; I never failed to notice it (though I never entered) when I walked by to visit girlfriends who lived on the block. I also took in the rich, visible Jewish ethnic and religious culture on the Upper West Side. Our family attended the Society for the Advancement of Judaism (SAJ) on west Eighty-sixth Street for Jewish holidays, joining my maternal grandparents, who were supporters of Rabbi Mordecai M. Kaplan and Reconstructionist Judaism, a small innovative religious movement with a radical theology and conservative observance. After services, we occasionally went to Steinberg's dairy restaurant on Broadway, or the Tip Toe Inn at the corner of Eighty-sixth Street. The many kosher bakeries, butcher shops, and small stores along Broadway registered in my consciousness. Occasional trips down to Orchard Street to buy yarn for hooked rugs added the Lower East Side to my urban Jewish geography.

Years of Hebrew school at the SAJ, including study for bat mitzvah, followed by four additional years of Hebrew High School, introduced me not only to Jewish religious life but also stimulated intellectual interest in studying Jews. Neither urban nor Jewish history appeared on the curriculum at the public High School of Music & Art (M&A) but Hebrew High School, a cooperative project supported by three congregations—the SAJ, Park Avenue Synagogue, and B'nai Jeshurun—encouraged me to study both. The Jewish labor movement—an urban subject if ever there was one—formed the topic of my first serious research paper, which I wrote for Paul Ritterband, head of the school and at the beginning of his illustrious career as a sociologist of American Jews. The opportunity to fuse the histories of New York and American Jews presaged my growing passions for both, and for their moral dimensions, especially the struggles to provide decent living conditions for working men and women.

As a teenager, I never questioned my life's particular urban ethnic synthesis or its association of aspects of my identity with different institutions. I absorbed the textured dimensions of New York society, noting how varieties of Jewishness appeared in public and private. In this way, I learned urban history together with Jewish history. By then I regularly traveled the length of Manhattan up to 137th Street and Broadway. I studied modern dance at Martha Graham's studios on Sixty-first Street by the East River and Israeli dance at the Ninety-Second Street YMHA on Lexington Avenue; I learned French at M&A and Hebrew at Hebrew High School; I lived downtown at the edge of the Village and went to high school uptown on the border of Harlem. Urban New York Jewishness could be found throughout the city as travels around town for my studies and various extracurricular activities demonstrated. When I encountered strangers, they occasionally took my combination of blue eyes and pug nose for Irish. Such mistakes amused me even though I usually sized up the city's residents according to a similar visual ethnic calculus. The notion that we were all White, as historians later taught, would have seemed irrelevant at the time. We were all different New Yorkers; we all picked up ethnic cues. The color line mattered on the subways and sidewalks, but not at M&A or Downtown Community School.

I left the city for college in 1963. Brandeis University in Waltham, near Boston, seemed to me to be almost rural. The campus had lots of trees, a couple of ponds, and winding paths from the dormitories to the classrooms. To reach the city of Boston required a train ride. Yet like New York, Brandeis allowed for uninhibited public expressions of Jewishness. One evening during freshman orientation, a large group of us formed circles for Israeli dances outside in the quad. I found it exhilarating. Brandeis closed for the Jewish holidays, not just the High Holidays of Rosh Hashanah and Yom Kippur as the New York City public schools did, but also the holidays of Sukkot and Shemini Atzeret. At Brandeis, I realized with pleasure, I could study French and Hebrew, and do both modern and Israeli dance all in one place.

Yet while Jewish studies and American history figured during my college years, they remained distinct as they had in high school. At Brandeis I gravitated to African American history (then called Negro history). Black history appealed to me. So did urban history. Both seemed to resemble my version of American Jewish history and provided an acceptable way to explore moral questions stemming from exploitation that I had plumbed in my paper on the Jewish labor movement in New York. My experiences at M&A and DCS heightened my consciousness of Black history. (I did a research project in sixth grade on

Frederick Douglass. My parents had never heard of him and thought I had been assigned Stephen Douglas.) My friendships crossed the color line and my politics impelled me to join boycotts of Woolworth's to support integration of their lunch counters in the South. Although marginally active in civil rights protests, I felt a deep commitment to integration and considered myself a liberal. I did a senior honors thesis under David Hackett Fischer's supervision on two cities during Reconstruction—Baltimore and St. Louis—paying attention to implications of their border status and the roles of free Blacks. When I returned to New York as a graduate student at Columbia University, I intended to focus on Black history during the era of Reconstruction. I did manage to complete an MA thesis on Robert Smalls, a Black politician from South Carolina during Reconstruction. I even got my first job teaching African American history.

Then politics intervened. The year 1970 was a year of upheaval on college campuses and students at Montclair State College in New Jersey, where I was teaching, wanted the history department to hire an African American. With only White faculty members in the department, my political sympathies lay with the students and their identity politics. So I switched my teaching to American history, including a course on the Civil War and Reconstruction. But the experience spurred me to reflect on my identity as a Jew, a woman, a New Yorker. The feminist movement had raised my consciousness, making me aware of how all my professors had been men.

Losing the opportunity to teach Black history after only one semester prompted me to reconsider my graduate studies. Perhaps it would make sense to turn to one of my enduring intellectual interests that actually coincided with my identity. I had claims on American Jewish history worth pressing. I had always loved studying Jews and identified Jewishness with scholarly rigor and excitement. Taking courses at Hebrew High School with such teachers as Paul Ritterband and the gifted historian Yosef Yerushalmi when he was a graduate student had been immensely rewarding. I had already met Gerson D. Cohen, the senior Jewish historian at Columbia, when I wanted to make Jewish history my minor concentration. In an intimidating interview, he nonetheless encouraged me to study American Jewish history at Columbia. Now I contemplated switching fields, making my minor the major, melding American history with Jewish history. I did not realize at the time that I was embarking on a project that would take decades: American Jewish history as a field did not exist. Yet the more I studied its complex and fascinating components, the more determined I became to give it legitimacy; just as African American history and Women's history acquired acceptance with significant political reverberations, so, too, could American Jewish history. Recognition would change how we thought about the American past. Gradually I realized that recognition would also change how historians thought about the Jewish past.

Only one book on American Jews ever crossed over into my history courses: Moses Rischin's *The Promised City*.[3] John A. Garraty assigned it as reading in his seminar on the Gilded Age. Rischin examined New York Jews from 1870 to 1914. He linked the history of Jewish immigrants with that of the city. My favorite chapter in the book—Chapter 5—presents his incredibly rich excavation of diverse residential patterns and quotidian life on the Lower East Side. It remains a fecund source of historical insight to this day. The diagrams of dumbbell tenements and maps of Jewish ethnic concentration within the East Side opened my eyes to dimensions of urban Jewish history. Rischin later explained that he had been influenced by the Annales School of historians, trying to integrate their insights and methodology.[4] I had not read studies by the Annales School, but *The Promised City* spoke to me as an exciting way to research and write American Jewish history.

Before I settled on a dissertation topic, David J. Rothman gave me a dissertation to read that had just won the Bancroft prize: Arthur Goren's study of the New York Kehillah (Jewish community), subsequently published as *New York Jews and the Quest for Community*.[5] Goren picked up the story of New York City Jews in 1908 and carried it through World War I to 1922. Using communal organization as a framework, he examined a number of topics that had never been studied, such as Jewish criminal activity. Although he focused less than Rischin on neighborhood ecology, he elucidated dimensions of communal culture that tested possibilities for urban democratic community, a concern he shared with Rischin. Invaluable pioneering models, both books pointed to New York Jews as a worthy historical subject and the interwar years as an ideal time period that had not yet been studied.

Here I entered virgin territory in the guise of following in the eminent footsteps of Rischin and Goren. Both had studied immigrants in the city, but in shifting my gaze to the period that saw the triumph of immigration restriction in 1924, I gravitated to children of immigrants. Thus, I conceptualized American Jewish history as an integral part of urban and social history, my first step toward establishing it as a separate field. Historians had ignored the second-generation; sociologists had dismissed it as a conflicted, weak cohort eager to escape immigrant neighborhoods and forget its foreign past in order to become American. Marcus Lee Hansen posited that only the third generation wanted to remember; Will Herberg popularized Hansen's "law" in his book, *Protestant Catholic Jew*.[6] The second generation lacked credibility and status, especially in the eyes of such second-generation writers as Nathan Glazer: one of the reasons he reprinted Hansen's essay in *Commentary* magazine was to assuage worried American Jews. "Hansen's essay threw a new light on the question of acculturation and assimilation," Glazer pointed out, "it suggested that not only was there no historical inevitability in the steady and monotonic decline of identity, allegiance, interest, commitment, but there was also reason to expect a change in direction in some of these features in the third generation."[7]

I intended to study not the storied, rich immigrant "ghetto," but what Louis Wirth called "areas of second settlement," neighborhoods that many didn't perceive as particularly Jewish.[8] Had I not been a New York Jew myself, I probably would have accepted Wirth and other sociologists at face value. But I knew that my grandparents had lived in a Jewish world in Brooklyn in neighborhoods Wirth would have considered "areas of second settlement"—the world my parents had grown up in. I had other authorities to which I could turn: second-generation Jews: they had reared a third generation. And that third generation, my parents, had raised my sister and me. Reaching back into the experiences of New York Jews in the interwar decades allowed me to reclaim my own history, revising the city's history in the process.

Of course, I didn't start there. As a good social historian, I started with numbers, specifically the 1925 New York State census. After poring over manuscript census returns, I discovered what a host of Jewish neighborhood surveys had demonstrated: Jews tended to congregate in certain sections of Brooklyn and the Bronx, as well as parts of upper Manhattan. This concentration posed a question: How did Jews get to these neighborhoods? The most straightforward answer came from urban historians who studied transportation networks and their role in dispersing populations. Sam Bass Warner Jr.'s *Streetcar Suburbs* helped me to account for such changes.[9] But why did Jews choose some neighborhoods and not others, although residential discrimination certainly prevented Jews from renting in some sections of the city? Neither Warner, nor Wirth's theories of urban migration, helped much. So I turned to my family, specifically my mother's mother.

Bella Lasker Golden had grown up in Brownsville, Brooklyn, and lived there as a young married woman until her husband's printing business began to prosper. Then she moved to other neighborhoods in Brooklyn, especially Flatbush, and continued to move as the business struggled during the Depression before recovering. A final move in 1939 carried her out of Brooklyn to Emery Roth's elegant *art moderne* apartment building in Manhattan, The Normandy, stretching between Eighty-sixth and Eighty-seventh Streets on Riverside Drive. Several brothers stayed in Brooklyn. One day, she asked her older brother, Morris, who lived in Sea Gate by Coney Island, to drive the two of us around the borough. I sat in the backseat as she pointed out tenements, apartment buildings, private houses, synagogues, and community centers—the diverse urban streetscape of Brooklyn Jews. And when I asked her why she picked one neighborhood over another as she moved, she described informal Jewish networks that connected those seeking a place to live with those building the homes. She even introduced me to some of these builders. They explained how they switched from the manufacture of buttons or blouses to apartments. I learned from them the ethnic calculus of the city's construction industry and how they assembled the pieces required for building an apartment house, from finance to designs, from scheduling contractors to ordering supplies. Newly attuned to these dimensions of urban ethnic behavior, I located books, articles, and newspapers that provided lively prose accounts. I called the chapter "Jewish Geography," punning on a Jewish practice of seeking to locate common acquaintances.

My focus on Brooklyn and Bronx Jewish neighborhoods drew upon Rischin's insights into the Lower East Side's physical world. Instead of dumbbell tenements, I described art deco apartment buildings (even including a blueprint of a typical layout).[10] Instead of immigrant ethnic groups, I mapped political and religious networks. The neighborhood emerged as the heart of my story, the place where Jewish and American features could get shuffled and sorted out, the space where Jews could leave their stamp upon the city. Later, I argued that these areas articulated a Jewish urban vision through their modern apartment houses on tree-lined streets.[11] I knew from experience how parochial a neighborhood could be even in the most cosmopolitan of cities. I knew, too, how one could cross invisible boundaries created by ethnic and other groups. I had learned to walk on the east side of Seventh Avenue and not the west to gain a bit of distance from the bars, and I also regularly took a more circuitous route to the public library on Thirteenth Street to avoid the technical high school on the block and the teenaged boys hanging out there. I possessed local knowledge.

Once I realized that I could talk to people and not rely exclusively on numbers and written sources, I conducted more interviews. Oral history was developing as a relatively new field in the 1970s. Herbert Gutman had initiated an oral history project with retired union garment workers, but most formal oral history projects targeted famous or influential people. I read a number of interviews, including one with Herbert Lehman, the Democratic Jewish governor of New York (1933–1942). However, I soon realized that if I wanted to learn about Jewish state assemblymen or local political figures beyond what the press reported, I had to speak with them or with sons who followed in their fathers' footsteps. Judge Nathan Sobel gave me an interview. Walking across Court Street to one of his favorite Brooklyn restaurants, we attracted looks—older man and younger miniskirted graduate student—and a few good-natured comments. Sobel told me about the first time he tasted clam chowder as well as the intricacies of running for office and choosing which synagogue to join. Stanley Steingut, state assemblyman from Brooklyn (1953–1978), received me in his assemblyman's office. Just seeing the long wooden table with him sitting at its head taught me something about expressions of political influence.

Political figures, public school teachers, and builders responded to my questions often from their own agendas. Most New York Jews knew why they moved where they did, why they took the jobs they worked at, why they pursued their politics, and why they joined or refused to join a Jewish organization. My interpretations, especially after they were published when I would give public lectures, often failed to match their own understanding of their Jewish experiences in New York City. To start with, they thought of themselves as first-generation Americans. The Jewish American story began with them, not their immigrant parents. They spun narratives of assimilation, whereas I emphasized enduring Jewishness. Some of what they perceived as American, I described as Jewish. And my account occasionally seemed to slight their achievements, though I had not intended to do so.

Academic audiences were different. By the time I finished my dissertation, called "The Persistence of Ethnicity," a title that reflected my explicit argument with social scientists, I discovered that I had entered a field that barely existed. I couldn't follow Rischin, who held an appointment at San Francisco State University as an American historian.[12] Nor could I follow Goren, who held an appointment at the Hebrew University of Jerusalem, in American Studies.[13] As scholars of Jewish immigration, both were recognized as American historians but both had traveled a significant distance from New York. In Jerusalem and San Francisco, New York City was hardly familiar territory. I, on the other hand, intended to forge a path as an American Jewish historian, despite the field's newness and the profound reluctance on the part of some Jewish historians even to consider American Jews worthy of historical attention. The brief American Jewish past warranted good journalism, they claimed, not serious historical study.

In the 1970s, social history, urban history, oral history, Black history, and women's history were reconfiguring historical study of the United States. As a young woman graduate student, I participated in these movements to rethink American history. For several years, I posted in my office a cartoon by Jules Feiffer portraying a befuddled hard-hatted man. First he describes the American history he learned as a child; then he describes what his son is learning. His conclusion: they're teaching his son some other country's history. I decided upon graduation to define myself as an American Jewish historian and agreed to start teaching the subject to graduate students at the Max Weinreich Center for Advanced Jewish Studies at the YIVO Institute for Jewish Research in Manhattan. Without realizing it, I had entered another intellectual world with deep roots in Eastern Europe and Yiddish culture. My association with the YIVO widened my perspectives on social science research and introduced me to new ways of studying immigrants. YIVO had pioneered in the use of autobiography by young men and women in order to elicit narratives of self-transformation as well as detailed descriptions of everyday life.[14]

The path from "The Persistence of Ethnicity" (1975) to *At Home in America: Second Generation New York Jews, 1920–1940* (1981) involved several additional way stations that modified my understanding of New York Jews. Most important,

I accepted a position in the Religion Department of Vassar College. It was an odd turn of events. Vassar had been my mother's dream school, the one that didn't admit her due to quotas for Jewish public school students from Brooklyn. Furthermore, neither Vassar nor religious studies had been on my radar. Considering myself an American Jewish historian, I assumed I would continue to live in New York City. Vassar, located seventy miles north of the city on the Hudson River in Poughkeepsie, appeared even more rural than Brandeis, though like Brandeis, regular train service connected it to New York. (I would become familiar with the vagaries of train travel when we moved to Poughkeepsie in 1976.) Indeed, I presented something of a leap of faith for my colleagues in the Religion department. In my job interview as I strolled in Vassar's Shakespeare Garden with a future colleague, a scholar and Christian minister, he asked if I would be happy as a historian in a religion department. I answered as a good New York Jew with my own question. Would he be happy with a historian in a religion department? Both answers turned out to be affirmative.

When *At Home in America* appeared as the first volume of a new series on urban history in New York City under the editorial direction of Kenneth Jackson, it seemed as if I had achieved my goal of synthesizing Jewish and American urban history. Jackson had encouraged me to publish in his Columbia History of Urban Life series because he felt that urban historians had not paid enough attention to New York, one of the world's great cities. Jackson's passion came at a particularly low point in the city's history. Teetering on the verge of bankruptcy, hemorrhaging population to the suburbs, plagued by wholesale abandonment of housing stock (especially in the Bronx, much of it owned by Jews), and a dramatic rise in crime, the city looked as if it were heading for disaster. Although a new publishing venture could hardly rescue New York, it could help contemporaries understand its past, both its mistakes and accomplishments. The series continues to publish impressive studies, many of them pathbreaking, and to exert an enormous impact on urban history by bringing New York into a position of central importance.[15] Jackson's prediction that my book would remain in print for many years proved true.

Yet synthesis eluded me for more than a decade. In 1994, I spoke as a professor of religion and the director of the American Culture Program at Vassar at a session on "Regional History as National History" under the auspices of the American Jewish Historical Society.[16] My paper mentioned barriers to acceptance still faced by American Jewish historians and employed urban metaphors to characterize modern Jewish historical studies. When I remarked that only one chair existed in American Jewish history in a non-Jewish university in the United States, the Salo Baron chair at Columbia University held by Arthur A. Goren, my audience gasped. Later, several men and women questioned me. They were surprised. They assumed that American Jewish history had entered the academic mainstream. Writing now as Frederick G. L. Huetwell Professor of History and director of the Frankel Center for Judaic Studies undoubtedly influences my interpretation. What seemed frustratingly impossible in 1994 has actually been achieved. American Jewish history is a field with several chairs, senior and junior professors, not to mention graduate students. The opposition of Jewish historians has faded. Some American historians ignore the field and others encourage American Jewish historians to devote less attention to communal issues and more to questions that animate scholars of American history.[17] Still, I consider the transformation significant.

At Home in America provoked diverse responses from scholars.[18] Some challenged my claims for the centrality of New York Jews in the United States. They rejected the idea that New Yorkers set a pattern recognized by other American Jews, what critic Robert Warshow called "the master pattern."[19] New York Jews made up 40 percent of the total American Jewish population in the middle decades of the twentieth century and formed a critical mass of two million in the largest Jewish city in history. How could these Jews not exert exceptional influence on other American Jews? I told a compelling history in At Home in America, but some argued it described only a particular, not a representative, group. Other scholars objected to "generation" as an organizing concept for a cohort. They noted, correctly, that large numbers of Jewish immigrants began arriving in the 1880s and 1890s and that a second generation emerged in the early twentieth century as well. Still others challenged my upbeat tone, my unwillingness to give antisemitism its due. They doubted my optimism.[20] What I characterized as being "at home in America," Jonathan Sarna called "a parallel universe that shared many of the trappings of the larger society."[21] Not attuned to New York's rambunctious urbanism, he failed to recognize how the city consisted of many parallel ethnic worlds that together created a larger whole. Like most New Yorkers, second-generation Jews found their paths into the city through their neighborhoods. Eli Lederhendler contended that the second generation's achievements collapsed after World War II under the twin impact of suburbanization and a growing African American population in the city.[22]

These critiques came later. When At Home appeared in January 1981, it managed to cross over into courses on American urban history, following in the footsteps of The Promised City, and occupied an important place in the still emerging field of American Jewish history. Reviewed widely by sociologists as well as historians, the book attracted attention in the Jewish press as well. Its title, At Home in America, articulated a powerful thesis that had sturdy legs, even when historians questioned it.[23] My title answered Irving Howe's last chapter query, "At Ease in America?" in his history of Eastern European Jewish immigrants in New York, World of Our Fathers.[24] It asserted the integrated Jewishness of New York Jews, a perspective informed not only by my understanding of New

York Jews' experiences in the interwar years but also by my perceptions growing up as a Jewish city girl.

One review of *At Home* recognized its intimate dimensions. Writing in *Commentary* magazine, David Singer bemoaned the "fair number of statistical tables," but he also remarked, "these are more than made up for by the abundant photographs, some of them charmingly amateurish, that dot the volume."[25] Singer was an astute critic. Photographs were a rarity in works of scholarship in 1981. Although he did not explicitly comment that I had used a number of family pictures, his characterization of them as "charmingly amateurish" recognized their snapshot attributes. When it came time to choose illustrations, I raided my family's collections. The cover photograph featured my grandparents as a young married couple in the back yard of their Brownsville Brooklyn home. Behind them appear flowering bushes and a six-story tenement looms in the background. They pose for the camera; my grandfather, standing behind my grandmother, leans over his wife's shoulder. Both are well dressed in stylish clothes. My grandmother wears a white dress that she sewed; my grandfather wears a suit, white collar, and elegant tie. Two of my grandmother's brothers, her oldest brother, Morris, and her youngest brother, Teddy, stand next to them. Morris, a big grin on his face, is dressed casually, his shirtsleeves rolled up. Teddy wears a sleeveless undershirt, a sign of his youth; a large cap shades his eyes. When the photo was taken, Morris was living with my grandparents, although I never determined whether he paid rent.

The photo conveyed to me important aspects of *At Home*. It pictured a Jewish tenement home in Brownsville (I included an interior shot inside the book). To the extent that one could glean emotion from a snapshot, it portrayed what Jews felt about living in this predominantly Jewish working-class neighborhood in the early 1920s. The photo had been sufficiently important to be placed in an album. As my book cover, it also hinted at insights I had gathered from family who lived as New York Jews. Finally, the photo gestured in gratitude to my family members for an introduction to their world. (Teddy always appreciated that he had appeared on the cover of a book. Many years later, at my younger son's bar mitzvah, he still talked about it.)

In some ways, the photographs constituted my version of manhole cover rubbings. I delighted in placing them in plain sight, properly titled and credited. They were visible markers of an infrastructure undergirding the book. That infrastructure that sustained my research, stimulated intellectual questions, and guided my commitments to become an American Jewish historian could be found in my family. I had learned in third grade history lessons on New York's sidewalks how to pay attention to ordinary dimensions of the urban world. Those lessons traveled with me on many trips to Brooklyn and the Bronx. They helped me recognize expressions of Jewishness throughout the city and encouraged me to seek critical ethnic connections fueling the growth of the metropolis.

FIGURE 2. Bella and Samuel Golden, the author's grandparents, outside their Brownsville, Brooklyn, home, with two of Bella's brothers, Teddy (on right) and Morris, circa 1920. Courtesy Bella Golden.

Notes

1. As Mimi Melnick writes, "Water, Power, Sewer, Gas, Telephone, Steam: each cover has a story to tell." In Mimi Melnick, *Manhole Covers* (Cambridge, Mass.: MIT Press, 1994), 1.

2. The sociologist Herbert Gans calls this "symbolic ethnicity." Herbert Gans, "Symbolic Ethnicity: The Future of Ethnic Groups and Cultures in America," *Ethnic and Racial Studies* 2, no. 1 (January 1979): 1–20.

3. Moses Rischin, *The Promised City: New York's Jews, 1870–1914* (Cambridge, Mass.: Harvard University Press, 1962). No book on American Jews ever appeared on the syllabus of Jewish history courses on modern Jewish history or Zionist thought that I took at Columbia University. These courses focused on European Jews.

4. This followed my discussion of that chapter; see Deborah Dash Moore, "The Ideal Slum," *American Jewish History* 73, no. 2 (December 1983): 134–141, in this issue of *American Jewish History* devoted to his pioneering book.

5. Arthur A. Goren, *New York Jews and the Quest for Community: The Kehillah Experiment, 1908–1922* (New York: Columbia University Press, 1979).

6. Will Herberg, *Protestant Catholic Jew: An Essay in American Religious Sociology* (Garden City, N.Y.: Doubleday, 1956).

7. Nathan Glazer, "Hansen's Hypothesis and the Historical Experience of Generations," in *American Immigrants and Their Generations*, ed. Peter Kivisto and Dag Blanck (Urbana: University of Illinois Press, 1990), 107. "The reprinting of Hansen's essay in 1952 was occasioned by the concern of a second generation Jew (and a journal edited by second generation Jews) about the coming third generation," Glazer explained.

8. Louis Wirth, *The Ghetto* (Chicago: University of Chicago Press, 1928).

9. Sam Bass Warner, *Streetcar Suburbs: The Process of Growth in Boston, 1870–1900* (Cambridge, Mass.: Harvard University Press, 1962).

10. Deborah Dash Moore, *At Home in America: Second Generation New York Jews 1920–1940* (New York: Columbia University Press, 1981), 37.

11. Deborah Dash Moore, "The Urban Vision of East European Jewish Immigrants to New York," *Proceedings of the Eighth World Congress of Jewish Studies, Panel Sessions: Jewish History* (Jerusalem, 1984): 31–38.

12. Rischin had not anticipated where his career would lead. See Moses Rischin, "Jewish Studies in Northern California: A Symposium," *Judaism* 44, no. 4 (Fall 1995): 417–419.

13. Arthur Aryeh Goren, "Epilogue: On Living in Two Cultures," *Divergent Jewish Cultures: Israel & America*, ed. Deborah Dash Moore and S. Ilan Troen (New Haven: Yale University Press, 2001), 333–350.

14. *Awakening Lives: Autobiographies of Jewish Youth in Poland before the Holocaust*, ed. Jeffrey Shandler (New Haven: Yale University Press, 2002).

15. Edward K. Spann's *The New Metropolis* was the second book published in the series. The next book on New York Jews in the Columbia History of Urban Life was by Andrew R. Heinze, *Adapting to Abundance: Jewish Immigrants, Mass Consumption, and the Search for American Identity* (New York: Columbia University Press, 1992).

16. Published as Deborah Dash Moore, "I'll Take Manhattan: Reflections on Jewish Studies," *Judaism* 44, no. 4 (Fall 1995): 420–426.

17. See David A. Hollinger, "Communalist and Dispersionist Approaches to American Jewish History in an Increasingly Post-Jewish Era," *American Jewish History* 95, no. 1 (March 2009): 1–32, and responses by Hasia Diner, Paula Hyman, Alan M. Kraut, and Tony Michels, 33–71.

18. See Deborah Dash Moore, "At Home in America? Revisiting the Second Generation," *Journal of American Ethnic History* (Winter–Spring 2006): 156–168.

19. Robert S. Warshow, "Poet of the Jewish Middle Class," *Commentary* (May 1946): 17.

20. Todd M. Endelman, "The Legitimation of the Diaspora Experience," *Broadening Jewish History: Towards a Social History of Ordinary Jews* (Oxford: Littman Library, 2011), 57.

21. Jonathan Sarna, *American Judaism: A History* (New Haven: Yale University Press, 2004), 222. As a second-generation Jew, Sarna also discounts the generational model as useful for understanding American Jewish history.

22. Eli Lederhendler, *New York Jews and the Decline of Urban Ethnicity 1950–1970* (Syracuse, N.Y.: Syracuse University Press, 2001).

23. Leonard Dinnerstein, *Uneasy at Home* (New York: Columbia University Press, 1987).

24. Irving Howe and Kenneth Libo, *World of Our Fathers: The Journey of the East European Jews to America and the Life They Found and Made* (New York: Harcourt, Brace, Jovanovich, 1976), 608.

25. David Singer, "Second Generation," *Commentary* (July 1981): 73.

4

Coal Town Chronicles and Scholarly Books

JOHN BODNAR

Growing up in Forest City in the 1950s, I caught a glimpse of a world that was rapidly vanishing. The once-booming anthracite coal industry of northeastern Pennsylvania was nearly at an end after reaching its peak around the time of World War I. I understand they still existed when I was a small child, but I have no conscious memory of seeing the actual mines or the large breaker erected by the Hillside Coal and Iron Company that shot nearly one hundred feet into the air and dominated the sky at the southeast end of town. I saw only remnants of an earlier time—a large slag heap at the end of the street where I lived, old people who spoke broken English, and ethnic churches built by newcomers from Ireland, Lithuania, Poland, Slovakia, and Slovenia.

Although I never saw the real fabric of this world, I heard about it all the time. The stories came typically from my father's parents, John Bodnar and Mary Matircho, who lived most of their adult lives in the shadow of the breaker and a bustling silk mill where they could easily walk to work. Even when I left Forest City in the 1960s for educational and professional opportunities they could never have imagined for themselves, I never forgot the stories they told me about their lives and the struggles they endured. Life in their corner of industrial America was never a simple account of getting ahead or—for that matter—falling behind.

Mary was born in Forest City in 1893, the daughter of a Slovak miner and his wife, both of whom had immigrated to America a few years earlier. She was feisty, energetic, and—I think—ambitious. Her sense of perpetual vitality was offset by my grandfather, who was one of the gentlest men I have ever known. Part mystic, part immigrant miner, he spent hours of his leisure time reading his well-worn book of prayers printed in Old Church Slavonic, a devotional practice he had learned from his father in Klecenov, a small village in what is now eastern Slovakia. Contrasting personas, however, did not wipe away the fact that both John and Mary lived within the confines of a tightly knit community where one's well-being was highly fragile and where individuals were expected to conform to the demands of family, work, and church.

Mary Matircho grew up in a small neighborhood at the bottom of a long hill near the railroad tracks that brought newcomers to the town and took out the coal and silk thread. The entire community, in fact, was laid out on a hill that stretched from east to west; people who lived in Forest City were always talking about going up or down "the hill." Slovak immigrant families were quite numerous in this small patch of ground along with their Irish, Polish, Rusyn (a small Slavic group originally from the same region as the Slovaks), and Slovene neighbors. Regardless of one's background, however, households were noticeably crowded with parents, children, and many boarders as newcomers continued to arrive from Europe. Homes were also money-making propositions as mining families divided them into apartments that they could rent to others. John Matircho, Mary's father, owned his home at the corner of Railroad and Center Streets by 1910 but the structure was divided in a way that allowed three families to occupy separate quarters. My grandmother told me that it was her mother who ran the finances of this domestic enterprise with income flowing from her miner husband, tenants, and the wages of Mary and her sisters who as teenagers had entered the Klots Throwing Mill where raw silk was turned into thread. Like many men in this mining town, her father never had a firm grasp on the family's finances. Women such as her mother, in fact, not only managed household budgets but also often stood in line with their men on paydays to ensure that precious wages were not squandered at local taverns.[1]

It was not difficult for the Matircho girls to find work at the Klots mill. Mining towns like Forest City were filled with factories that wove silk and made cigars because entrepreneurs—usually located in eastern cities such as New York or Philadelphia—wanted to take advantage of the huge pool of inexpensive female labor. A government study of immigrant workers around 1910 found that these *throwing mills* were heavily populated by young women described as being from "inferior groups" such as Poles, Slovaks, Magyars, and Lithuanians, who lacked the technical skills of the Irish, Germans, and Welsh. Mary entered the mill after about five years of schooling for about $1.25 per week and remained there for the next ten years, turning most of her earnings over to her mother. She told me when I interviewed her in 1976 that she rather liked the mill. The 1910 census listed both Mary and her sister Anna as weavers, a job that suggests that they were performing tasks that were highly repetitive and required little expertise. The Klots mills in Forest City and in nearby Carbondale and Archbald were throwing mills, which concentrated on winding filaments of silk when it first came into the country. At Forest City, women tended machines that entwined a lower grade of

FIGURE 3. The author's grandmother, Mary Matircho Bodnar, second from left, and aunt, Emma Bodnar, back row, third from left, on his great-grandmother's porch in Forest City, Pennsylvania, 1922.

tussah silk in contrast to more lustrous and expensive (*bombyx*) grades and wound it onto cones that were then shipped to finishing mills throughout the East, where products such as shirts and rugs were produced. Company records suggest that the Forest City mill had an especially strong link to the factories of Ipswich, Massachusetts, which made women's hosiery.[2]

So many women toiled long hours—sometimes sixty hours a week—in these noisy mills, twisting strands of silk and seeing that they were properly wound around bobbins, that they became an object of concern for reformers and journalists seeking to improve the treatment of workers in industrial America. Reformers not only criticized wealthy mill owners such as Henry Klots, who had started his company after graduating from Princeton in 1888, for exploiting these girls but also immigrant parents for forcing their offspring to perform such tedious work at a young age. Florence Lucas Sanville, who toured the anthracite region's towns in 1910 to report on child labor conditions, was struck by how much dirt she saw not only in the coal breakers where boys worked but in the silk mills as well. She actually felt that the boys had it a bit better because the hours they worked were partially regulated by a strong miners' union. Most mill girls like Mary had no such protection and often labored for ten hours a day. Sanville was especially worried that many of these girls were tempted to seek a release from the drudgery of the silk mills by eagerly hurrying into early marriages.[3]

Critics like Sanville also noted the crowded conditions in which these girls lived. They were horrified that young women usually witnessed adult men in their household taking daily baths where they were scrubbed by their wives and older sisters. And they especially worried over the tradition of heavy drinking that characterized towns like Forest City, which had numerous taverns and raucous wedding celebrations. This concern was reflected in 1908 when the National Board of the Young Women's Christian Association included Forest City in a sociological investigation they made of Pennsylvania coal towns; they concluded that there were "lax moral conditions" in such places because most families slept in one room and young girls were exposed to the miner's daily bath ritual and their heavy drinking. Mary herself told me that there was a time when her mother would wrap a burlap bag around her as she slept to protect her from possible sexual advances from boarders. The report even singled out Forest City as a place where the chief amusements for young women included dances and saloons and claimed the town had a reputation of drinking more beer than any other in the area.[4]

While Mary toiled at the Klots mill, my grandfather John began to think about joining a vast emigrant stream of Rusyns and Slovaks that was leaving the farming villages of the eastern regions of the Kingdom of Hungary. His father owned a modest-sized farm in Klecenov, but the family lived on a narrow economic margin like most of their neighbors. At age seventeen John took a job with a local railroad company and turned his wages over to his mother, whom he recalls as being sickly a good deal of the time. Railroad work took him away from home, but this was now possible because his younger brother Mike was able to help with the farm chores along with cousins who shared the same property. Watching so many of his peers leave for America, however, caused him to think about joining the vast emigrant stream. And he had already been in contact with an uncle, George Yacoob, who had left in 1899, and was now working in the mines of Forest City and living with his own family just steps from the Matircho homestead. John said his mother was opposed to the idea and his father thought he was "crazy" but "I just made up my mind. That's all." I can still recall him telling me one evening when I was about six or seven years old the story of his journey. He set out with a group of about twelve men from his village and "walked" to Germany. The group was turned back at the German border because they lacked the proper papers. They soon got some legal assistance, however, and set out again, arriving in the port of Hamburg in December 1911.[5]

My grandfather marveled at what he saw in the German city. He told me that he was amazed at the size of the port and the sight of so many ships and all of the activity. He had never seen anything like it. And he was amazed that German officials provided housing for him and his companions in fine quarters with his own bed; it was a far cry from the life he had known in his village, where he shared one half of a house with his parents and three siblings. His father's sister's family occupied the other half.

Although my grandfather did not know it, I suspect the quarters he was referring to were in Hamburg's emigrant village, a vast facility the city built in 1901 to house the throngs of people—especially Jews from Eastern Europe and Slavs from the Austro-Hungarian Empire—that were using the port as a point of departure to the United States. The village was, in fact, a sprawling complex containing some twenty-five buildings and designed to keep this mobile population separated from the main part of the city for fear they might bring unwanted diseases, a concern rooted in the experience of a cholera epidemic in 1892. Separate quarters for emigrants were also provided in order to keep them from dealing directly with local merchants who were prone to overcharge them. The emigrant trade was important to the economic lifeblood of both the port and shipping companies, and Hamburg's city fathers were intent on regulating it as best they could.[6]

This vast movement of people was stimulated, moreover, not only by emigrant desires but also by eager ticket agents who worked throughout Eastern Europe drumming up business for shipping lines such as Hamburg-American. My grandfather actually recalled the agents well and said he saw them everywhere. He appreciated the fact that they could provide him with essential information about when boats left and how much he had to pay for his trip. But he was not happy with his shipboard accommodations on the *Prinz Adelbert*, where he recalled being packed along with friends into third class like bugs or horses on a sixteen-day voyage to Philadelphia during which he felt sick and exhausted all of the time.[7]

My grandfather's story was not unique for young men living in Eastern Europe at this time. Louis Adamic, a Slovene immigrant who in the 1930s became something of a literary celebrity in America and a left-wing activist, remembered as a boy listening to the stories that men told in his village of Blato after they had returned from laboring in the United States. In his autobiography Adamic wrote about one of them, Peter Molek, and recounted how Molek coughed incessantly and had difficulty breathing. "This is what America did to me," Molek told Adamic. The returned miner even had a photo he showed the young writer of a huge coal pile in a town in Pennsylvania named Forest City, where Slovenes constituted the largest immigrant group and where he had lost his health. Although his mother disapproved as well, Adamic's desire for new experiences was not to be deterred, and in 1913 he arrived in the United States.[8]

The region my grandfather left was a particular center for emigration to industrial America early in the twentieth century. Pennsylvania mine owners had actually begun to recruit men from Saros and Zemplin Counties (in what is now eastern Slovakia but was then part of northeastern Hungary) as early as 1877. As farming became more mechanized in northeastern Hungary by the late nineteenth century, poverty intensified and work opportunities eroded. Men and women from hundreds of Rusyn and Slovak settlements (Klecenov had a mixture of both groups) in this region now began to look for jobs in the industrial sectors of the United States, a fact that resulted in a continuing close association between these groups in America itself. Estimates of as high as fifty thousand people emigrated from northeast Hungary in 1904 alone. Large landowners in the region were not pleased with this exodus of cheap labor and frequently attempted to pressure the government in Budapest to regulate this outward flow. Such efforts proved futile, however, because people like my grandfather found ways to move anyway, and many officials in the government realized how important the money immigrants sent back to their villages was to the local economy.[9]

Although my grandfather originally intended to join his uncle in Forest City, a traveling companion persuaded him to try his hand at a job unloading ships in Port Chester, New York. Working on the docks proved disappointing, however, because employment was sporadic. When I sat down to interview him in 1976, my grandfather told me about this particular stop on his journey. "We were about two days without work. Then a big boat would come in and we would unload it. After that we were without a job again. We'd ask the boss when we were going to work again and he said, 'I'll let you know.'"[10]

After several weeks of the uncertainty of Port Chester, my grandfather decided to catch a train to the steel town of Homestead, Pennsylvania, where a relative of his mother lived who had already written him in Europe about employment possibilities. The year he spent in the mill town, however, proved unsatisfying as well because he could find only occasional day jobs outside the mill itself. Frustrated, he finally contacted Yacob, who encouraged him to come to Forest City. From the start, he found what he was looking for—steady work. "By gosh I come here and I could work the same day. Yacob took me into the mines and the boss asked only what was my name," he explained. He worked first as a helper to Patrick Cleary, a contract miner who taught him to drill holes for explosives, build roof supports, and work with dynamite. Cleary lived with his wife and eight children, including a son who picked slate in the large breaker in the same neighborhood as Yacob and Martircho. By 1914, after a two-year apprenticeship, John was able to earn his certification as a miner. Eventually, he kept the family immigration network alive by bringing his brother, Mike, and his younger sister, Mary, to Forest City in the early 1920s. Mary stayed and married in Forest City. Mike eventually returned to Europe because his wife would not follow him to the United States.[11]

In the year he qualified to be a miner, he married Mary Matircho. He had come to know her because she delivered milk to Yacob's house, where he boarded when he first arrived. She was supplementing her wages in the silk mill by selling milk produced by a cow that her mother owned; such was the resourcefulness of these immigrant women. The marriage ensured that John probably would never return to Klecenov, a fact he regretted because it prevented him from seeing his mother before she died. He explained to me that my grandmother, who was raised in this country, had no interest in going to Slovakia and that after a number of years he felt he would just be lost over there. John and Mary quickly moved into one of the apartments her parents had carved out of their homestead. One year later their first child, a daughter named Emma, was born and my grandfather went to the courthouse in Scranton to declare his intention to become an American citizen, with his father-in-law and his brother-in-law serving as witnesses. The 1920s census indicated that three families lived in the Matircho home. My grandmother's parents were in one unit with five children still at home, although a younger sister was now a "floor lady" in the silk mill and a son was in the mines. Another Slovak immigrant miner lived with his wife and six children—the oldest toiling as a breaker boy—in another apartment. John and Mary resided with their daughter Emma and a son, Joseph, in a third unit. The census was taken early in 1920, however, and by March of that year my father was born into this household. This meant that twenty people lived in a very modestly sized structure of three households all headed by males from Slovakia with one more baby about to join them. In the house just up the hill toward the silk mill, Mary's sister Anna was now married as well and lived with her husband and two offspring.

Heartbreak, however, loomed for the young couple as they settled into their adult lives. In 1922, when Mary gave birth to her fourth and last child, her father was killed in an accident in the Erie mine when he was caught under a rock fall. John Matircho's American dream ended at age fifty-four; he left a widow with five young children at home. Anna could still rely on the income from at least two children who now worked; she also got a modest financial settlement from the mining company. But the 1930 census showed she was still scrambling for dollars, since it indicated that she had taken a boarder into her household to help with expenses.

Studies of workingmen's compensation from the coal companies at the time suggested that payments in the anthracite region were actually better than in many other industries because of the power of the United Mine Workers. Many immigrant families usually carried some form of life insurance with their ethnic fraternal society as well. It is possible that Anna received as much as several thousand dollars in benefits from her husband's death. The local newspaper noted that John Matircho was a respected member of the Slovak community and was affiliated with several fraternal societies. He had also been on the committee that built a Slovak Roman Catholic church in Forest City after

Slovaks tired of attending services at the Irish parish. My grandmother recalled that her mother had insisted that she did not care what funeral director the family secured for her husband as long as he was not Irish. I suspect that these insurance payments represented something of a modest windfall for the Matircho household because Anna was able to give some of what she received to my grandparents so they could buy a home of their own nearby; she would recoup these funds by gaining another apartment to rent when they moved out. My grandfather recalled that the home cost about $3,500 but they felt it was big enough to house several apartments that could also enhance their own family budget. This was the house in which both my father and I were raised.[12]

Mining deaths and crippling accidents were common occurrences in mining towns. Forest City witnessed about four or five per year in a work force that averaged around twelve hundred in the late teens and early twenties. In 1921, some nine hundred men died in the mines of Pennsylvania alone. Just a few weeks after John Matircho's death, two more men died in the town's mines. One was hit by a coal car in the Clinton colliery, which broke the victim's neck, and another lost his life at the Hudson Coal Company when he was buried under a rock fall.

Four years later, my grandparents experienced the greatest sorrow of their lives when their oldest child died from an accident in a nearby rail yard. In the summer of 1926, just as the family was getting back on its feet after a long strike by the United Mine Workers Association, their eleven-year-old daughter, Emma, was injured on her way to swim with friends in a nearby river. As the group of girls crossed the railroad yards on the eastern edge of town at the bottom of the hill, they attempted to walk under some standing railcars. At that moment a switch engine in the yards bumped one of the cars, setting it in motion. Unfortunately, a projection from the moving car happened to catch Emma, severely lacerating her thigh. Her companions quickly pulled her to safety and took her to a neighboring house where a flagman applied a tourniquet, stopping the flow of blood. Others were able to run to a nearby lumberyard where the owner put the young girl in his truck and drove her to a hospital in Carbondale, about seven miles away. Doctors acted quickly to save her by amputating the injured leg in order to stop the spread of a blood infection.

When an account of the tragedy was first reported in the *Forest City News* on July 29, 1926, readers were told that Emma's life hung in the balance. The paper expressed sympathy to the family and retold the details of the accident, indicating "that the condition of the little girl was serious." One week later a front-page story told readers of the *News* that Emma's leg had been badly "mangled" and that she died after the amputation. The article also noted that she would have been in the sixth grade that fall and that the members of her Girl Scout troop carried floral pieces at her funeral mass. My cousin Harry told me as I was writing this that he recalled the entire family—Mary and John and all their relatives—standing in the hospital parking lot crying after they learned of her passing. As at many anthracite region wakes, Emma was laid out in her home where funeral services started before the congregation of mourners moved to the church for a formal mass and interment at a local cemetery, where many Rusyn and Slovak setters were buried.

Emma remained very much on her family's mind after the 1920s. In an old album that I still have, I found traces of Emma's life that had notations in my father's handwriting. They included photographs, a poem written by a friend titled "The Passing of Daughter Emma," and small postcards that Emma loved to collect, according to my father's captions on them. The cards—labeled magic pictures—were distributed by the Henry German bakery in Scranton, and allowed the child to imagine what distant parts of the globe might look like from an airplane—a prospect that must have captivated her. My mother recalled that several decades after Emma died, my grandfather would often knock on our door on his way to work to remind her to watch her children carefully that day. He was always worrying that something might happen to me and my siblings as well. Years later, when my father had me tend to the family burial plot just west of town, I would often look at the tombstone marked with the names of John and Anna Matircho and the very small marker next to it—no more than a foot or two high—inscribed with the name of Emma Bodnar. It was impossible to stand there and not think about the tragic stories I had heard so often.[13]

The Great Depression brought more turmoil to John and Mary. Forest City's mines worked only sporadically during the early thirties. Mine workers at the Hudson and Clinton collieries each lost about one hundred days of work in 1932, a reduction that directly affected my grandfather and his brother Mike. The town received a devastating blow in March 1932 when the Hillside Colliery was shut down and the miners were ordered to remove all their tools. The News proclaimed that the announcement came as a "hard blow to local residents" as word spread quickly throughout the entire vicinity. It would be seventeen months before Hillside would call men back to work and the local paper could proclaim that "the dark cloud of unemployment that has hung heavily over the community is about to be lifted." But mines that are closed quickly fill with water and it would take months to pump them out before the entire workforce could return. In fact, the 1930s were a period of overall decline for the entire anthracite industry as hard coal lost out to its competitors in the home heating market. Employment in the area mines dropped from 175,000 to only 99,000 from 1927 to 1937. Absent the renewed demand created by World War II, the anthracite mines might have closed sooner than they did.[14]

Mining families had always proved to be resourceful in finding ways to survive, and this proved to be the case again during hard times. Unemployment and underemployment continued to hurt. In the southern parts of the anthracite area north of Allentown, Pennsylvania, miners launched a strong effort to equalize work and insist that various collieries spread their work opportunities on a more evenhanded basis so more families could have a slice of whatever employment was available. Indeed, Franklin Roosevelt's National Recovery Administration was besieged with letters from the region—now suffering unemployment rates of more than 30 percent—with appeals for distributing work as widely as possible.

In northern fields around Scranton, coal companies were stronger and able to blunt the formation of strong alliances between employed and unemployed miners who might clamor for equalization as well. Here families responded to hard times by launching bootleg coal operations. Men and women trekked to the *culm banks* or breakers to pick any coal they could find. In some cases men drove shafts of their own on company property and mined anthracite in order to heat their homes or sell. This bootleg coal operation became, in fact, a major political issue in the state. When Louis Adamic visited the region that he had first heard about as a boy in Europe and interviewed many of the residents in 1934, he wrote a piece for *The Nation* that expressed sympathy for the mining families and explained how many were forced by necessity and unemployment to drill tiny shafts of their own and sell whatever coal they could. Coal companies continually tried to force the state government to restrict this illegal practice and protect their property, but officials refused to order police into the area to arrest bootleggers because it was widely known that grand juries in the region empathized with the workers and would not prosecute these struggling citizens.[15]

In Forest City the unemployed mobilized to press for public works projects. At a mass meeting in 1933, citizens confronted the director of the local Emergency Relief Committee and insisted that the county government launch a project to build a road from Forest City to a nearby lake to create more jobs. The year before, the town's poor board had reported that some 225 families were getting food subsidies and that applications from another fifty families were pending. Given the size of most families at the time, this probably represented about one quarter of Forest City's population.[16]

My grandfather took a different approach to hard times. Thinking back to his boyhood on the farms around Klecanov, he sought out farmers in the hills surrounding the town and asked them for work. He told me he was missing so many work days in the early thirties that he thought he "would get crazy." He recalled periods when he would make only five dollars from the mines during a two-week period. He knew an agent who worked at the rail station in Forest City who had a summer cottage at a nearby lake and the man hired him for a time to paint it. He felt he "got lucky," however, when a neighboring farmer saw him painting and asked him if he would be interested in helping to cut his hay. He recalled that the man was a "German and had a lot of money." He distinctly recalled the fact that the man paid him thirty-five dollars, which was a big help at the time. Soon afterward, the German farmer recommended him to a rich farmer who asked my grandfather if he was hungry and if he could help cut hay as well. My grandfather was in awe of this man, who not only owned a large farm but also cottages at a lake that he rented to people from New York City. The man even offered my grandfather one of the cottages to live in if he would come to work for him on a regular basis, a proposal that he felt he had to run by his wife. After being away for several weeks, the wealthy farmer brought my grandfather home and handed him fifty dollars. The immigrant miner was simply overwhelmed. "You could not make fifty dollars no place in those days," he exclaimed. Soon he was called back to the mines, but whenever they shut down he returned to the farm and the man who had impressed him so much with his wealth and generosity.[17]

John and Mary saw their economic situation stabilize during World War II. The mines worked steadily and the demands of war production actually prolonged the life of the anthracite industry itself. The couple worked diligently, moreover, to ensure that their three sons would not work underground, a sign that their life experiences had extracted a toll on them they did not want their offspring to bear. In the late thirties my grandfather, then out of work for a time, took his two oldest boys with him to work on a construction site in New York State but quickly sent them back home when he saw how arduous the conditions were under which they were expected to toil. Mary encouraged her oldest son to enter the priesthood and derived pride from the fact that he did. To her—as with other women in Catholic communities in the industrial towns of the time—a religious vocation actually brought some prestige to the family and represented at least a small step out of the depths of the laboring class and the shadow of the breaker. In this particular case, the Greek Catholic Church in America even paid for the college training for young men before they entered the seminary, an opportunity she felt that could not be missed. After the war, their sons established independent lives of their own and the mines and the culture it generated faded away. John and Mary worked less and began to enjoy their grandchildren, although I can still see my grandfather picking up stray pieces of coal near the railroad tracks. I did not realize until writing this piece that this was probably a habit born in the 1930s.

My grandparents bore witness to the experience of living and working in one part of industrial American in the period before I was born in the mid-1940s. Scholars would say that such testimony is driven partially by a desire by the narrator to defy the flow of time and the myriad forces that tend to erase things that were said and sentiments that were felt. Yet, I believe they were doing more than resisting a process of forgetting. Their remembrances were never articulated in a coherent story that was essentially progressive or even tragic. There were elements of both genres in what they said. They certainly provided proof that working people like them had setbacks, but their tales continually affirmed that they were resourceful people who found ways to negotiate the unpredictable nature of their economic and family life. Whatever attachments they had to higher ideals—to America, to Catholicism, to the Rusyn or Slovak communities, to the United Mine Workers—counted for less in the way they retold their lives than their insistence that they were self-directed individuals capable of confronting hardship and surviving tragedy. I think it was this sense of strength and the independence they projected—as limited and exaggerated as it might have been—that explained why they told the stories they did. Beyond the felt need to retard erasures from family memories was the effort they mounted to claim a degree of dignity and respect. The basis of their claims was not that they were good citizens, heroic veterans, or exploited workers but that they were autonomous actors who had suffered and struggled but found a way to endure. And to the extent that that point was valid, they made an argument that was actually quite universal in its import and that could reverberate with individuals nearly everywhere.

It was obviously easy for me to react to what my grandparents told me with compassion and sympathy. In his insightful book, *The Ethics of Memory*, Avishai Margalit discusses the power and pervasiveness of the recollections and sentiments many of us have for those we know and hold near and dear. Such feelings can actually provide the "cement" for many social groups, in part because they have a capacity to foster solidarity with those we know well and hold in high regard. The larger problem that Margalit addresses, however, is how to generate some level of connection to strangers and extend the circle of our empathy and respect. What sort of remembrance could prompt us to at least look with some understanding toward those we hardly know at all? Since our relations with such outsiders would be "thin" when compared to the "thick relations" we share with those with whom we are familiar, Margalit argues that such ties could only be based on the more general "attribute of being human." Thus, he insists that we all have an obligation to remember instances when people were victimized by forms of evil or misfortune, if only to make the case that such things should not happen again and to remind us that we all endure hardship no matter our group. He particularly noted the role of "communities of memory" in helping to maintain recollections capable of inducing a sympathetic human response in others. Thus, a community of Jewish Holocaust survivors could encourage people everywhere to recall human distress and thus share in calls that such a disaster not happen a second time. He also saw that New York City firemen played a similar role after 9/11 in shaping the response of a larger public to that tragedy and the view that their sacrifices not be forgotten.

Certainly the struggles of my grandparents were not the equivalent of the narratives of mass death represented by the Holocaust or 9/11. They were tales that resided in the smaller and more personal realm of memory that I carried into my adulthood but were never going to claim any significant degree of public attention. Amy Schuman has explained, however, how stories can travel across time and space as listeners appropriate them for a variety of uses. Thus, she suggests that one person's tragedy can become another's inspiration. She notes that this is how stories can do "cultural work." The chronicle of John and Mary clearly traveled with me to graduate school and was very much a part of my private thoughts when I began dissertation research in the early 1970s. Despite their personal nature, however, I think at their core they did convey a larger point that merited public exposure; they were, in the end, not only tales of ancestors in a coal town but accounts of "dignified conduct"—illustrations of ordinary people relentlessly exercising their autonomy to act and fashion lives in the face of powerful forces that sought to use them for other ends. And to that extent they were capable of reminding anyone of an "attribute of being human."[18]

The idea of dignity I have in mind in this case is described well by Peter Lawler. In the modern era, Lawler argues, individuals tend to insist that they not be reduced merely to "ends that are not their own." His point is that at its core, the modern idea of human or personal dignity is rooted not in performance of roles one undertakes in behalf of a family, nation, religion, or ideology or even in the extent to which one may have been victimized, but in the extent to which individuals make choices or direct their behavior toward ends they may embrace. Richard Miller has reminded us that humans derive respect ultimately from their capacities to act as "moral subjects" who make choices with whatever degree of personal sovereignty they can muster. What we all do, regardless of our race, creed, or nationality, is to attempt to use our individual abilities to resist the many forces—economic, biological, ideological—that seek to determine our fate. Thus, even as we accede to the forces of destiny, to the call of duty, to the horror of tragedy, or to the dislocations of the economy, we can still "order our actions toward ends that we may embrace" and take action to adjust, resist, or move beyond "all the cruel indignities nature randomly piles upon us." For Lawler, our dignity is manifested in these actions or, in his terms, "the orders we're really capable of giving to ourselves." Lawler's argument adds an important dimension to Margalit's, for he moves beyond assertions that humans deserve respect simply because there is an intrinsic value in the very fact of being human and adds that they merit admiration by constantly striving to find ways to handle adversity. I would suggest that this means that we not only have an obligation to remember crimes against humanity or the plight of victims—which by and large historians have done well in recent decades—but the less dramatic but more common endeavor to affirm personal freedom in the face of the many forces that threaten to over-whelm it.[19]

In graduate school, the family stories I carried with me as a young man met the New Social History, an exploding scholarly paradigm that took aim at an older view of the American past that was oriented more toward explain-ing the nation's progress and the faith so many had in it. This older consen-sus view of the American story had proved powerful in the 1950s, when the nation basked in the glow of its victory in World War II and often induced some citizens to conclude that the United States was a special place blessed by God and free of the violence, discontent, and inequality that marked life in other nations. Emerging from the political climate of the 1960s, the New Social His-tory rejected sentimental notions of the American past, however, and began to stress the many fissures that divided America over time and the widespread quarrels that had marked the course of its development. In a particularly strik-ing way, its insistence that history was studied best from the bottom of society or from the viewpoint of people from many types of backgrounds—exploited workers, dispossessed minorities, and abused women—actually pointed toward a more human-centered account of the past. Scholars such as Margalit have cer-tainly endorsed this perspective on the past and raised concerns about histories that were highly nation-centered and patriotic because they tended to foster gratitude toward "heroes" more than a concern for victims and were often filled with accounts of a nation's enemies or objects of hatred. But the stories I car-ried not only raised questions about a sentimental view of the American past and expressed concern for those generally hidden from scholarly view, but had much to say about the agency or "dignified conduct" undertaken by the types of people who were at the center of the New Social History itself.[20]

I found it instructive to reread my early scholarship in preparing this essay to see just how thoroughly I was motivated by the synergy that resulted from the intersection of my family stories with a fresh scholarly paradigm. Clearly, the scholarly world was opening up rapidly to students like me who were interested in aspects of their own past and who came from social groups that had not had extensive access to higher education before the 1960s. Thus, many in my age cohort began to address questions about Black history, family history, immi-gration history, labor history, and (a bit later) women's history. More specifi-cally, I was undoubtedly moving toward a research paradigm that was rejecting not only nationalistic myths and politics (like most other practitioners of these new approaches) but also one that was more willing to register the feelings and struggles of people from the lower orders of the social structure.

This was evident in my 1982 book, *Workers' World: Kinship, Community, and Protest in an Industrial Society, 1900–1940*. This study was grounded almost entirely in oral histories I conducted in the 1970s with people very much like my grandparents and in communities like the one in which I was raised. Obviously the life I lived as a boy—and the politics of the '60s—had piqued my interest. And it was clear to me at the time I was doing this research that it was still possible to talk with many of the immigrants and working people who were at the heart of my scholarly concerns. The core of my interest was expressed at the time in points I made about the importance of ethnic, family, and communal networks determining the way working people met the economic challenges before them.

This rendition of daily life was at the heart of much of what I had heard as a youth, but I see now that I was trying to elevate it to something more—to a perspective that was actually more cosmopolitan than histories grounded in national or even group uniqueness. The book also devoted much effort to contesting the influence of theoretical models that historians had already brought to the study of working people that stressed the influence (determinism) that large structures or ideologies had over my historical subjects. Thus, I challenged scholars who said workers were tradition-bound mostly because they felt they had to stem the onset of widespread mechanization and specialization in their work lives. I also took issue with labor historians who cast the thought and behavior of workers into an ideological frame that suggested they were all militant activists who sought equality with capital and power in the workplace. I certainly saw that many of these scholarly arguments had validity. I just did not think they squared completely with the framework I had heard about from a wide body of oral testimony: these testimonies suggested that the people who interested me were constantly taking steps to manage their lives somewhat on their own terms, regardless of who they were or what they thought. Indeed, right after *Workers' World* I coauthored a book, *Lives of Their Own: Blacks, Poles, and Italians in Pittsburgh*, that attempted to explain the way both Black migrants and European immigrants develop strategies to gain work and establishhomes in the face of powerful forces of racism and urbanization.

The Transplanted: A History of Immigrants in Urban America (1985) allowed me to advance my model further and apply it to the broad sweep of immigrant history in the century before the 1920s. In looking at the book again after so many years, I am struck by how much I stressed several points. Although the book challenged an earlier synthesis of immigrant history by Oscar Handlin, I see now that I reached certain conclusions similar to his. Both Handlin and I agreed that immigrant adaptation to industrial America was difficult and could be painful. I differed mainly on the point that it was destructive to these newcomers. Clearly, I wanted to stress the ability of newcomers to adapt and endure, which was certainly at the core of what my grandparents' tales and oral histories said and what Lawler would suggest was the basis of their pride. David Gerber caught a glimpse of this when he wrote that I had tried to "impart dignity" to ancestors whose voice had yet to penetrate America's historical literature. But he also felt this effort ultimately led to an overly positive assessment of the process by which immigrants became Americans. That is to say that my work expanded the historical vision of how diverse the process of nation making was but sadly obscured the devastating impact of racism and the reality of enduring divisions in American life.[21]

Yet, I was striving continually in the book—perhaps, too much so—to assert the shared dimensions of immigrant adjustment in several ways. *The Transplanted* consciously tried to jump over the ethnic boundaries that had dominated the field and the conventional model of immigrant scholarship at the time of looking at one group in one place. More important, it sought to affirm the universalism of meeting the challenges of everyday life—played out in this book in a pattern of personal decision making in the realm of the family household—as the key common denominator that explained how people adjusted to the vagaries of economic and cultural change regardless of where they came from or who they were.

One central critique of *The Transplanted* was that it failed to adequately explore the topic of assimilation. A number of scholars noted not only how this book and even much of the scholarship of the New Social History was so absorbed in exploring the interior of working-class lives or featuring conflict that it neglected to explain how immigrants and other ordinary historical actors ultimately made their way into the American mainstream. In a careful analysis of the changing historiography of assimilation, Russell Kazal felt my stress on the "struggle to maintain the family household" had prevented me from explaining how these working people might have attached themselves to the larger culture of capitalism and its possibilities. Historian James Barrett echoed this contention when he wrote that the larger political level of the immigrant experience was missing from the study. Gerber also acknowledged that the New Social History tended to promote contention and struggle in American life instead of agreement and a steady march into the American mainstream, but he actually detected an inference in this scholarship that suggested that Americanization did in fact take place but in a way that was more democratic and pluralistic. In other words, the many subjects of the New Social History eventually found their way through a maze of political parties or unions or even educational opportunities into the life of the American nation and in so doing reinforced an underlying belief that historians like me had in the democratic possibilities of the nation itself. Regardless of the direction these comments on assimilation took, however, it was clear to me that I could have explored more than I did the larger problems of Americanization and nationalization.[22]

Eventually assimilation and the process of creating American identities did garner the major focus of scholarly attention as the impetus of the New

Social History began to subside. In part, this alteration was focused to a considerable extent on the problem of race in America and its ability to explain how American society was structured and the paths newcomers followed to settle in it. The turn to racial divisions and the complex manner in which Americans crafted racial identities as a way to explain the making of the nation had a distinct bearing on the interpretation of immigrant and working-class history. The type of people that had drawn my early scholarly attention—White European immigrants and their children who generally lived and worked in industrial areas—were now less likely to be seen as workers struggling against oppression or economic setbacks. Any sense that they were victims or losers in the larger society was diminished by the realization of the massive exploitation of racial minorities. Indeed, European immigrants were now often cast as beneficiaries of a pervasive system of racial privilege that facilitated their absorption into American society under the guise of being "White"; the scholarly assumption now is that they passed through doors closed to those with darker skin. Admittedly European immigrants often faced derision and ridicule, but they were never mistreated as much as African Americans, for instance, and there was evidence that they often rallied to racist beliefs to advance their own progress.

Thus, Thomas Sugrue's research documented the mobilization of workers in Detroit after World War II who used a "newly assertive working-class whiteness" to block the aspirations of African Americans for equal work opportunities and housing. Others noted in the revival of White ethnic consciousness in the 1970s another manifestation of the gulf that now separated the children of the European immigrants from Blacks and their rising expectations. As Peter Kolchin remarked in 2002, "suddenly whiteness studies were everywhere." Kolchin readily admitted the pervasiveness of racism in America but worried that this new historical trend was inclined to indict White Americans to such an extent that it often lost sight of intricate contextual variations that marked the real histories of the people who had commanded the attention of what was by now the old New Social History. And others cautioned that whiteness studies might have diminished historical understanding of other self-conscious categories or identities such as family and community, which people used to understand who they were and how they would shape their lives.[23]

The New Social History not only came under attack by scholars who felt it had not sufficiently addressed the impact of a cruel racism in America but also by conservatives in the larger society who railed against its tendency to criticize what were deemed to be ideals of national unity and patriotic virtue. In revisiting the preface to a book I published in 1992, *Remaking America: Public Memory, Commemoration, and Patriotism in the Twentieth Century*, I noticed that I made it clear that the process of crafting national unity was driven in part by this conservative critique and an effort I felt was grounded in the attempt to restore a more mythical view of national history. I wrote that I had always assumed that social history—the study of the small worlds and individual lives of working people—had contributed much that was new to the field of American history and admitted that I empathized with the struggles and goals many of the subjects of my interest pursued. The growing criticism that social history received in this country by the 1980s, however, actually caused me to move away from some of my earlier topics to explore instead the history of this conservative and more mythical perspective on America.

Remaking America was an attempt on my part to look at the history of patriotic rituals and commemorative events—many of which drew in large number of immigrants—and suggested that their proclamations of patriotic duty were continually contested by a variety of group and regional remembrances. In a recent book on the way Americans recalled the "good war," I continued to explore the determined effort by many to fashion highly patriotic and mythical views of Americans. The book attempted to say that individual citizens struggled considerably with the realities that World War II brought and constantly sought ways to deal with its horror and tragedies in spite of constant efforts to efface them. Thus, some Americans would come to see the war not as a human tragedy but as a national victory that revealed the exceptional nature and loyalty of the nation's people. In this case human dignity was grounded not in a constant effort to make choices or order one's life—something Americans could share with strangers around the globe—but in the fact that one was an American and the belief that one was blessed with traits that few others anywhere else could possess.[24]

Myths, of course, permeated the life and times of my grandparents. *The Spirit of the American Doughboy* statue that stands in Forest City today and that I passed daily when I went to grade school was erected just after World War I and enshrined the ideal of patriotic sacrifice for the nation. The *Coal Miner's Memorial* that stands just a few feet away and was dedicated in the 1990s basically turned the town's immigrants into timeless archetypes of hard-working and family-oriented people who seemed to lack any sense of self-determination or personal autonomy. This is not to say that my grandparents and the people who inhabited the coal town with them never felt the pulse of patriotic fervor or the pull of family obligation. They did. At some level they may have even benefitted from larger racial injustices that shaped the nation in which they lived (although I think my grandparents would not have understood that point very well). But local memorial builders, historians of whiteness, and the conservative defenders of myth never really listened to what people like my grandparents had to say about how they made pivotal decisions to leave home, carry on after profound losses, and find ways to make ends meet. They were not perfect people and they were not among the most victimized people that American society or world history created over time. They told another story, however, that carried broad implications because it was about the human effort to make personal choices in the face of overwhelming forces that sought to regulate their lives. My grandparents and others like them were telling me that they warranted respect not because they were heroes, victims, or even my grandparents but because they were ordinary people constantly trying to preserve some degree of independence. In this regard, they affirmed not their difference but their similarity to everyone else.

Notes

1. Interview with Mary Matircho Bodnar, November 25, 1976, by author. Bill Feddock, "Our Coal Miners and Their Family Life Remembered," pamphlet in author's possession. I would like to thank Sophie Snider and Francesca Snider for their help in researching this paper.

2. *Reports of the Immigration Commission, 1907–1910, Part 5: Silk Good Manufacturing and Dying* (Washington, D.C., 1910), 97, 105. Bonnie Stepenoff, *Their Father's Daughters: Silk Mill Workers in Northeastern Pennsylvania, 1880–1960* (Sellingsgrove, Pa.: Susquehanna University Press, 1999), 29, 41, 75. Klots Throwing Company Records, box 1, Hagley Museum and Library, Wilmington, Delaware.

3. Florence Lucas Sanville, "Home Life of Silk Mill Workers," *Harpers Monthly Magazine* (June 1910): 22–31.

4. Annie Marion McClean, "Life in the Pennsylvania Coal Fields with Particular Reference to Women," *American Journal of Sociology* 14 (November 1908): 329–351. Peter Roberts, *Anthracite Coal Communities* (New York: Macmillan, 1904), 234, also lamented the fact that young boys were leaving school early to work in the breakers and that Forest City seemed to have a high percentage of taverns for its size.

5. Interview with John Bodnar, November 25, 1976, by author. Interview with Andrew Bodnar, 1974; tape no. 25, Pittsburgh Oral History Project, MG 409, Pennsylvania Historical and Museum Commission, Harrisburg.

6. Edwin Jones Clapp, *The Port of Hamburg* (New Haven: Yale University Press, 1911), 67.

7. Interview with John Bodnar, November 25, 1976, by author. Interview with Andrew Bodnar, 1974; tape no. 25, Pittsburgh Oral History Project, MG 409, Pennsylvania Historical and Museum Commission, Harrisburg.

8. Louis Adamic, *Laughing in the Jungle: The Autobiography of an Immigrant in America* (New York: Harper, 1932), 12–20.

9. Julianna Puskas, *From Hungary to the United States, 1880–1940* (Budapest: Akademiai Kiado, 1982), 21–39; Konstantin Culen, *History of Slovaks in America* (St. Paul, Minn.: Czechoslovak Genealogical Society International, 2007 reprint of 1942 edition published in Bratislava), 31–43; Paul Robert Magoci, *The Shaping of a National Identity: Subcarpathian Rus', 1848–1948* (Cambridge, Mass.: Harvard University Press, 1978), 41–78.

10. Interview with John Bodnar, 25 November 1976, by author.

11. Interview with Mary Timko, 25 November 1976, by author.

12. Interview with John Bodnar, November 25, 1976, by author. Mary K. Compton, "Effects of Workmen's Compensation Laws in Diminishing the Necessity of Industrial Employment of Women and Children," *Bulletin of the U.S. Bureau of Labor Statistics*, no. 217 (1918).

13. *Forest City News*, July 29, 1926, 1; August 5, 1926, 1.

14. *Forest City News*, March 10, 1932, 1; August 3, 1933, 1. For days worked and mine accidents at each colliery in the state, see the annual reports of the Commonwealth of Pennsylvania, *Report of the Department of Mines* (Harrisburg, Pennsylvania).

15. *New York Times*, March 26, 1936, 41; November 20, 1936, 34. Adamic, "The Great Bootleg Coal Industry," *Nation* (January 9, 1934); Thomas Dublin and Walter Licht, *The Face of Decline: The Pennsylvania Anthracite Region in the Twentieth Century* (Ithaca, N.Y.: Cornell University Press, 2005), 58–84.

16. *Forest City News*, July 21, 1932, 1; February 23, 1933, 1.

17. Interview with John Bodnar, November 25, 1976, by author.

18. "Dignity, Human Rights, and Human Genetics," *Modern Law Review* (September 1998): 665–666.

19. Peter Augustine Lawler, *Modern and American Dignity: Who We Are as Persons and What That Means for Our Future* (Wilmington, Del.: Intercollegiate Studies Institute, 2010), 11–18; Richard Miller, *Terror, Religion, and Liberal Thought* (New York: Columbia University Press, 2010), 54–56, 100.

20. Margalit, *The Ethics of Memory* (Cambridge, Mass.: Harvard University Press, 2002), 13–73.

21. John Bodnar, *Workers World: Kinship, Community, and Protest in an Industrial Society, 1900–1940* (Baltimore: Johns Hopkins University Press, 1982); John Bodnar, Roger Simon, and Michael Weber, *Lives of Their Own: Blacks, Italians, and Poles in Pittsburgh, 1960* (Urbana: University of Illinois Press, 1982); Bodnar, *The Transplanted: A History of Immigrants in Urban America* (Bloomington: Indiana University Press, 1985).

22. David Gerber, "Forming a Transnational Narrative: New Perspectives on European Immigration to the United States," *History Teacher* 35 (November 2001): 64–66; Russel Kazal, "Revisiting Assimilation: The Rise, Fall and Reappraisal of a Concept of American Ethnic History," *American Historical Review* 100 (April 1995): 437–471; James Barrett, "The Transplanted: Workers, Class, and Labor," *Social Science History* 12 (Fall 1988): 227.

23. Thomas Sugrue, "Crabgrass-Roots Politics: Race, Rights, and the Reaction against Liberalism and the Urban North, 1940–1964," *Journal of American History* 82 (September 1995): 551–578; Daniel T. Rogers, *Age of Fractures* (Cambridge, Mass.: Harvard University Press, 2011), 126; Peter Kolchin, "'Whiteness Studies': The New History of Race in America," *Journal of American History* (June 2002): 154–173; James R. Barrett and David Roediger, "Inbetween People's Race, Nationalism, and the 'New Immigrant' Working Class," *Journal of American Ethnic History* 16 (Spring 1997): 3–44; Eric Arnesen, "Whiteness and the Historians' Imagination," *International Labor and Working Class History* 60 (Fall 2001): 25.

24. See John Bodnar, *Remaking America: Public Memory, Commemoration, and Patriotism in the Twentieth Century* (Princeton: Princeton University Press, 1992), and Bodnar, *The "Good War" in American Memory* (Baltimore: Johns Hopkins University Press, 2010).

5

Ethnic and Racial Identities

A Polish Filipina's Progress in Chicago and the Profession

BARBARA M. POSADAS

How did I become a historian of American immigration and ethnicity? Perhaps I should begin at the beginning with other questions. How did I get to college in the first place? How and why did I become a historian? As with so many others who came of academic age in the 1960s and 1970s, the answers to these questions were never self-evident. Born and raised in a White, multiethnic, working-class neighborhood, Wicker Park, on Chicago's near Northwest Side, I grew up in an interracial home in a tiny, two-and-a-half room, third-floor apartment and fulfilled my parents' ambitions for me by earning a bachelor's degree and, subsequently, a PhD.

My parents, Estelle Hazack Posadas and Alipio Gutierrez Posadas, met at a dance in Chicago sometime in 1931 and eloped with another mixed-race couple later that year to a wedding chapel in Crown Point, Indiana. Their marriage lasted for forty-seven years until my father's death in 1979, the event that propelled me into the subfield of immigration and ethnicity.

My father hailed from the city of San Carlos, in Pangasinan, a northern Philippine province on the island of Luzon. His father, Felipe, died shortly before his birth in August 1901, apparently in a cholera epidemic raging amid the dislocation caused by the war between Filipinos and their new American colonial rulers. During the next decade, his mother remarried and bore three daughters before dying of tuberculosis. By age ten, my orphaned father lived with his half sisters in the home of his maternal grandparents, looked after by maiden aunts, his security ensured by the substantial income that came to him from his wealthy, landowning paternal grandfather's estate. He finished the primary grades at the local English-language grammar school before relocating to the Philippine capital, graduating from Manila North High School in 1923, and enrolled in the ten-year-old University of the Philippines, where he completed three years, majoring in electrical engineering. By the mid-1920s, the lure of an American college degree, with its promise of enhanced prestige back at home, took hold. With parental blessing and support, his best friend from San Carlos, Venancio Lim, had already left for Purdue University in West Lafayette, Indiana, keen on becoming a Big Ten "Boilermaker." In June 1926, my father followed. His camera recorded a slender young man rather formally dressed in a white tropical suit, wearing a hat, and standing proudly on the deck of the ship at anchor, surrounded by his half sisters, aunts, and other relatives.

Unfortunately, as his ship readied to sail across the Pacific, a Posadas cousin convinced him to sign a revised power of attorney he did not understand, and through which his income would be cut off and his land mortgaged to finance the cousin's venture into politics. With only the money with which he embarked, my father soon found himself stranded—without funds to pay for a second term at Purdue. Unable to complete his degree and return home—as he always called the Philippines—my father moved to Chicago, where a few thousand other Filipinos already lived, and began scrambling to earn his keep, perhaps intending to return to school, but soon intent only on surviving the Great Depression. He never returned to the Philippines.

My mother, Stanislawa (Anglicized to Estelle), entered the world in Chicago in 1910, the third of seven children born to Josef Hazack, who immigrated from Rzeszów in the then Austrian province of Galicia in Poland, and Apolonia Kemp, from near Łódź in Russian Poland. Josef worked as an iron molder in Chicago, making streetcar wheels, intending to stay only long enough to earn money to buy land near his father's farm. In 1912, he sent his wife and three small children back across the Atlantic to await his return in a year's time. Rumors of the coming war altered his plans and, as he instructed, my grandmother and the children returned to Chicago. Thereafter, the family focused on building a secure life in the Second City with a succession of houses that always contained at least one income-producing rental apartment. Like her sisters, my mother left school after her eighth-grade graduation. Though her parents expected the girls to turn over their pay from their factory jobs, they did not oversee them closely, enabling my mother to meet and marry my father and to incur parental wrath that did not abate for five years. By the time I came along in 1945, almost fourteen years after their marriage, my father worked with other Filipinos as an attendant for the Pullman Company on club cars along the great passenger rail routes stretching out of Chicago to the East, West, and South, while my mother kept our tiny apartment immaculate.

I remained an only child and especially relished time spent with my father during layovers between his Pullman runs. We played rummy and board games— Monopoly, Sorry, and Dixie. Every December, he set up my Lionel electric trains on a large wooden platform on which they circumnavigated our Christmas tree.

FIGURE 4. The author and her parents, Estelle and Al Posadas, Chicago, Illinois, circa 1949.

My parents sent me to the Annunciation Parish Elementary School, and then to the Catholic, all-girls Josephinum High School, where I thrived and became the student newspaper editor and valedictorian. In my earlier childhood, as they had before my birth, my parents kept up an active social life among interracial and Filipino couples, some of whom lived nearby. Their gatherings typically featured Philippine dishes that the men cooked and sex segregation by language, as the Filipinos spoke Tagalog or the Pangasinan dialect to each other, while their multiethnic White wives chatted in English. Outings consisted of picnics, birthday parties, and holiday gatherings with those of my mother's siblings who accepted my father, as well as overnight stays with my father's younger cousin, who worked as a machinist in Elgin, Illinois, had married a local German American woman, and had three children near in age to me. As our neighborhood sank into disrepair and families moved, race kept my family place bound until 1965, when we rented the second-floor apartment in my aging grandfather's two flat (a building with one apartment on each of two floors); after his death two years later, we paid my mother's siblings for their shares. As my father reached retirement age, my parents finally owned their own home.

Fortunately, both of them, especially my father, believed in college for me. By contrast, higher education had no place in the lives of my female cousins on the Polish side, who thought of work after high school only as a prelude to marriage, although circumstances kept all of them in paid employment throughout their lives. Initially, I wanted to be a civil engineer, but DePaul University's downtown campus, where I had worked part-time since my senior year in high school, did not offer the prerequisite math and science courses. I gravitated instead toward high school history teaching, inspired by DePaul professor Margaret (Peggy) Mulvihill, whose every course I took. A PhD in U.S. foreign relations from the University of Chicago, she was smart and dynamic, and by my sophomore year also engaged to be married to an attorney. But student teaching—which I loathed but aced—convinced me that there *had* to be another career path, and I decided to go to graduate school. After I told DePaul's history department chair of my plan, he looked at me with dismay and with what I *expect* was sincere concern, and blurted out, "Oh, Barbara, why do you want to do that? You'll never get a husband."

That fall, in September 1967, I entered Northwestern University on a fellowship, driving from home for classes. Following on Peggy Mulvilhill's example, I intended to study diplomatic history. At Northwestern, the climate differed significantly from DePaul in many ways, including the lakeshore campus and the elegant homes on Evanston's tree-lined streets. I was one of two women in an entering graduate history cohort of twenty-eight, swollen in numbers by male students escaping the Vietnam War draft. The other woman did not survive into our second year. A sole persistent woman per cohort remained the norm for several years—from the previous year, Melitta Cutright, whose dissertation examined the life of a Tudor era noblewoman, and Anita Clair Fellman, who had entered in 1965 and now pushed a baby carriage to Deering Library in good weather, where her then husband Michael met her at the door and pushed the carriage home while she studied. Anita ultimately became director of Women's Studies at Old Dominion University in Virginia. None of us could then conceive of asking to do a field in women's history. When I suggested in Robert Wiebe's seminar that the "family" might be an appropriate topic, the male students around the table—but not Bob—simply looked puzzled, or dismissive.

Northwestern's history department did not seem a promising place for the study of immigration and ethnicity either. Although I did not take note of it at the time, gender being more salient, I was the only person of color in my entering class. Several others made clear their Euro-American working-class backgrounds— I would have defined myself similarly as part Polish and part Filipino—but most of us seemed content to study traditional topics in traditional specialties within U.S. or European history. Somewhat aloof from the rest of us in methodology and mystique stood a number of returned Peace Corps volunteers, all White males, in African history, a few African American students, notably the substantially older Sterling Stuckey, who joined the faculty soon after finishing his graduate work, and John Bracey, who maintained a dynamic presence, especially in faculty newcomer George Fredrickson's seminar on slavery.

Though I was not particularly aware of it at the time, I now realize that ferment in the profession as well as the upheavals of the late 1960s and early 1970s significantly influenced the Northwestern program. For one thing, the department experienced persistent turnover, as eminent or soon-to-be eminent historians such as Fredrickson, Christopher Lasch, James J. Sheehan, and Conrad Totman came and went. Visitors such as Peter Novick, John Hemphill, and Jesse Lemisch brought new perspectives during their short stays. In 1972, long after I had finished classes, the department hired its first female faculty member, Joan Wallach Scott, who stayed two years before decamping to Chapel Hill.

Apart from rare moments at graduate seminars, late night student parties at which wives hung out together in apartment kitchens in neighborhoods where I could never find parking, and bag lunches in the library lounge with history students who favored sports over ideas as subjects for discussion, I found little opportunity for intellectual camaraderie among my peers, probably because I commuted daily from home. Social highs came when one of us passed the oral comprehensive exam, and we gathered for a lively Mexican group dinner at La Choza, just over the border from Evanston in Chicago's increasingly unsafe Juneway Terrace neighborhood. Although we loved the food, none of us ever wondered aloud or probably gave a second thought to the origins and experiences of the men who waited on tables and made our meals.

In 1971, I completed my comprehensive exams in U.S. foreign relations with Richard W. Leopold. I don't really know what Mr. Leopold thought of me as a student, but he did once pay me what I'm sure was a sincere compliment. He had hired me to type the mammoth joint AHA/OAH investigative report responding to the charges by historian Francis L. Loewenheim that the Franklin D. Roosevelt Presidential Library had withheld from him documents made available to other researchers. "Barbara, you would have made a wonderful executive assistant!" I lacked the courage to ask if he was also making a suggestion. Now an ABD, I began researching a dissertation on FDR's ambassadors to Latin America, a topic that soon became profoundly boring to me.

Increasingly, I found myself captivated by the "new" social history, a rapidly emerging field that took historical study away from past politics. Suddenly, my work in African American history, with its emphasis on the lives of slaves and freedmen, my longtime fascination with my hometown, Chicago, and the New England town studies introduced in John Hemphill's Colonial America seminar came together to point me in a new direction. Abandoning diplomatic history, I regrouped and completed a dissertation on Jefferson Township—now Chicago's Northwest Side where I had lived all of my life—from the mid- to the late-nineteenth century, a period including its annexation to Chicago. During my search for a new dissertation topic, I did tentatively suggest that researching Pullman's Filipino workers might be a worthwhile topic, but was quickly cautioned about the probable unavailability of sources—and filiopietism. In the course of writing my dissertation, Henry Binford arrived at Northwestern and became my adviser; Bob Wiebe, although never my dissertation director, remained supportive. The dissertation put me in touch with patterns of settlement, housing, and family structure that, little did I know, would help inform my work on Filipino immigrants and their families.

Even as I labored away keypunching IBM cards to create a statistical portrait from the 1880 census of patterns of nationality and residence, I found my ongoing interest in the family. Each year a *very few* more female graduate students arrived, including Ellen Carol DuBois, whose dissertation on the mid-nineteenth-century women's rights movement was the first Northwestern product that, to my knowledge, focused directly on a women's history topic. In 1973–1974, I cotaught Northwestern's first-ever U.S. women's history course in the Evening School for part-time students on the downtown Chicago campus.

In 1972, the Newberry Library became central to my academic self-transformation. I participated in Richard Jensen and Daniel Scott Smith's Newberry summer seminar in social history and met the first two women, both University of Illinois at Chicago graduate students, whose research targeted women of color. Jacqueline Peterson investigated American Indian women, their mostly French trader partners and husbands, and their mixed blood—*métis*—offspring in the Upper Midwest in the eighteenth and earlynineteenth centuries. Louise Año Nuevo Kerr, known for her Mexican heritage but also half Filipino, researched Mexican ethnic-group formation in Chicago. They were the first whom I knew personally who combined gender and race in their inquiries. But these subjects had not yet secured the foreground, for most of us in that seminar obsessed over using the census to track occupational and spatial mobility, à la Stephan Thernstrom and Peter Knights.

What produced my turn away from quantitative urban social history and toward the study of Filipino immigrants and their interracial families in Chicago? Having published several articles from my 1976 dissertation following my hiring as an ABD history instructor at Northern Illinois University (NIU) in 1974, I concluded that the absence of qualitative sources for my project precluded producing a publishable monograph. Presumed lost in the Chicago Fire, not even the Jefferson Township government records were available, although they would ultimately be found years later. Thanks to supportive colleagues in Northern Illinois's history department, including Alfred Young, who encouraged my decision to change my research focus before earning tenure, I decided shortly after my father's death in February 1979 that if someone did not interview the Filipino immigrants of my father's generation soon, no one would capture their experiences in the Second City, where many of them, like my father, had lived for more than fifty years. Through oral interviews with the men, and research at the Chicago Historical Society in the Brotherhood of Sleeping Car Porters papers and at the Newberry Library in the then unorganized Pullman Company papers, I began research on Filipinos who migrated to the Chicago area before passage of the Tydings-McDuffie Act in 1934 virtually halted migration from the Philippines until after World War II. My father had become one of the "unintentional immigrants," young men who hoped that their sojourn in the United States would help them surpass others when they returned to their homeland. En route to realizing their dreams, plans changed. For some, job security and a better income in the United States trumped loneliness for family back home. For others, including my father, marriage to a White woman and the formation of a family transformed them into the settlers who established a Filipino presence in Chicago before 1935.

The interview project aimed to give "voice" to what the Brotherhood and Pullman records revealed, and to a remarkable extent the elderly men whom I interviewed spoke candidly to me, the adult daughter of a countryman with whom they had worked or socialized. Their stories helped create a vivid picture of work lives in what I conceptualized as a "hierarchy of color." Initially given a separate, racially defined classification as attendants, the Filipino presence in Pullman's dining, club, and observation cars constituted a sharp warning to the African American porters who had long comprised most of Pullman's service employees: unionize with A. Philip Randolph and you can be replaced. Between the mid-1920s and the early 1930s, Pullman work became a Filipino niche in the Second City, employing as many as three hundred of Chicago's estimated two thousand Filipino residents. Ranked higher on the hierarchy than African Americans, the Filipinos nonetheless could not advance at Pullman based on performance or seniority, for the company reserved conductor positions for Whites. Filipinos also faced a myriad of regulations, violation of which readily led to docked paychecks or to suspension. My interviewees made clear the ways that they and their countrymen had engaged in passive resistance against harsh treatment. For someone who had read Kenneth Stampp on slave behavior, I did not need an elaborate notion of "agency" to help tell the Filipinos' story.[1]

But I soon discovered more than work lives, sometimes very directly from the elderly wives who sometimes sat in on the interviews and supplied added details and perspective. Given my longstanding interest in women's history, the path to a portrait of the interracial community in which these women had long participated emerged right away. A second article, "Crossed Boundaries," took that direction.[2] In ways about which I was not fully conscious when I wrote, my subject became a study of the women's self-marginalization when these White, ethnic women chose to marry Filipino men stigmatized by race and ineligible for citizenship. When they married across the color line, the women were amazingly naïve about the burden of race and often sacrificed, at least at first, their own family connections with parents and siblings who opposed their marriages. They found it difficult to find housing when landlords would not rent to inter-racial couples—much less purchase homes, even if they had the money for a down payment—and they lived their lives with the daily prospect of racial or ethnic slurs.

As I had done with the Filipinos in "Hierarchy of Color," I followed that aspect of the new social history that stressed agency and denied victimhood. I presented the women of "Crossed Boundaries" as rational actors and survivors, and possibly underestimated the costs of their decisions, even though the costs to my mother for having married my father should have been apparent to me as I grew up.

Before I entered my teens, I formed a personal understanding of my own racial identity, of being neither White nor Black, but part Filipino,[3] not on the basis of exclusion—indeed, in the absence of *any* students of another color, my grammar school friends were all White—or because of insults hurled by strang-ers, but rather because of my emerging awareness of how race shaped the fear with which my parents lived throughout their lives together. In the 1950s and 1960s, apart from our attendance at Catholic mass or a rare dinner excursion to Chinatown with other interracial couples, my parents avoided being seen together in public. I knew that they feared verbal abuse, and that my mother feared worse for my father. I regularly went out with my mother *or* my father—shopping at Marshall Field's, eating hamburgers at Wimpy's, going to the local park—but never with *both* of my parents. Hence, two rare exceptions remain clear in my mind. In the late 1950s, after my parents learned that Marlon Bran-do's film *Sayonara* dealt with interracial love between American airmen and Japanese women, we saw it together in a neighborhood theater. Almost twenty years later, in 1976, my husband, Roland, and I took my parents to a fancy Scan-dinavian restaurant for my father's seventy-fifth birthday as our way of assuring them that they no longer had to fear being seen together in public.

By the early 1980s, I had become something of a pioneer in unexplored territory. My first two articles had pointed out the differences between the small Filipino community in Chicago, which originated in the transition from sojourner to settler of relatively well-educated young men who found steady work in the service sector and often married interracially. They contrasted markedly with the typically less-educated Filipinos laboring in agriculture on the West Coast who could not marry because of antimiscegenation laws that "my" Filipinos did not face. At this point, as throughout my subsequent career, I benefited greatly from mentorship. Roger Daniels, on his way to being a pre-eminent historian of immigration and ethnicity, had agreed to read my early work and began what is now more than thirty years of advice and encourage-ment. Closer to home, Northern Illinois University history department col-leagues C. H. George, J. Carroll Moody, Mary Furner, and Al Young had recently assisted me to earn tenure when the dean opposed it. The founder of NIU's interdisciplinary Southeast Asian Studies Center, anthropologist and Philippine specialist Donn V. Hart, helped me win a Senior Fulbright Research Fellowship at the University of the Philippines for the fall semester of 1982. My newly acquired spouse, historian Roland L. Guyotte, a fellow Northwestern alumnus, who had concentrated up until then in the history of U.S. higher education, came along on the trip, and we began an academic collaboration that has endured for three decades.

Our time in the Philippines proved to be a scholarly turning point. Although it may have seemed unlikely to go overseas to learn about the American experience of Filipino immigrants, the American Historical Collection, then located in the U.S. Embassy, held important published materials unavailable elsewhere, including Philippine magazines containing articles written by Filipinos in America. Some of them, especially about Filipino undergraduate life overseas in the 1920s, piqued Roland's curiosity and contributed to our joint work on the student origins of the Chicago Filipino community. Though the term itself would not surface for more than a decade, we became premature "transnationalists" by interviewing Filipinos who had completed their studies in the Midwest in the 1930s and returned home to successful careers in the Philippines. The widow of one of them—like my mother, of Polish origin—had been one of the few White wives to accompany her husband. In addition, a few Filipinos had lived out their working lives in Chicago and had retired to the Philippines.

The Fulbright research became the primary source of "Unintentional Immigrants," our first cowritten article.[4] Both it and "Aspiration and Reality" took the story back in time from the 1930s, the primary focus of "Hierarchy of Color" and "Crossed Boundaries."[5] As I moved further into the lives of the Filipino Chicagoans, I found additional topics to write about, and the social history triad of the 1980s—race, class, and gender—helped organize most of them, especially "Ethnic Life and Labor" and "Filipinos and Race in Twentieth Century Chicago."[6] The Fulbright research-based articles on the student community emphasized the role of higher education as a means for social mobility in a Philippine society modernizing under the tutelage of American rule. Though some of the Chicago students hoped for lives in politics or private enterprise, far more envisioned themselves as credentialed professionals using their American college degrees to advance their homeland through contributions in scientific agriculture, engineering, education, and medicine. They thus fit well into the land grant mission of Midwestern higher education, and embraced more of the American project in the Philippines than they rejected. In comparison with subsequent harsh critics of imperial rule who viewed the students from the perspective of a nationalist Philippines dissociating itself from the American era, I have tended to accept these Filipinos at their word. They saw themselves as nation builders forging the only feasible path to independence.

Yet the central story of the Filipino community in Chicago had much to do with disappointment largely influenced by factors beyond its residents' control. How might these young men imagine that the success of the early government-sponsored *pensionados* reflected an American commitment to the Philippines that would later wane, that this first generation of American-trained college graduates would take up most of the civil service positions in the Islands and stifle their mobility, or that continuing economic troubles back home would intensify during the Great Depression? Thus, the work they found, whether they had completed their schooling or not, was almost invariably at a lower level than that for which they had trained. Though many forged lasting unions with American-born wives, many did not, either staying single or becoming divorced. Race determined where they could work, where they could live, and, in the transition period after the 1934 law (which virtually halted immigration from the Philippines), whether they could safely visit the Philippines and then reenter the United States to reclaim their jobs or rejoin their families.

Our next project somehow belied this gloomy view. I had long remembered the community's major holiday celebration, an annual banquet held on December 30 to honor Philippine national hero José Rizal, executed by the Spaniards in 1896. Rizal, a polymath ophthalmologist, poet, novelist, and anthropologist, had been a convenient hero for Americans because he predated the Philippine-American War. He had been a special hero for the Filipino student community because his accomplishments gave the lie to American claims that the typical Filipino wore a breechcloth and ate dogs. I had seen my parents' copies of the huge, panoramic photographs of downtown hotel ballrooms filled with Filipino men and their American-born wives or girlfriends, almost all formally dressed, without ever thinking of their Depression era context! When Roger Daniels helped us get an invitation to a conference on "Feasts and Celebrations in North American Ethnic Groups," held in Paris in December 1989, we eagerly accepted. Roland had read Eric Hobsbawm and Terrence Ranger's collection, *The Invention of Tradition*, and this helped structure our essay, which turned into a survey of the changing ways Filipinos had commemorated Rizal, from an earnest early student ceremony at the University of Chicago in 1906, to the downtown galas of the 1930s, to celebrations at suburban hotels in the 1980s. Rizal Day began as an argument demonstrating the worthiness of Filipinos for independence, but morphed into an ethnic festival, special to Filipinos, but similar to those of other American immigrant groups, a rite of symbolic ethnicity. Most important, though I did not know it then, the Rizal article pushed me to think about the future, the post-1945 and eventually post-1965 immigration from the Philippines.[7] On a personal note, we were made both happy and sad several years later to discover that our late mentor

Bob Wiebe had chosen to include the Rizal article in the bibliography of his post-humously published *Who We Are: A History of Popular Nationalism.*[8]

If thinking about Rizal Day moved me to consider a longer time frame for Filipino American history, association from 1987 onward with the Filipino American National Historical Society (FANHS) convinced me to take on the spatial range of the immigrants' experience in the United States as well. Much of my early work had been devoted to explaining how Midwestern Filipino Americans of the "old-timer" generation had differed from their counterparts on the West Coast and in Hawaii. This did not change, but interaction with this newly founded group of nonprofessional historians helped me rethink my own work. FANHS was the brainchild of Fred and Dorothy Cordova, second-generation Filipinos from California and Washington State and community leaders in a vibrant multiracial Seattle neighborhood. FANHS members of their generation had become successful professionals, especially in the public sector, who coexisted gingerly with some of the post-1965 immigrants, also professionals but Philippine-trained before immigrating to the United States. Typically more culturally and politically conservative than American-born Filipinos, the newcomers seemingly viewed themselves as the only authentic Filipinos. "You don't speak Tagalog?!" They often displayed little sympathy for the legacy of workers who struggled for livings in the fields and canneries and as barbers or café operators in the "little Manilas" of the 1930s and 1940s—or for the accomplishments of the old-timers' children. FANHS members set out to reclaim and instill pride in that legacy. And, for my purposes, class differences among Filipinos, and the legal regimes that had governed both earlier and later immigrants, entered the narrative.

Ronald Bayor's invitation to contribute *The Filipino Americans* to his series "The New Americans" brought me foursquare into the study of the post-1965 Filipino immigrants. I drew upon my earlier work in women's history and the history of specific communities, as well as my newer interest in law and policy, to examine occupational preferences, family reunification, and paths to citizenship.[9] The book also covered topics such as Filipino values and customs in an American setting, generational challenges, and continuing ties to the Philippines. Though many of the specifics were relatively new to me given that I had little day-to-day contact with recent immigrants, I found that my historical background helped me express my findings clearly. As I came to understand the centrality of family for post-1965 immigrants who sought to take advantage of the reunification provisions in the 1965 law, I developed the concept of "strategic citizenship" and have applied it in subsequent research and writing.[10]

One contemporaneous project that interrogated the larger story laid out in *The Filipino Americans* became "Filipino Families in the Land of Lincoln," a case study of a modestly sized Filipino community, composed almost entirely of post-1965 immigrants, in Springfield, Illinois.[11] Roland and I scrutinized more than twenty years of local Filipino organizational records and publications provided to us by physician Virgilio Pilapil. Then we interviewed representatives of two generations of Springfield's Filipinos—the earlier immigrants, largely physicians who arrived in the late 1960s and 1970s to practice medicine in Springfield, in small neighboring communities facing a doctor shortage and at the local V.A. hospital, and the more recently arrived Filipinas who came to central Illinois in the 1990s as "pen-pal brides" married to typically older American-born White men. Despite their lack of professional status, the newcomers could win acceptance and incorporation into the existing Filipino community *if* they conformed to the relatively conservative social order that had evolved among the professionals who organized themselves through Catholic devotions and charities, annual celebrations showcasing the scholarly achievements of their children and grandchildren, the Knights and Ladies of Rizal, and the local Filipino Historical Society of Springfield. The earlier professional cohort regularly returned to the Philippines to visit family and friends, as well as to provide medical care for poor Filipinos, and thus might be termed *translocal* as defined by Elliott Barkan.[12] However, with the older immigrants largely on the cusp of retirement and their adult children mostly married to non-Filipinos, it was the newcomers who showed more interest in sending remittances to those at home and using their citizenship to eventually bring family members to the United States.

With the new century, such powerful paradigms as transnationalism, globalism, and state policy have found echoes in our recent work. In 2006, "Interracial Marriages and Transnational Families: Chicago's Filipinos in the Aftermath of World War II" appeared in a special issue of the *Journal of American Ethnic History* edited by Elliott Barkan.[13] Originally presented to a University of Minnesota Conference honoring Rudolph Vecoli on his retirement, it scrutinized the naturalization petitions of 444 Filipino Chicagoans who rushed to become citizens in the six months after July 4, 1946, the date when they ceased being "aliens ineligible to citizenship." This project brought me full circle—back to my father and his generation—as I viewed a Chicago *Sun Times* photograph of Filipinos taking the citizenship oath that included my father. These documents confirmed our long-held hypothesis about the significant differences between prewar Chicago and West Coast Filipino communities, and also highlighted the old-timers' continuing connections to the Philippines, which had remained implicit in earlier publications. A subsequent article took a longer view of U.S. government policies originating in the 1940s that affected not only the old-timers but also war brides and fiancés, nurses and other specialized professionals, and most recently the Filipino veterans of Philippine units mobilized during World War II.[14] Strategic citizenship provided the linkage for otherwise disparate events across two generations, as Filipinos utilized legislation to assist family members to migrate to the United States both before and after 1965.

These activities included the efforts by family members of the aging veterans in the Philippines who were promised citizenship decades earlier, and Filipino American activists in the United States, to short-circuit the long waiting lists for entry. Again, Filipino agency in response to the cards the legal system dealt them shaped the story.

Though I certainly still consider myself a U.S. historian, in recent years I have recognized the global context of Philippine migration. As its postwar economy faltered, the Philippine government systematically encouraged Filipinos to work overseas so the remittances they send home to their relatives will help sustain the nation. Probably a greater percentage of Filipinos labor overseas—in Hong Kong, the Persian Gulf, Nigeria, Italy, Canada, and on ships plying the world's oceans—than any other country's nationals. Because these Filipinos, like those who migrated to the United States after 1965, are far more likely to be female and already married, they do not especially resemble the young male colonials of the old-timer era in the United States. Nor are they routinely eager or able to become citizens of the countries in which some of them work for decades. Our 2003 article, "'Life Is a Gamble,'" emphasized gender, and most recently, "Sending Money 'Home,'" a tentative comparison of remittance policies and practices, compared the Philippines and Mexico among other nations.[15] That piece originated at an international conference in Krakow, where I surprised the multinational audience by mentioning my Polish grandfather from nearby Rzezsów, who contributed only modestly to my mostly Filipina features.

Over the last thirty years, my work has evolved in new directions but has also retained significant continuities. I remain a fairly unrepentant "new social historian," suspicious of the sometimes empty theorizing that is often ungrounded in primary research or historical context. Long ago, I also abandoned that part of social science history that saw people primarily as numbers. Though I am as happy as anyone to deploy census data or construct tables from naturalization petitions, the stories of individuals, with all their variability, remain central to what I write. From my earliest days in the field, I have wanted to invite the previously excluded into the conversation. Over time, I have discovered even more complexity in that endeavor than I originally expected.

Notes

1. Barbara M. Posadas, "The Hierarchy of Color and Psychological Adjustment in an Industrial Environment: Filipinos, the Pullman Company, and the Brotherhood of Sleeping Car Porters," *Labor History* 23 (Summer 1982): 349–373.
2. Posadas, "Crossed Boundaries in Interracial Chicago: Pilipino American Families since 1925," *Amerasia* 8 (Fall–Winter 1981): 31–52.

3. I made an early attempt at exploring these issues in "Mestiza Girlhood: Interracial Families in Chicago's Filipino American Community since 1925," in *Making Waves: An Anthology of Writings by and about Asian American Women*, ed. Asian Women United of California (Boston: Beacon Press, 1989), 273–282.

4. Posadas and Roland L. Guyotte, "Unintentional Immigrants: Chicago's Filipino Foreign Students Become Settlers," *Journal of American Ethnic History* 9, no. 2 (Spring 1990): 26–48.

5. Posadas, "Ethnic Life and Labor in Chicago's Pre-World War II Filipino Community," in *Labor Divided: Race and Ethnicity in United States Labor Struggles, 1835–1980*, ed. Robert Asher and Charles Stephenson (Albany: State University of New York Press, 1990), 63–80; Posadas and Guyotte, "Aspiration and Reality: Occupational and Educational Choice among Filipino Migrants to Chicago, 1900–1935," *Illinois Historical Journal* 85, no. 2 (Summer 1992): 89–104.

6. Posadas and Guyotte, "Filipinos and Race in Twentieth-Century Chicago: The Impact of Polarization between Blacks and Whites," *Amerasia Journal* 24, no. 2 (1998): 135–154.

7. Guyotte and Posadas," Celebrating Rizal Day: The Emergence of a Filipino Tradition in Twentieth-Century Chicago," in *Feasts and Celebrations in North American Ethnic Communities*, ed. Ramon A. Gutierrez and Genevieve Fabre (Albuquerque: University of New Mexico, 1995), 111–127.

8. Robert H. Wiebe, *Who We Are: A History of Popular Nationalism* (Princeton: Princeton University Press, 2001), 265.

9. Posadas, *The Filipino Americans* (Westport, Conn.: Greenwood, 1999).

10. Posadas, "Strategic Citizenship: Filipino Migration and Filipino American Ethnicity in an Age of Globalization and Transnationalism" (paper presented at the 93rd annual meeting, Organization of American Historians, St. Louis, Mo., April 2, 2000).

11. Posadas and Guyotte, "Filipino Families in the Land of Lincoln: Immigrant Incorporation in Springfield, Illinois, since 1965," in *From Arrival to Incorporation: Migrants to the U.S. in a Global Era*, ed. Elliott R. Barkan, Hasia Diner, and Alan M. Kraut (New York: New York University Press, 2007), 143–162.

12. Elliott R. Barkan, "America in the Hand, Homeland in the Heart: Transnational and Translocal Immigrant Experiences in the American West," *Western Historical Quarterly* 35, no. 3 (Autumn 2004): 335–341.

13. Posadas and Guyotte, "Interracial Marriages and Transnational Families: Chicago's Filipinos in the Aftermath of World War II," *Journal of American Ethnic History* 25, nos. 2–3 (Winter–Spring 2006): 134–155.

14. Posadas and Guyotte, "Strategic Citizenship and Immigration from the Philippines," in *Immigration and the Legacy of Harry S. Truman*, ed. Roger Daniels (Kirksville, Mo.: Truman State University Press, 2010), 96–119.

15. Posadas and Guyotte, "'Life is a Gamble': State Policies, Gender, and the Global Context of Filipino Migration to the United States," in *Remapping Asian American History*, ed. Sucheng Chan (Walnut Creek, Calif.: AltaMira Press, 2003), 153–169; Posadas and Guyotte, "Sending Money 'Home': Toward a Transnational History of Immigrant Remittances," in *Between Old and New: Studies in the History of World Migrations*, ed. Agnieszka Malek and Dorota Praszalowicz (Frankfurt am Main: Peter Lang, 2011), 11–26.

6

From Back of the Yards to the College Classroom

DOMINIC A. PACYGA

Historians think of themselves as objective observers of the past, but like all human beings our points of view are largely shaped by our experiences. We began our journey as students of the past at a very young age as we took in our circumstances and understood our environment. These influences cannot help but impact our worldview. This is especially true for those of us who grew up in tight ethnic communities and then went on to write about the history of those communities. Ethnic families and neighborhoods shaped many of the immigrant, ethnic, and working-class historians who came to adulthood in the 1960s. This insider knowledge hopefully gave us a deeper insight into the historical experience. Certainly it shaped my approach to immigrant/ethnic and urban history.

My career as a historian began as I observed life in the legendary Chicago neighborhood, the Back of the Yards. Located to the south and west of Chicago's Union Stock Yards, a sense of history filled the neighborhood. Its streets literally told the story of American immigration, while the stockyards spoke volumes on industrialization, labor history, and social class. Twelve Catholic churches could be reached within a fairly easy walk from my house. Irish, German, Polish, Lithuanian, Czech, Slovak, Ukrainian, French, and Mexican Catholic churches rang their bells three times a day for the Angelus prayers.

Ethnic businesses filled the main thoroughfares and Polish, Lithuanian, and Russian Jewish merchants dealt their wares all along Forty-seventh Street and down Ashland Avenue. The Goldblatt Brothers and Meyer Brothers department stores dominated Ashland Avenue and marked the early boundaries of my life. Bakeries abounded on the main and side streets, selling their German, Czech, Polish, Lithuanian, and Mexican cookies, cakes, *kolaczki* (cookie-like filled pastries), *pączki* (jelly-filled doughnuts), and excellent rye bread. Delicatessens and meat markets offered their products to fit nearly every ethnic taste. The

Vitak-Elsnic music store was a great depository of East European music, although I went there to listen to the latest rock and roll records. Jasinski's music store sold hard-to-find East European instruments and sheet music as well.

Neighborhood churches were always paired with a local funeral parlor. Sacred Heart parish had the Wolniak Funeral Parlor, located across the street, but many of the Polish highlanders, or *gorale*, preferred the Bafia Funeral Parlor on Forty-seventh Street, as the family that owned it was active in the Polish Highlanders Alliance. The Lithuanians at Holy Cross parish took their deceased to the Eudeikis Funeral Home. Every family wanted its dead cared for by one of their own, someone who understood the long-established ways of sending their relatives and friends properly to their own God. Adding to this diversity were the everyday crowds of African Americans who rode streetcars and later buses through the neighborhood to reach their jobs in the packinghouses and other local industries that made up the core of our neighborhood.

My family history had paralleled a large part of the American experience of the twentieth century. Immigration, labor strikes, the Great Depression, and World Wars I and II made up much of the talk around Babka's (Grandmother's) kitchen table. My father had served in World War II and was a highly decorated veteran of the European Theater. My uncles had all been in the service and the youngest, Chester, whom everyone called Lefty, went to Korea. Uncle Lefty had been seriously wounded early in the Korean War, and when he came home he continued his struggle to become a working-class intellectual. He read voraciously and did his best to get me interested in a mix of Marx, Nietzsche, Aristotle, Plato, and Buddhism.

One of the two high school graduates in the family, Lefty faced the problems associated with the self-educated thinker. He wandered from one philosophy to another, never finding a home, but encouraging me to read and try to understand great books. Talking with him was fascinating, and his quest to learn inspired me. Lefty introduced me to geography and classical music, especially Tchaikovsky. His was a particularly Slavic gloom, inspired by his traumatic experience in the Korean War and the frustration born of his inability to find an intellectual home. He once told me that my grandfather, himself an avid reader of Henryk Sienkiewicz, Adam Mickiewicz, and other Polish authors, had told him to write a book only after he had accomplished the impossible task of reading all the books published. When Lefty died, he was still reading.

Babka's green kitchen proved to be a wonderful place to hear stories. She sat magisterially in the center of her domain, watching everything and commenting on everyone. My maternal grandmother left Poland in the company of cousins before the age of twenty, had her first taste of ice cream in Bremen, Germany, while waiting to board the ship for America, and soon married my grandfather, Stanisław Walkosz. They were both *gorale* from the same village,

Szaflary, in the Tatra Mountains of southern Poland and met here in Chicago. My grandfather, or Dziadek, went to work in the packinghouses east of Ashland Avenue like the other *gorale* of Back of the Yards. They raised seven children in an intensely Polish American household. Dziadek died after a packinghouse accident in 1948, less than a year before I was born, but his memory and spirit seemed always to be nearby.

While Babka ruled over her domain, the radio was always tuned to Chicago's Polish station. Marysia Data would awaken me through the radio every morning either at Babka's or in our family's close-by four-room flat with her piercing Polish yodel that announced the start of the day. Father Justin's Rosary Hour was often heard at night. The hilarious Siekierka family, with their son Junior—played by Bruno Zielinski—ruled Polish American radio comedy. Meanwhile, Chicago-born Little Wally Jagiello created the Chicago Polka Sound and was always a favorite both on local radio and television. Classical music meant Chopin and the celebrated Ignace Jan Paderewski. In Babka's kitchen, General Jozef Pilsudski would always remain a hero and General Władysław Sikorski, a martyr for the cause of Polish freedom.

Outside of Babka's kitchen, the most Polish space in the neighborhood was Sacred Heart Church on Wolcott Street. A three-story multiuse building with the church on the second floor, Sacred Heart provided the heart and soul of our community. Here I went to daily Mass with the other students of Sacred Heart Grammar School. The Felician Sisters taught us and watched carefully so that their working-class charges did not get out of control. Once or twice a month the sisters taught us Polish, but by the 1950s and early 1960s few of us except those recent immigrants who had been displaced by the war spoke the language. I, because of family gatherings in Babka's green kitchen, did and do speak the local patois we called *po Chicagosku* or in the Chicago manner, the usual mixture of Polish and English words with Polish endings attached. It was the lingua franca of West Forty-seventh Street in the 1950s and 1960s. It also brought me closer to those displaced Polish students at Sacred Heart who had been born after the war in Germany, Poland, or England and were allowed into the United States under the Displaced Persons Act or as political refugees because of the communist takeover of Poland in 1945. We became fast friends on the streets of Back of the Yards and in each other's homes: their parents happy that they had an American friend who spoke enough Polish to be understood, my parents pleased to have Polish-speaking children coming in and out of our apartment.

I served as an altar boy during Mass and the various Polish language Rosary Hours, Forty-Hour Devotions, Holy Hours, and Lenten rituals. Funeral masses were especially moving, as the organist sang traditional Polish hymns. Wedding parties and wakes were the two most important neighborhood rituals that surrounded these various church events. Just about every tavern had a banquet hall behind the barroom. These provided public places of celebration. After the wedding ceremony in the church, family and friends would gather at a local hall to feast on Polish sausage, chicken, and roast beef accompanied by salads, green beans, potatoes, and plenty of talk and drink, and then dance the night away. Polish weddings were memorable events with bands playing heart-pounding polkas well past midnight. All of this was accompanied by an open (free) bar, which more often than not fueled fights among the younger men. An off-duty Chicago cop usually sat at the door to break up arguments and scare the legion of children who ran about the hall playing tag or hide and seek.

Funeral masses were somber events accompanied by the singing of religious hymns that would often cause mourners to weep and occasionally pass out, but wakes were always more communally joyful events. Old people gathered to tell stories during each of the then three nights of a Polish wake. In 1966 some two hundred people came nightly to honor Babka and laugh as well as cry at her wake held at Bafia's on Forty-seventh Street. A wake was a natural event that community members and their children were expected to attend to pay their condolences. After a while the men would make their way to a nearby tavern to drink and tell more stories.

Whereas life in Back of the Yards was a series of communal events, high school meant leaving the comfort and protection of my Polish American world and entering a larger arena. De La Salle Institute located on Thirty-Fifth and Wabash, a good forty-minute, two-bus ride away was hardly Polish in its educational culture. Located in the heart of Bronzeville, the African American neighborhood about two miles to the east of Back of the Yards, De La Salle, an all-boys Catholic school, was taught by a primarily Irish American group of La Sallean Christian Brothers and lay teachers. The heavy, gray, nineteenth-century building stared down Thirty-fifth Street looking like a fortress. Founded the same year as Jane Addams's Hull House, De La Salle had educated the then mayor, Richard J. Daley, and his son, the future mayor Richard M. Daley, who had graduated just a few years before my arrival. It was the first time I met someone who could not pronounce my last name correctly—or at all for that matter.

This was definitely not a Polish world. In fact, it was a very diverse world of students from across the South Side. Black, Chinese, Hispanic, and White ethnic students mingled in the corridors and classrooms. They competed on the athletic fields, and Latin, Spanish, or French replaced Polish in the foreign language classroom. No one mentioned Poland in a history class unless I did. Chicago's diversity was on display at Thirty-Fifth and Wabash. De La Salle taught us about loyalty to church, family, neighborhood, city, and by extension to the nation and the Democratic Party. It was the most American place I had known up to that time. At De La Salle I met a cadre of teachers who would be the first to inspire me to stay in school and go on to college and graduate school. One learns from bad teachers as well, and there were a few. I learned how to teach and not to teach from my time as a student at De La Salle.

What I ended up studying and teaching came from the streets of Chicago's neighborhoods. It seemed that I had always worked. One year, I sought out a job at Meyer Brothers and there met Harry, who became my Yiddish uncle. Harry had been born in Ukraine and told fascinating stories as we worked in the shoe department. He could sell a pair of shoes to just about anybody. Harry spoke more than twelve languages and began peddling as a small boy. He traveled throughout Europe selling and learning. By the time he made it to Meyer Brothers he had invaluable skills, especially in a neighborhood like the Back of the Yards, where a proficiency in various Eastern and Central European languages came in handy. Harry's stories brought the larger immigrant world to me, a world that included more than Polish packinghouse workers. He opened my eyes to a wider world, a world that would eventually lead me to read a whole new literature ranging from Alfred Kazin to Saul Bellow to Philip Roth to Bernard Malamud and Isaac Bashevis Singer. Here I would find, through Harry and through Jewish writers, an immigrant group not like us, but not so unlike us either. We had shared the same space both in Europe and America.

I read Upton Sinclair's *The Jungle* for the first time in high school. Although I understood his radicalism—most of my relatives were liberal Democrats if not closet socialists—something about the novel felt wrong. The Back of the Yards I knew, while it still smelled, or rather stank, of the stockyards and fertilizer plants just the other side of Ashland Avenue, was not such a desperate place as Sinclair portrayed. It bothered me that none of the characters in *The Jungle* enjoyed themselves even briefly; disaster seemed the natural outcome of their lives, and a desperate struggle for existence marked them. Why had my grandparents stayed in the neighborhood? They had arrived shortly after Sinclair's book appeared. Had it changed that much in a few years? The people I knew were not straw men and women blown this way and that by capitalism or anything else. The neighborhood's many taverns hardly seemed to be dark and evil places, but rather places frequented by men and women I knew and loved—a place to hear polka music on the jukebox or watch the White Sox on a black and white TV set hung on its perch in the corner of the room above the bar. Father Francis Karabasz, our parish's founder and pastor, who might have met Sinclair while a young priest in another Back of the Yards Polish parish, remained a venerable figure in the neighborhood and Sacred Heart Church the center of a vibrant community.

Nothing like this appeared in *The Jungle*. Had my grandparents and their generation lived such bleak lives? Why did my parents, aunts, and uncles stay in the neighborhood? Why did we still live in the neighborhood? The stories I heard as the old folks spoke at wakes or in the bars or in my Babka's green kitchen were not dire ones. When I got to college I quickly noticed that these same images of helpless forlorn immigrants appeared in my history books. These were not the people who watched over me as I made my way down the side streets of Back of the Yards. Those people, many of whom had arrived in Back of the Yards around the time Sinclair had written his novel, were strong individuals empowered by a sense of their place in the world and not shy about telling you about it. They had struggled, but had not been destroyed, and they built churches, fraternal organizations, unions, and even political machines in order to have what I would later, borrowing a term from John Kenneth Galbraith, call countervailing power. These people were my childhood heroes, but I did not see them either in *The Jungle* or in my American history classes. Instead, I found the huddled masses, the forlorn, the jetsam and flotsam of an ancient backward peasant Europe.

After graduating from De La Salle Institute in June 1967, I enrolled at the University of Illinois at Chicago Circle (UICC). The Circle, as it was generally called, was the first four-year public university in the city. The place was built on the West Side of the city and had displaced much of an old Italian neighborhood. The first time I walked onto the grounds in the fall of 1967, I realized I had entered another world. The huge, cold, gray campus seemed a daunting place for a freshman, and the times were tumultuous. Change was in the air. I came as a first-generation college student with some vague idea of majoring in history and becoming a high school teacher. The diversity of the city I had grown up in filled the place, as did the controversies of that turbulent decade. Students stood around small tables representing various organizations outside the then huge Pier Room dining hall and argued about the Vietnam War, the civil rights movement, racism, sexual liberation, and other topics. The Students for a Democratic Society (SDS) had a large contingent that called out to those entering the cafeteria to get involved, help stop the war, and create a new society. Professors practiced yoga on whatever small grassy areas they could find among the huge concrete slabs of this very urban campus. Jane Addams's Hull House looked out of place in front of the modernist student union; no longer a settlement house serving immigrants, it simply reminded persons walking by of its once noble existence and acted more as an outdated appendage rather than a symbol for the new university.

It was in the Pier Room that I came to find myself as a student of the city and its ethnic groups and eventually began to mature as a historian. Some working-class students came to claim one corner of the dining hall. Somehow we found each other among the twenty thousand or so Chicago Circle students. As I recall, a friend from my neighborhood told me he had met a wild poet and I had to meet him too. Before I knew it we had a group of friends from across the working-class neighborhoods of Chicago eating lunch regularly and just hanging out. Young men and women whose Polish American fathers worked in South Chicago's steel mills, along with Italian immigrants and Czechs from the Lower West Side, Irish and Jewish Chicagoans from South Shore, Mexicans from South Deering, and our small contingent from down by the stockyards gathered to talk about war, the Black civil rights movement, freedom, philosophy, poetry, religion, and history. I began to recognize the great weave of history while arguing about politics and life in the Pier Room. Coming from the Back of the Yards, I knew plenty of young men who were in Vietnam. I also hated the war that I felt was wrong, and yet I was torn as I felt a great loyalty to my buddies from the neighborhood who were now putting their lives, often against their wills, on the line in Southeast Asia. For both the answers to my questions and, frankly for relief from the troubled present, I turned to the past and immersed myself in the study of history.

In the summer of 1969 I worked in a steel processing plant on Fifty-first Street and California Avenue. I hated the job and quit after a few weeks. Afterward I began to search for employment and found myself walking east of Ashland and looking at old abandoned packinghouses. There was a small Swift & Co. sausage plant that was still operating, but it displayed a "no help wanted" sign. I had some vague idea that I might find a job in the old meatpacking district that my grandparents, mother, uncles, and aunts had worked in, but all the packers I knew of were gone. As I walked aimlessly east, I came upon the Union Stock Yard, which I had thought was also closed, but in fact the market for livestock still operated east of Racine Avenue. On a lark I walked into the employment office, a small office built under an abandoned livestock viaduct formerly used to move animals from the pens to the once-mighty kill floors to the west. That night I began my job as a livestock handler in the hog house, a one-story concrete and metal barn that could hold perhaps ten or fifteen thousand hogs if it had to. My job was to drive hogs back and forth from truck docks to sale pens. I unloaded hogs arriving for the next day's market and drove those purchased by packers to the truck dock pens to be loaded on outgoing trucks. We usually had between fifteen hundred and thirty-five-hundred hogs unloaded a night, although at times the numbers would reach nearly five thousand. I felt the reality of history especially on a ninety-degree day when dust would cover me as I drove several hundred hogs down the hog alleys armed with a slapper, a long piece of canvas on a stick that would make a firecracker sound on the back of a recalcitrant hog without leaving a bruise on its precious meat.

The voice of Sinclair echoed in my mind, and at times I felt like a concentration camp guard as the hog squeals told me the animals knew exactly what their fate was. The men I worked with were a cross section of Whites from the South Side; few African Americans worked for the Union Stock Yard & Transit Co., although they had dominated the mostly defunct packinghouses that surrounded the market. Polish and Irish Americans along with southern Whites and non-ethnic Whites who referred to themselves as mongrels worked the hog dock while one lone Mexican labored on the day shift. Some first came to the yards at the age of twelve or thirteen and loved telling stories about big cattle runs, strikes, or the big 1934 fire that burned down the yards and jumped across Halsted Street to savage part of Canaryville, the Irish neighborhood just to the east of the yards.

One of the younger livestock handlers turned out to be a university student like myself, but he had arrived on a mission. Sent by the SDS, he came to radicalize this small group of men who worked the hog dock from 5:30 P.M. to 1:30 A.M. I gather he had read *The Jungle*. When business was slow, we would sit on the benches by the dock or in the little dock office and eat our lunch. The SDS worker would stand on a bench and read from Mao's *Little Red Book*. The men listened politely and went back to work. Old Firpo, who was nicknamed after a famous prizefighter in the 1930s, would listen, chew tobacco, and ask me what I thought. I just laughed and would read my history book.

I came from the same neighborhood as these men and I knew they would have nothing to do with the SDS or Mao's *Little Red Book*. They especially would have no use for a rich kid in pre-med at the University of Chicago whose blond wife drove him to work each day in a Triumph Six, while the rest of us took the bus or drove tired old Chevies. The day before he was to be made permanent, someone fooled with his sandwich and the young radical fled the hog house vomiting. One of the men then turned to me and asked me if I was a revolutionary; I just shook my head and walked away. After my thirty days, I joined the union. Later, when the fall came, I left the yards for a while, as I could not work the late shift and go to classes at UICC, but I returned in the summer of 1970 and stayed on as a guard until the yards closed and were demolished in late 1971, working a shift from 2:00 P.M. to 10:00 P.M. I was able to work, take classes, and begin to understand how the stockyards and the Polish community had fit together. Ferpo, whose real name was Walter Konkol, became a friend and a source as I began to write about the Back of the Yards. When the stockyard closed, I saved primary sources sent to the dumpster and they eventually landed in the UICC special collections.

Working in the yards piqued my interest in social class, ethnicity, the Industrial Revolution, and the impact of technology. A child of the railroads that made Chicago a major transportation center, the stockyards fell prey to the interstate highway system, trucks, antiunion rules, and a shifting economy. Put simply, their time had passed and I had the privilege to be there as it happened. When the yards closed, I entered graduate school determined to write about Poland, but soon realized that what I really wanted to write about was Chicago's Polish working-class community, especially in Back of the Yards.

As an undergraduate in the late 1960s, I felt the waves of change riding across academia. Students wanted to know their own histories. Blacks demanded Black studies. Women wanted Women's studies. I did not feel part of the White majority, but I certainly was not Black. I felt drawn to Polish history, and Polish history in turn led me to seek out Professor Edward C. Thaden, the Russian historian at UICC. Dr. Thaden, a truly witty and humane man, encouraged me to study Poland's past. He and Professor Samuel Sandler in the Slavic Languages Department helped me to explore a language, history, and culture outside of the typical Western canon. Thaden suggested graduate school and in the fall of 1971, instead of going off to teach high school, I continued on at UICC in the graduate history program. I knew at that point that, if I could help it, I would never leave the academy.

It was the streets of Chicago and not those of Krakow or Warsaw that called to me. The smells of the stockyards, the glow of the open hearths in the steel mills, and the busy streets of Chicago's neighborhoods seemed to dare me to tell their story. Before I received my master's degree, I left Russian and Polish history with the blessing of Ed Thaden to explore the immigrant's role in American history. It was then that my own work experience as a livestock handler and security guard in the Union Stock Yards began to influence me as a historian. How did my family's history fit into the larger issues of the times? I wondered how and why I had ended up in Back of the Yards.

Graduate school was a truly enlightening and also, in some ways, discouraging experience. My working-class education had not prepared me as a writer. The need to work in order to pay for school weakened my focus on my studies all through high school and into college. Still, a working-class stubbornness made me resilient even after my graduate advisor told me I should take my master's degree and go home. It was then I met the immigration historian Leo Schelbert, thanks to an introduction by Ed Thaden, who once again came to my aid. Thaden suggested Schelbert take me on as a student and here I found what every graduate student must find in order to succeed, a true mentor and friend. Schelbert took me under his wing and I began to take the disparate ideas in my head and focus them to form a thesis and tell the story that I wanted, even needed, to tell. I began to write the history of the Poles who worked in the stockyards. A young urban historian at UICC, Perry Duis, warned me not to just focus on one Chicago neighborhood or one industry, but to look at South Chicago as well. The connections of neighborhood life in Chicago soon formed my approach. I would write about both packinghouse and steelworkers. I found two neighborhoods that were startlingly similar and began to look at all Chicago neighborhoods from the inside and wondered how they were put together.

Always the smells and bells of Catholicism, the raging discussions of Babka's green kitchen, the diversity of Forty-seventh Street, and my experiences working in local stores, factories, and finally the Union Stock Yards shaped my sense of history, justice, and even my approach to teaching. Over time what I saw as conventional neighborhood life began to seem a tale of historical importance.

The stories I heard around Babka's kitchen table started to make sense. History came alive as my parents, aunts, and uncles recounted tales of the neighborhood when they were growing up. While writing my first conference paper and then turning it into an article, I realized that a story I had heard years before about Babka hiding a striker under a bed as police searched for him had taken place during the 1921–22 strike in the packinghouses. In putting together the final version and adding photographs to it for *Chicago History*, I came across a photograph of a man running into a building chased by police. Then I realized he was a striker seeking refuge in the very building my grandparents lived in at the time. I had accidentally come across a photograph of a legendary event in my family's history! Other stories of neighbors and relatives involved in the strike leapt from the pages of Chicago's Polish newspapers as I continued my research.[1]

My upbringing in Back of the Yards prepared me to study the trinity of immigration, the working class, and Chicago. These subjects have dominated my academic life. In the late 1960s and 1970s, many younger historians embraced social history and began to explore the lives of those either not covered in traditional classrooms or bypassed quickly with a brief reference to Emma Lazarus's poem on the base of the Statue of Liberty or to the work of Oscar Handlin or perhaps to the Haymarket Riot or the Pullman Strike. If Polish immigrants were mentioned

FIGURE 5. Union Stock Yards, circa 1900. The Chicago Stockyards provided the economic heart of Chicago's Back of the Yards neighborhood for over one hundred years.

they were often referred to as one of the "New" immigrant groups that entered the country after 1880. Of course there were several books, the legendary William I. Thomas and Florian Znaniecki's sociological study of the Polish peasant in Europe and America, some amateur filiopietistic studies, institutional yearbooks, and so on. Some of them were rather well done and sources of long lost information, but it was not until Victor Greene's path-breaking work that true historical scholarship begin to shape the study of Polish Americans. Soon labor, urban, and ethnic historians began to uncover the immigrant past, and journals such as *Polish American Studies*, the *Polish Review*, the *Journal of Urban History*, and the *Journal of American Ethnic and Immigration History*, among others, began to shape the field. In addition to Victor Greene, Stephen Thernstrom and others opened up the study of these communities for us and profoundly influenced our generation of scholars. They of course had built on the solid foundation that Oscar Handlin and other historians had laid before them. In many ways this was also a logical progression from the work of African American historians, especially John Hope Franklin, who widened the scope of American history through their pioneering work. African American historians did for social history what the civil rights movement had done for society as a whole. For myself, my time in the racially integrated classrooms at De La Salle Institute and later UICC had transformed me both as a person and as a student of history. Once again my experiences on the streets of Chicago and its neighborhoods merged to create my personal approach to history.[2]

In graduate school I encountered Thomas and Znaniecki's classic study *The Polish Peasant in Europe and America*, along with Frederick M. Thrasher's *The Gang* and Clifford R. Shaw's *The Jack-Roller*. These founding documents of the Chicago school of sociology depicted a Polish community that was disorganized, under stress from modernization, and in decay. Although the Polish American community denied such claims, these studies, like Sinclair's portrayal of Chicago's immigrant ghetto, were widely accepted in academe. Here my life experience and my studies again began to clash. Even though I cherished the approach of the Chicago school and the many interviews, letters, and reports issued by Florian Znaniecki, W. I. Thomas, Ernest Burgess, and the others, their interpretations did not ring true to me. I had grown up in a community that was highly organized and supportive. Had it changed so much in a period of about fifty years? My research into the primary sources of Polish society in Chicago told me it had not. The Polish parish and the Polish family provided a strong basis for adjustment to modern capitalist society. A *gemeinschaft* response was perhaps more appropriate than a modern *gesellschaft* one given the poverty and biases faced by the immigrant generation. Indeed, it seemed that the resulting countervailing power had proven crucial for upward mobility. The Catholic parishes of the Back of the Yards and South Chicago, with their parochial schools, fraternal organizations, and ability to organize large numbers of immigrants and their children, empowered Polish Chicago. Those Catholic parishes built for worship proved to be engines of upward mobility. In a way their success meant the long-term destruction of those very neighborhoods they served. They allowed the children of immigrants to eventually move out to better, more middle-class neighborhoods and to more education and thus better employment. In short, they provided for upward mobility. My experiences on the streets of the Back of the Yards proved to be a valuable source for interpreting those historical events in the history of the Chicago Polonia (Polish ethnic community).[3]

In 1973 I became involved with the Polish American Congress (PAC) through a young activist who recommended me to President Aloysius Mazewski as someone to study poverty in Chicago's Polish community. In 1944 several Polish American organizations had created PAC as an umbrella organization to support a democratic Poland in the aftermath of World War II. Over the years, it attempted to influence American foreign policy and to advocate for Polish American interests. Mazewski, president of the Polish National Alliance as well as the PAC, took a liking to me and sent me to President Nixon's Washington to learn about the project. Al Mazewski was a wily politician, who, while a Nixon supporter, knew that his constituency was mostly working-class Democrats.[4]

The Chicago Polonia, even though ideology sometimes pulled it apart, was always about community. Mazewski wanted me to get a doctorate because he felt it was good for both the larger community and myself; he also knew that as a graduate student I was often in need of money. Over the years Mazewski arranged to fund various projects for me to work on for the PAC. I wrote a report on Polish American participation in Chicago area professional schools. Mazewski introduced me to Victor Greene's book and told me to write one about Chicago's working-class Polonia. He knew where my interests were and encouraged me as his "house" radical.

My work with PAC resulted not only in meeting Mazewski and allowing me to financially support the pursuit of my degree but it also gave me a wider knowledge of Polonia, including the post-1945 refugees, of which I knew little. These immigrants had been displaced by war and then by the imposition of communism on Poland after the Yalta Conference; many had fought in the underground Home Army, or in the Polish Army in the West. They were generally of a different social and cultural class than those immigrants of my grandparent's generation, and while they disagreed with me politically, again they fostered my career. In turn they taught me the value of community and institutional life, a valuable lesson for any historian, especially one interested in immigration, ethnicity, and cities. When doing my research and writing, I thought often of these postwar immigrants and the men I worked with in the stockyards. They gave me a perspective that would allow me to understand Chicago's neighborhoods and their often difficult-to-interpret political, social, and economic realities.

In the mid-1970s, while doing research at the Chicago Historical Society, I met Glen Holt, a young assistant professor at Washington University. We quickly became friends and began to give tours of Chicago's neighborhoods for the Newberry Library. Shortly thereafter Father Andrew Greeley, the notable sociologist, generously quoted my work in his book *Neighborhood*. At the same time, the irrepressible Fannia Weingartner, editor of publications for the Chicago Historical Society, took me under her wing and published my first article about the 1921 Packinghouse Strike in *Chicago History*, and then, thanks to the encouragement of Richard Jensen, Glen Holt and I coauthored what would be my first book in 1979, *Chicago: A Historical Guide to the Neighborhoods (Loop and South Side)*. I finally received my PhD in 1981 thanks largely to the patience of Leo Schelbert and the encouragement of my future wife, the historian Kathleen Alaimo. By that time I had been hired as associate director of Columbia College's Southeast Chicago Historical Project. My work on the steel mills paid off as I began to work on a very successful public history project that centered on the city's Steel Mill District. In South Chicago, my Polish language skills and knowledge of Polish American culture came in handy and opened doors for the project to collect a valuable archive that now sits in the James P. Fitzgibbons Museum in Calumet Park. We collected more than five thousand photographs, created a twenty-five hundred square foot historical exhibit for the Museum of Science and Industry, a Public Broadcasting System film, and a photo book of the district's history.[5]

Over the years, I have come to realize the impact of my childhood and young adult experiences on my role as a historian. I was shaped by the talk in my Babka's green kitchen as well as on the hog dock and in the cattle alley of the Union Stock Yards. My experiences at De La Salle Institute, at UICC—now renamed the University of Illinois at Chicago (UIC)—and on the streets of Chicago helped me to both appreciate and understand the impact of events and cultures around me. My life experiences helped to free me from the negative and inaccurate paradigm established by the Chicago school of sociology, particularly by Thomas and Znaniecki, and later by Oscar Handlin. The people and institutions of the Back of the Yards gave me a greater insight into the historical processes I wrote about in my dissertation, which later evolved into a book, *Polish Immigrants and Industrial Chicago: Workers on the South Side, 1880–1922*. The men and women of Polonia gave voice to the historical record that I researched. My work, not only on the Polish community but also on Chicago, would have been the lesser without their help in understanding the historical events I explored. Graduate school sharpened the tools and gave me a wider view of the world and the historical trends that shaped it. In the end we are all the product of thousands of occurrences both big and small, both under our control, and wildly out of it. To be able to search the past to understand the present is indeed a privilege.

Notes

1. Dominic A. Pacyga, "Crisis and Community: The Back of the Yards 1921," *Chicago History* (Fall 1977): 167–176.
2. Victor R. Greene, *The Slavic Community on Strike: Immigrant Labor in Pennsylvania Anthracite* (South Bend, Ind.: University of Notre Dame Press, 1968); Oscar Handlin, *The Uprooted: The Epic Story of the Great Migrations That Made the American People* (New York: Grosset and Dunlap, 1951); John Hope Franklin, *From Slavery to Freedom: A History of Negro Americans* (New York: Alfred A. Knopf, 1947); Stephen Thernstrom, *The Other Bostonians: Poverty and Progress in the American Metropolis, 1880–1970* (Cambridge, Mass.: Harvard University Press, 1973).
3. William I. Thomas and Florian Znaniecki, *The Polish Peasant in Europe and America*, 5 vols. (Chicago: University of Chicago Press, 1918–1920); Frederick M. Thrasher, *The Gang* (Chicago: University of Chicago Press, 1927); Clifford R. Shaw, *The Jack-Roller* (Chicago: University of Chicago Press, 1930).
4. For a history of the Polish American Congress, see Joanna Wojdon, *W Imieniu Sześciu Milionów: Kongess Polonii Amerykańskiej w Latach 1944–1968* [In the Name of Six Million: The Polish American Congress, 1944–1968] (Toruń, Poland: Adam Marszałek Press, 2005), and Joanna Wojdon, *W Jedności Siła: Kongess Polonii Amerykańskiej w Latach 1968–1988* [In Solidarity Is Strength: The Polish American Congress, 1968–1988] (Toruń, Poland: Adam Marszałek Press, 2008). See Also Donald Pienkos, *For Your Freedom and Ours: Polish American Efforts on Poland's Behalf, 1863–1991* (Boulder, Colo.: East European Monographs, 1991).
5. Andrew Greeley, *Neighborhood* (New York: Seabury Press, 1977); Glen E. Holt and Dominic A. Pacyga, *Chicago: A Historical Guide to the Neighborhoods; Loop and South Side* (Chicago: Chicago Historical Society, 1979). My dissertation was published as *Polish Immigrants and Industrial Chicago: Workers on the South Side, 1880 to 1922* (Columbus: Ohio State University Press, 1991; reissued by the University of Chicago Press, 2003).

7

Why Irish?

Writing Irish American History

TIMOTHY J. MEAGHER

He is a tiny figure in the photograph, so small that his features are hard to discern. In life, he had a long, thin face and nose, but in this photograph it is hard to see anything but a bowler hat, a snowy patch of white beard on his chin, a thin frame, and bowed legs. Yet the pose and the photo were important to him, because the place and the time were important to him. He is standing next to the door of a whitewashed cottage in Ireland. It was 1905, and he was home for the first time in a half century. He had left that cottage, left Ireland, left his childhood and his family's past for America in 1853. His wife left a similar cottage, not too far away—there is a photograph of it too. He is Henry McDermott and she is Bridget McDermott, born Bridget Hagan, my mother's paternal grandfather and grandmother, thus my great-grandfather and great-grandmother.

The house and the surrounding farm still stand today in Bellurgan, County Louth, at the beginning of the Carlingford or Cooley Peninsula, where Irish myth says the great Irish hero Cu Chulainn roamed and fought his battles. Irish, English, and Scottish armies battled, marched, and countermarched for centuries through the "gateway to Ulster," the Moyry Pass, nearby. Edward Bruce, brother of the great Scottish king, Robert Bruce, was killed in a battle for dominion over Ireland in the fourteenth century in Bridget (née Hagan) McDermott's townland of Faughart, and Bruce's body lies in the same graveyard there as some McDermott ancestors.

The farm sits on low ground next to Dundalk Bay and is surrounded by the River Flurry, which snakes around its fields. The neighborhood is called "the Marsh"—you get to it today on the Marsh Road leading from the highway—but it has been scraggly pasture and farmlands for centuries now, reclaimed perhaps long ago from wetlands created where the river met the Bay. Stand on the property now with your back to the water and look landward and you see grasslands and cultivated fields that slowly, then quickly, rise to the red and brown slopes of the Cooley Mountains.

There is little doubt that Bellurgan was still home to Henry McDermott even after all those years. His son, James A. McDermott, my mother's father, accompanied him on this trip and left an account of it. Though sparse, that account, nonetheless, makes his father's feelings clear. Henry walked through the house, James wrote, warmly noting furnishings still there from his childhood, and rode through the village and its environs in a horse-drawn trap shouting greetings to men and women, old neighbors, whom he had not seen for a half century.

Back in 1853, when he saw them last, however, Henry had been eager enough to leave. His brother James was already in America and begged Henry to join him. Yet more than James's entreaties or talk of a new world, it was the collapse of the family's fortunes at home that must have made up Henry's mind, and, indeed, had probably pushed James out earlier.

The McDermotts and the Meaghers

In the early decades of the nineteenth century, and perhaps for many years before that, the McDermotts of Bellurgan seemed to be doing quite well. A mix of evidence suggests this prosperity. They did not own their land—few Catholics did in nineteenth-century Ireland—but their landlord's rent roll in 1830 reveals that the McDermotts's property was one of the most valuable in Bellurgan or on the estate that extended beyond it. No one on the roll was charged a higher rent. A gravestone erected in the Faughart cemetery in 1818, large and elegant with carved angels, was another sign of their prosperity. More intriguing, just a few yards from where Henry stood for his photo, connected to "his" house, was another one, grand by the standards of Irish tenant farmers in the nineteenth century, two storied, and with minor decorations that hint at Georgian elegance. Evidence suggests that the McDermotts owned that house in Henry's youth.[1]

Henry did not stand beside the grander house for his photograph on his return in 1905. It no longer belonged to the McDermotts. It had been lost a half century before, part of the final crushing economic blow that broke his family and sent him and James to the United States. After 1815, falling agricultural prices, rising rents, and the contraction of the linen industry wreaked havoc with many Irish peasants, including the McDermotts. The same rent rolls that revealed the value of their property also recorded that they were chronically behind in paying their rent in the 1830s and 1840s. James's account of his father Henry's life also suggests the family's difficulties. Henry was born in County Dublin in 1828, about fifty miles south of Bellurgan, where, his son explains, Henry's father had gone to find work. Presumably, he found nothing lasting, as the family returned home to Louth soon thereafter.[2]

Somehow, the McDermotts managed to survive, despite these difficulties, until the late 1840s, when the potato blight finally pushed them and most of the country into the suffering and chaos of the Famine catastrophe. They were listed on a rent roll paying a rent of only four pounds in 1851, about one-sixth of what they had paid in 1830, and they did not appear in and around Bellurgan on the official Griffiths Valuation conducted in the early 1850s. Later in that decade, they finally popped up on legal records that showed them as joint tenants with another family, the McEvoys, on the lands the McDermotts had rented on their own. The McEvoys moved into the grander house, and their descendants live there today. May Mulligan, who married into the descendants of McDermotts still on the land, spoke vaguely in the 1980s about the Famine, when "the McDermotts gave land to the poor people."[3]

So Henry and his wife Bridget left for America and met up with Henry's brother, James, in Auburn, Massachusetts. Henry and Bridget later moved to Worcester, Massachusetts, where Henry found a job as a tanner, and they raised five children in an Irish neighborhood on the slopes of Vernon Hill on the city's East Side.

He sits in the photo posed like some icon of martial bearing: a formal, steady gaze, neat brass-buttoned uniform, and perched on his chair as if he were some French officer on a camp stool in a campaign. Yet the hair sprouting out from under his kepi cap and the youthful, dewy cheeks belie the military formality. The picture was taken some time between 1861 and 1864, when he fought for the Union in the Civil War as first a private then a corporal in the Second United States Cavalry, a regiment in the Army of the Potomac. His discharge papers list the battles he participated in during the war and they read like a list of the major engagements on the war's Eastern Front: Second Bull Run, Antietam, Fredericksburg, Chancellorsville, Gettysburg, the Wilderness, and Spotsylvania, among others. It was probably in the smaller cavalry fights, Brandy Station, Aldie, Middleburg, Upperville, Williamsport, however, when his unit plunged into the midst of charges, countercharges, and deadly volleys with Confederate cavalry that he been in the greatest danger. He was Dennis W. Meagher, my father's paternal grandfather and my great-grandfather.

And he was hardly more than a boy then. Sources disagree over how old he was. Irish baptismal records, his gravestone, census manuscript schedules, and his naturalization papers, suggest he may have been anywhere from fifteen to eighteen when he joined the army—perhaps eighteen, at most twenty-one, when the picture was taken. Dennis would marry Margaret Foley, an Irish immigrant, my father's paternal grandmother and my great-grandmother, after the war.

Unlike Henry, Dennis never went back to Ireland. Few Irish immigrants actually returned to their home and very few to stay. Yet Dennis had especially good reason not to go "home," because there was no home to go back to.

The Meaghers were from the townland of Moyneard, next to the village of Moyne or Moynetemple, near Thurles in northeastern County Tipperary. This is not the tourists' Ireland, with crashing waves on rocky coasts or craggy mountains dotted by waterfalls. It is Ireland's Iowa, green as much of the island is and not unpleasant, but flatlands with only slightly rolling hills, occasional copses of trees, and the Devil's Bit and other mountains eight or nine miles away on the horizon. There had been no Cu Chulainn there, but the Irish had handed the Normans their first defeat in Ireland not far away in 1174. In the half century before Dennis was born, its history was no less tumultuous, if less grand, filled with faction fights and highwaymen and agrarian secret societies such as the Whiteboys. Until recently, there was a memorial in the local graveyard to all the natives of Moyne who had gone—or been shipped as prisoners—to Australia.

Like the McDermotts, the Meaghers or Mahers of Moyneard appear to have been prosperous in the early nineteenth century. Dennis's grandfather or granduncle, Michael, held more than forty acres of land in the 1820s in Moyneard and paid a substantial five pounds for a pew in the local Catholic chapel. By the 1840s, he had disappeared from all land and church records and presumably was dead, and Maher land in Moyneard was divided up among three men, Dennis's father, Michael, and Anthony and Edmond, the latter either Michael's brothers or cousins. Dennis's father, Michael, wound up with only seventeen acres, too few to stave off economic troubles even in good times. It was not good times. After five years of famine, Dennis's father had lost his land and an 1850 ratepayers' list records his only holding as a tiny house. Dennis was one to four years old at the time.[4]

What happened to Dennis and his family in the next decade or so is not entirely clear. His father remained in the ratepayers' records holding only a house until 1856. Dennis, his mother, and his five siblings might have lived with him, spent time in a workhouse in Thurles, or boarded with their relatives, Anthony and Edmond in Moyneard, who still held their land—at least for the moment. But Dennis's siblings slowly began to dribble away to America. Con, the oldest brother, called Cornelius in America, went first in 1850, soon after his father had lost his land. Con's grandchildren believed that he went back, possibly several times, to bring his brothers and sister over to the United States. Several times seem unlikely, but he did go back to Ireland and he did bring others, Dennis among them, to America in 1857. In America, the siblings scattered, but not randomly: Dennis went with Conor (later called Cornelius) to Worcester, Massachusetts; Mary and John went to Chicago; and William and Michael to Missouri. Michael stopped in St. Louis; William ventured the farthest west of all his siblings, out to Boonville on the Missouri River.

Dennis would become a boot maker after the war, a member of the shoe and boot makers union, the Knights of St. Crispin, and was active in the great

Massachusetts Crispins strike of 1870. At some point in the late 1870s, he used some of his veteran's pension to buy a saloon in downtown Worcester. He had already married Margaret Foley, pretty, bright, and alert, from a photograph that remains of her. She may have come from Tipperary as well. The Meaghers had a number of children, though only three, including my grandfather, John Henry, survived to maturity.

Moyneard and Moyne meanwhile were lost, forgotten. Dennis himself claimed to be from Thurles on his gravestone, perhaps because it was a big, noteworthy town but a few miles from Moyne. (As people from Worcester will sometimes say they are from Boston: it is easier to explain.) Con more accurately listed the parish of Moyne on his memorial.

Yet the dispersal of Dennis's family and the "forgetting" of his family home had not broken his ties to kin and country. In 1912, his brother Michael visited him and Con in Worcester, the first time they had all seen each other in forty-seven years. Dennis died shortly thereafter, as if he were ready now to go. Long before that, he had fixed the spelling of his name. Various public records had listed him as Dennis Maher, but, at some point, after the Civil War, he began insisting on his last name being written Meagher. That is the more authentically Irish version; it had been replaced by the more Anglicized spelling of Maher during the spread of the English language in Ireland in the eighteenth and nineteenth centuries. Dennis, so the family story goes, had become enamored of Thomas Francis Meagher, once an Irish rebel, later an Irish American hero (of sorts). Thomas Francis Meagher was a brigadier general in the Union Army and commander of the Irish Brigade in many of its legendary battles in the Civil War, but critics claimed he was often drunk in combat, and, whether drunk or not, some Irish Americans thought he recklessly and needlessly endangered his troops on the battlefield.

My Family and Ethnic Identity

So that was where it began for me as a historian of Irish immigration to America and Irish American ethnicity—with Ireland and the migrants who left it for America.

Or was it?

In an obvious way, yes, as Ireland is the origin of "my people" in America. Yet, why are they, the Irish, Irish Americans, my people? I am many things, have many identities, and thus many pasts that mean a great deal to me, so why study this one?

The story I have told is not so much a beginning as an end. It is a history I have researched in the last twenty years and constructed in print here for the first time. Very little of it, just snippets really, came down to me through my family. My aunt Louise was the only one of my mother's siblings to remember my great-grandfather, Henry McDermott, but all she could recall was an old man who seemed rooted to a seat next to the stove in his family's kitchen. No one in my mother's family went back to Bellurgan after 1905, or, to my knowledge, even communicated with the McDermott descendants who still lived there until I went there with my aunt Katherine, Kitty McDermott, in 1987. My mother's siblings did not know where they came from, despite their father's account; some thought it was Howth, a neighborhood of Dublin, not Louth, the county. Members of my father's family knew even less about their origins. My aunt Peg, my father's sister, had hazy memories of Dennis, a diamond stickpin on his tie and an arm that hung listlessly at his side, which she thought was the result of a war wound. In the 1970s, my father asked Peg to write to Ireland, searching for the Meaghers' home, but without much result. From Peg, I inherited hundreds of family photographs from the nineteenth and early twentieth centuries neatly pasted in several fancy velvet- or leather-covered albums. Almost none of the pictures is identified, however, or ever will be.

My family's "forgetting" of its Irish origins was but part of a broader cultural forgetting of the Irishness my great-grandparents brought from Ireland. Not only were there few stories from Ireland, but also there were few artifacts, no crafts or skills, no foods, no music, no sports, no language. Roast beef was Sunday dinner for us in the 1950s and 1960s, and unless pouring a lot of red wine on it is somehow Irish, there was nothing to that meal that harkened back to the "old sod." My father thought Irish music was noise—I remember him complaining when I played a record of the famous traditional music group, the Chieftains. He preferred to listen to classical music (any kind—he was no connoisseur) while he raced through his Mickey Spillane novels after dinner. My mother was more sympathetic to Irish music, but had no real interest in it. We had some Bing Crosby records filled with Irish American Tin Pan Alley tunes then, but I can't recall my father and mother listening to them.

I grew up in Worchester, where my immigrant great-grandparents had settled. The American trinity of sports—baseball, basketball, and football, but especially baseball and the Red Sox—ruled in our house (one brother, who played most things well, also dabbled in hockey and excelled in tennis). I wouldn't see Irish hurling until it became a signature piece of ABC Television's old *World Wide World of Sports'* famous opening montage—striking because it showed a hapless hurler crumple, after blows from hurley sticks to his head, front and back—and I would not see Irish football until I came to Ireland many years later. I sometimes thought that phrases in my parents' or aunts' and uncles' language might have had roots in the Irish language or in "Irishized" English, but that was simply my own speculation; they never understood it as Irish. Last year, a researcher, Dr. Miriam Nyhan, assistant professor and faculty fellow in New York University's Irish

Studies program, came to interview me for the University's Irish American oral history archive. After moving through several questions for more than an hour or more, she seemed puzzled by this apparent total absence of cultural influences inherited from Ireland: "No music? No stories? Nothing?"

Yet it was not just Irish culture, old or new, but Ireland itself that was scarcely present in my childhood household. There were few discussions of its economic fortunes or its politics, even after the Troubles broke out in Ulster. Only my aunt Kitty went back to Ireland (although not to Bellurgan) when I was growing up. It was a special tour for her in the 1960s, but only one of her many trips to Europe then. I don't believe my father and mother ever thought of going to Ireland.

Perhaps this forgetting is not surprising. On the whole, the McDermotts and Meaghers got on very well in America. James A. McDermott, Henry and Bridget's son and my mother's father, became one of Worcester's leading contractors, building apartment buildings, churches, libraries, schools, and houses all across the city, owning city blocks in Worcester, and big tracts of real estate in Florida. He planted his family in a big beautiful house, formerly owned by a mayor of Worcester, on the city's Old West Side, its toniest neighborhood. John Henry, Dennis and Margaret's son and my father's father, never accumulated the same riches, but he was accomplished in his own right: an excellent trial attorney, president of the county bar association, part owner of a minor league baseball team, and president of a nationally prominent rowing club. My mother's family summered in Newport (not, of course, on Bellevue Avenue, where the millionaires lived, but in a big, pretty, airy house, nonetheless) and my father went to his first date in a handsome Packard. My mother was an athletic star in high school, All-City in basketball and field hockey, and vice president of her class and went on to Rosemont College in Pennsylvania. She was elegant, and artistic, and settled only uneasily into the limited roles permitted wives in mid-twentieth-century America's married domesticity. My father could only wish for his wife's athletic ability, but went to Georgetown, transferred to Harvard, then to Harvard Law School. He would become a judge of the Superior Court of Massachusetts.

Their lives were nothing like those of their grandparents'. Some would say that they had assimilated. Maybe. But I have spent a lifetime writing about Irish Americans, at least in part because I think, and have always thought, I am an Irish American. And I think that because my family thought that.

And yet, as important, I think and have always thought, I am Irish American, not Irish, and thus have written about Irish Americans, not Ireland. I have visited Ireland often in the last quarter century, and have come to love and know it and to appreciate, as I never did before, its subtle influences on my family's history and the history of Irish Americans generally. My familiarity with the Irish in Ireland, however, has only reinforced, not diminished, my sense that I am not them, that they are different, that I am Irish American and not Irish.

As I recall, my father did so more than my mother, but my father's identification as Irish American not only prompted my interest in Irish American history, it also helped define the central intellectual problem for that work ever after. He was also much better educated and far more successful than they had been. Why did he think he was Irish American after all this time? From the very beginning of my work, therefore, I have been less interested in immigrants than in American-born, ethnic generations, and that was my question: Why and how does ethnicity survive after the immigrants? It would, I think, have been hard to identify my father, the Harvard-educated judge, as Irish or even Irish American. He hated professional Irishmen and Irishwomen, people who paraded their Irishness in a cloying sentimentality at every opportunity. He suspected them of being phonies and scam artists, exploiting such sentiment for their own political or economic gain. He loved to wear Brooks Brothers suits and to eat at fancy men's clubs founded by Yankee elites, such as the Worcester Club, a privilege awarded all judges.

But my father knew he was not a "Yankee." He was not a member of such clubs or socially exclusive country clubs. He knew he was different from Worcester's Protestant elite of British ancestry: Irish, Catholic, something, set him apart. As far as I know, he was never anything but gracious and polite with the Yankees that he knew and those he worked with on the court or in civic organizations. I remember once, one such colleague on the court needed a place for his son, captain of his prep school rowing team, to hold the team's farewell dinner after they had competed in the New England interscholastic rowing championships on Lake Quinsigamond in Worcester. My father arranged through a Lithuanian American court officer to hold the dinner at the Lithuanian American club (where the court officer in a relaxed moment of familiarity turned to the Yankee judge and asked, "I know where the Lithuanians come from and I know where the Irish come from, but where do the Yankees come from?").

Yet, though my father did not speak often of his feelings about Yankees, he was not shy in telling stories of slights that he or his family had suffered, slights by the members of that elite that still burned forty or fifty years later. I also do not remember that my father had any close Yankee friends. In 1980, when I went off to teach at Worcester Polytechnic Institute—the city's fine engineering college founded by Worcester's Yankee industrial elite in the nineteenth century—he told me to be careful: "That's the Yankee school." There was a boundary there for him, between them and people who, like him, "came from somewhere."[5]

Perhaps he was or had been a "wannabe," like a character in a John O'Hara novel: wanting in, coming so close, but ultimately excluded and thus frustrated and angry. Yet I did not get the impression that that was the only, or even principal, cause of his sense of difference. He displayed, as I have said, little interest that I could see in Ireland, even the later conflicts in the North, when I knew him. Yet as a younger man, fresh out of Harvard Law School in the 1930s, he had become a member of the Clan Na Gael, the American support organization for the Irish Republican Army (IRA). They were banned in 1936 by their old leader Eamon De Valera, but in 1939, tiny in number and severely weakened, they, nonetheless, still undertook a brief and ultimately pointless bombing campaign in Britain, which resulted in seven deaths, two hundred wounded, and the capture and execution of two IRA men.[6] That association with the Clan caused him trouble, he told me, when he was commissioned as an officer in the U.S. Army Air Corps during World War II and assigned to its intelligence service. Our British allies were concerned. The Clan would give him a pretty clock when he became a judge in 1952, which was prominently displayed in our living room—I have it now.

I never knew whether he had joined the Clan Na Gael because he had a hidden, passionate interest in Ireland or, as my Uncle Charlie described the local Clan, because it offered opportunities for Irish Americans in Worcester to network and mobilize against their ethnic rivals. Maybe both, but I think the latter, at least, was important. I think my father was Irish because it was his people, his team, in an inevitable competition among rival ethnic teams.

Ethnicity was about contesting groups and boundaries more than about the food you ate, the clothes you wore, the songs you sang, or even much about the old country you came from—only that you came from one. Food, clothes, songs, holidays all became important as markers of those boundaries, but they could be invented, not inherited. So my family did those Irish American things, like wearing green pins or ribbons and eating corned beef and cabbage on Saint Patrick's Day. But politics and power were different, more serious. My father once told me that he always voted for the Democrat in a general election and the Irishman in the Democratic primary. That may have been aimed at a son aspiring to an intellectual life and thus whose credulity knew no bounds—a target too inviting not to tweak. Irish love. Yet he also made clear to me that he was stung when other Irish Americans criticized his participation in bringing city manager government to Worcester. They believed that it was a betrayal of Irish American interests in the city. He insisted that more Irish Americans had been elected under the new municipal government than under the old one.

The root of his ethnicity then, I think, lay in this sense of group competition. It fired ethnic identity, gave it an edge, and nourished its dynamism. It was where my ethnic identification began then as well, and thus, where my interest in American ethnic history, and more specifically Irish American history, began, too.

Yet that is hardly the entire story. Culture was not as irrelevant as such an interpretation may make it seem. It just was not an identifiably Irish culture, and, as important, it did not just survive from the past; it was invented or remade in the present. As Gary Wills once wrote about his own childhood in the 1940s and 1950s, "we grew up different," but he meant not because of some kind of ethnic loyalty (I don't know that Wills has any sense of an ethnic identity) but because of his religion, Catholicism.[7]

Catholic culture was as thick and present in our everyday life in the 1950s as anything specifically Irish was absent. It was a Catholic calendar: fish, meatless spaghetti, or cheese sandwiches on Friday; confession on Saturday; mass on Sunday; holy days of obligation, such as daily mass during Lent (my most vivid memory of those Lenten masses was the sight of Bob Cousy of the Boston Celtics at the back of the church, as he lived in our parish); Holy Week services on Thursday, Friday, and Saturday nights; ashes on Ash Wednesday; and blessing of throats on the feast of Saint Blaise. At school we had processions in May, gathering at a shrine to Our Lady of Fatima on the grounds of the church. At home we prayed the rosary some evenings, led by a bishop or a priest on the radio. We did this together in the living room and every member of the family knelt, leaning on a piece of furniture as we recited the Hail Marys and Our Fathers. (One of my brothers, distracted by the elaborate floral patterns of the upholstery, would later recall those rosary sessions as "reading" the furniture.)

Whatever Irish edge this Catholicism once had, most of it seemed to have been shorn off by the time I grew up. There were no Irish-born priests in my church and no Irish-born sisters or religious brothers in my Catholic primary or secondary schools, and neither my church nor my schools did much to promote Irish culture. I remember once when I was an altar boy serving mass on a Saint Patrick's Day, the pastor of my parish, American-born of Irish ancestry but old by my time, had the church organist bang out the Irish tune, "The Garryowen," at the end of the service. As he lumbered out of the church, the priest proclaimed, "I'm glad I did that." But it was because it was such an uncommon event that I remembered it.

It was a social as well as cultural world, tied together and bounded by an extensive network of institutions and clubs and associations. All but the oldest two siblings in my family went to Catholic school for our entire primary and secondary education and those two went to Catholic high school. My Cub Scout troop met in the parish hall when I was in primary school and my Catholic Youth Council basketball team played in the same hall when I was in high school. This was hardly the Jim Crow South and a society divided between racial groups. We lived in a multireligious neighborhood. Greek Orthodox, Jews, Yankees, and other Protestants and I played on a Little League team with enough Jewish kids about to make their bar mitzvah that we had to schedule our practices around their after-school Hebrew lessons. Parochial school and the multiple activities centered on the Church, however, dragged me back toward a Catholic world, and my close and enduring friends from childhood were Catholic. Many of my siblings were less insular and had Jewish or Protestant childhood friends that they remain close to today. Nevertheless, I don't think I ever knew a Protestant as more than a passing acquaintance until I went to graduate school.

Both my parents were committed to Catholicism, but religion meant more to my mother, I think, than to my father. When we were downtown with my father, he often took us to a shrine to Saint Anthony, established in 1899 in his old parish. He remained committed to that devotion until he died—a hard-bitten tough guy, known as "Black Jack" on the judicial bench to quaking lawyers, but dutifully saying his prayers to Saint Anthony every night. It was my mother, however, who was devout, religious to the core, not in a fierce, domineering, or unyielding way, but a believer for whom religion was a constant. She went to mass as often as she could and prayed often. She spent a number of years tutoring poor kids and that, I think, flowed naturally from her religious commitment. And she set a tone in the house. Our home was no chapel, but she was responsible for many of the religious pictures and crucifixes there. We said prayers before and after meals, and she painted the words for "Grace" on the kitchen walls in a stylish script.

Finally, we were a big family, six children. It was the baby-boom era, but this number still seemed a dramatic contradiction of what demographers might expect of a college-educated wife and her Harvard-educated husband. When I looked at the number of children in the families of my Catholic friends' families, some of them headed by doctors, accountants, lawyers, or successful civil servants, however, that did not seem so remarkable—five, six, or even more did not seem like so many.

Religion, then, I believe, defined us as Catholics with Protestants as the principal "others." Jews, Greek Orthodox, and Armenian Orthodox stood somewhere in between, but we viewed them, in many ways, as more like non-Irish Catholics, Italian, Polish, or Lithuanian Americans than like the Yankee Protestants who dominated Worcester. That meant that Jews, Greeks, and Armenians could be competitors and were different and bounded, but, like us, they were outsiders, peoples from "somewhere." If we had friends on the other side of the Catholic boundary, then, they were more likely to be Jews, Greeks, or Armenians than Protestants. Catholic-Jewish relations in Boston or New York were often tense, poisoned by Father Charles Coughlin and kept alive by political rivalries, but my mother and father had Jewish classmates from their high school days who remained lifelong friends. One Jewish couple and their children (and later their grandchildren) spent almost every Christmas with us. My aunt Kitty spent every Christmas Eve with Armenian friends.

What is missing here is class. My father had a prestigious job and a powerful position in the community. He knew it, and my siblings and I and most people I came into contact with knew it as well (Worcester is not a big city). Most of the people my parents chose to socialize with, that I remember, were college educated, and lawyers, doctors, or businessmen. My parents did not, however, belong to a country club or other kinds of social or recreational clubs so we children did not either. Much of their social life outside of our home, particularly my mother's, was spent with their own families, their siblings. Her father, James A. McDermott, as noted earlier, had been very successful: in my father's words, "the richest Irishman in Worcester" in the 1920s. Yet by the time he died in the early 1930s, almost all that wealth was gone, the heavily mortgaged real estate holdings foreclosed by the banks (including a bank he had helped found forty years earlier), and the once-profitable construction firm shut down because it could find no business during the Depression. Most of my mother's sisters and brothers, the ones I saw often, had respectable but not prestigious jobs: clerk at the courthouse, agent for the state Veterans' Administration, bookkeeper for the state tax department. My father's sister had married a man whose family auto supply business had flourished through the 1940s and early 1950s but was declining when I was growing up.

David Doyle argues that because they were so spread out throughout all levels of the American economic hierarchy, Irish Americans were more likely to have family members from many classes. That was true of my family but to a limited extent; I had no uncles, aunts, or cousins who were blue-collar workers. Almost all of my friends came from my school, and some were the sons of doctors or managers of businesses, but of my two closest friends through high school, one was the son of a foreman at a plant that manufactured steel wire and the other was the son of a police patrolman. Class prejudices did exist among the children in my school. I remember a classmate, maybe in third or fourth grade, who had a birthday party and invited everyone in the class to attend. Few of the wealthier kids showed up, as I recall, because he lived in a "three decker," a tenement.[8]

What is also missing here is race, whiteness set against African Americans, which several scholars have argued defined Irish American identity. So prevalent has this argument become that one historian has suggested that it is now a cliché.[9] Racial issues became controversial in our parish in the early 1960s, when a young priest gave a passionate sermon on behalf of Black civil rights, including intermarriage with Whites. One family walked out. Eventually, the priest was transferred. I do not remember any organized protests or broad talk against him, or even conversations among my friends about his sermon, but I assumed then that some parishioners had complained about him. Some members of my extended family talked in racist terms about Blacks, but not often. More to the point, I do not remember my father and mother ever doing so. In the midst of the country's racial turmoil in the late 1960s, my father pointedly called in the local newspaper to report that most crimes in Worcester were committed by Whites. My mother and father had no close Black friends that I recall, but my father often invited judges, who were from other parts of the state but sitting in Worcester, to our house for dinner. I remember when I was in grade school, he brought home Judge Edward Gourdin, the 1924 silver medalist in the long jump in the 1924 Olympics and the first African American appointed to his court. When I was a freshman at my Catholic high school, my homeroom debated creating a scholarship for African American students and voted overwhelmingly to do so. About the same time, one of my brothers became very active in civil rights locally in the early sixties, working with our former curate and others at a settlement house that served Worcester's Black community. Another brother would later serve on Boston's Human Rights Commission.

Why race did not become critical, or at least consciously critical, to our definition of identity perhaps deserves some explanation given the power of the whiteness argument. My mother and father were no radicals; both were staunchly anticommunist. My father was a New Deal and Fair Deal, northern liberal Democrat. My parents attended Harry Truman's inauguration in 1949, but my father also had great admiration for Adlai Stevenson. My mother was probably most influenced on racial issues by her religion, often citing it to criticize racist speech or behavior. Recent research has revealed the limits of such Democratic Party liberalism and mid-twentieth-century Catholicism on racial issues. That being said, I think both my parents believed racism was wrong. My family, however, was probably also insulated from racial tensions in critical sites, such as workplaces, schools, and neighborhoods, in large part because of my father's status and how much money he made, but also because of the city in which we lived. Worcester had a small and long-settled African American population that did not grow much in the 1950s and 1960s and an even smaller Puerto Rican population that increased at only a slightly higher rate. There were no African Americans or Asian Americans in my Little League that I can remember, and few who came to the basketball court where I played in the summer. There were two African American students, a brother and sister, in my grammar school in the eight years I was there, and none in my high school over my four years there.[10]

Whiteness scholars often suggest that becoming White for European immigrants and their children was a kind of assimilation, erasing the boundaries that divided them from other Whites. That did not happen in Worcester throughout my childhood in the 1950s and 1960s. Certainly the division between Blacks and Whites was deeper there, as elsewhere, than conflicts among Whites, but differences among Whites were significant enough to shape social life and politics. For all its strengths, I believe that whiteness scholarship ignores or overlooks religious difference, but in Worcester religious difference did not disappear over years and generations.

If anything, Catholicism was stronger in the 1940s and 1950s than it had ever been, but it had also changed. The Catholicism at the center of my growing up may have seemed a simple and obvious legacy of an Irish past. Some Irish and other Catholics today often think that, bemoaning its decline as an aberration, a failure. The Catholic world I grew up in, however, was not some simple inheritance from the immigrants, but something that had been made and remade over time. It did, of course, derive from an older Irish and Irish American Catholicism, yet the way it dominated my childhood was significantly different even from the role it played in my parents' growing up. They went to public school, not parochial school (my father spent six months at a Catholic high school to "straighten him out" before college).

Moreover, their large brood of kids was not a continuation of an old trend, but a change in an older pattern. A good friend and colleague at Catholic University, who is Catholic of German origin, likes to point to the steadily declining number of children in his family over several generations as a neat encapsulation of its steady and inevitable assimilation. Yet my family growing up in the 1950s was larger than my parents' families in the 1910s and 1920s, or, for that matter, the ones in which my grandparents were raised by their immigrant parents. Those big Irish Catholic families in the 1940s and 1950s, and the high proportion of them sent to parochial schools, reflected a self-consciously revived Catholicism that was strongest at that time among the growing Irish American Catholic middle, not working, class. Neither that Catholicism, nor the big families it produced would last, as my brothers' smaller families today reveal. As I have grown older, my siblings and I have had more contact, taken more time to visit, and when we do, I am reminded how growing up in such a crowded household was such a unique experience, not likely to ever return.[11]

The collapse of that Catholic world began as soon as the next decade, the 1960s. Some Catholics have blamed the Vatican Council for changing the Church as if it had not already changed often. To me the more important factor was the failure of the Church to follow through on the Council than the changes that gathering made. Yet given the broader impact of change in America in the 1960s, it may not have mattered what the Church did. During the sexual and social revolutions of that decade, it suddenly seemed obsolete, irrelevant, to many. More important, in the tumult of that decade, Catholic identities no longer seemed forced or determined; Kennedy's election and death, the Vatican Council, and most important, the civil rights movement smudged or erased the boundary that separated Catholics and Protestants.

Neither Irishness nor Catholicism seems forced, determined, nor locked in by a competition among groups now. Ethnic or religious identities for Whites have become optional, and for some of my siblings they have only episodic importance today. For others in my family for whom an Irish American identity still has meaning, the focus of that identity has now shifted to culture, not the popular culture Irishness invented in America, but a search for a more authentic, traditional Irishness. Music is a small but telling example of that change, I think. As part of the broad national trend toward interest in the authentic, I had become a fan of folk music in the early 1960s. Someone in our family, probably one of my older brothers, bought Clancy Brothers and Tommy Makem records then, and I played them constantly. Later I would become a devotee of the Chieftains and other traditional music groups from Ireland. Bing Crosby and his Tin Pan Alley tunes were long gone.

For some of my siblings, it was not music but academic or literary interests. A brother and my sister took Celtic Studies courses at Harvard from the legendary John Kelleher, and my sister made images of our family's Irish heritage the focus of her visual studies senior thesis. I often buy books on Ireland for one of my brothers, and steal from his own excellent collection of Irish books. Another brother, an academic, has done research on Irish and Irish American literature. Finally, and perhaps most important, I had grown up in a mid-twentieth-century Irish America, "without Ireland," but that changed in the 1960s for me, my siblings, and many more in my generation. One of my siblings went to Ireland in the 1960s and went back twice thereafter, and two went in the 1970s, and one of them went back twice as well. I first went to Ireland in 1983 and have been back at least eight other times, twice traveling with siblings. It is hard for me to think of an Irish America without Ireland now.

If many of my siblings remained vitally interested in "Irishness," I made a career of it in researching and writing Irish American history. For much of that career, it has been the question of my childhood that nagged at me and became central to my work: How and why do ethnic identities persist after immigration? In this case, how and why did my family continue to think they were Irish Americans through the best of American educations and significant upward mobility? Inevitably, then, my dissertation and later my first book were about Irish Americans in Worcester. They focused on the turn-of-the-twentieth-century period, the emergence of second-generation children of the Famine immigrants.

I believe that immigrants like Henry McDermott and Dennis Meagher knew who they were and their sense of "Irishness" was easy and natural, but their American-born children had to work out who they were. This story turned out to be more complicated than I thought, and some of it contradicted the received wisdom of my childhood: most notably, that the mutual hostility between Yankees and Irish in my own time had not been a given since the Irish first arrived in the city, that there had been significant episodes of cordial collaboration between them amid the longer periods of enmity. Yet some of the broader lessons of my growing up, my father's understanding that ethnic loyalties were rooted in the rivalries and jockeying of group competition and my mother's appreciation of religion's significance, figured prominently in my thinking for that work.[12]

If, after rediscovering Ireland I might have been seduced into believing that Irish American and Irish were simply interchangeable versions of the same thing, I realized on my first trip to the old country more than thirty years ago that this was not true. It became clear to me early on in that visit that my ethnic identity had been made in America, forged in an interaction among American ethnic groups, and that Irish people had very different notions of where their Irishness came from. At one point on the trip, I turned to an Irish American friend and lamented, "Where are the Italians?"—or just as easily the Armenian, Polish, African, or even Yankee, Americans?

Yet engaging with Ireland and its history over the three decades since that trip has raised new questions for me about the long-term, if subtle, influences that an old country's culture can have on multiple generations of descendants in a new land. I became interested, in particular, in why Irish Americans have long been so prominent in American politics (if now as Republicans more often than Democrats), and if there were an enduring Irish American political "style" that accounted for this prominence. These questions, too, had roots in my own experience: my father's passionate interest and participation in politics that seemed to pervade the household and dominate conversations not taken up by the Red Sox or the Celtics. I still believe that Irish American politics has been made largely in the challenges and opportunities of American urban life, yet I have come to believe that certain Irish American attitudes, such as suspicions of elites, and skills, such as talents for political mobilization, have important roots in Ireland's past.

As I write this now, I sit in an apartment, but a block from Dublin Castle, the seat of government in Henry McDermott's and Dennis Meagher's Ireland, the seat of British colonial rule, a principal cause of Irish rebellion, political resentment, and, for some, emigration. I am in Ireland to investigate the political culture of pre-Famine Ireland as a precedent for Irish American political experience. I have thus begun to dig into Dennis's and Henry's world, a world long forgotten in the Irish America of my childhood, but now, I believe, a world that has exerted powerful influences on Irish America, and still does even today.

Notes

1. Rental referred to in the "Annexed Account, 1830," James Tipping, Tipping Papers, Public Record Office of Northern Ireland.
2. Kerby Miller, *Emigrants and Exiles: Ireland and the Irish Exodus to North America* (New York: Oxford University Press, 1985), 193–344; Raymond D. Crotty, *Irish Agricultural Production: Its Volume and Structure* (Cork: Cork University Press, 1966), 35–65.

3. Rental referred to in the "Annexed Account, 1830," James Tipping; "Rental for the Bellurgan Estate for the Half year, Edward Tipping 1851," and "Estate and Business Correspondence," Tipping Papers, Public Record Office of Northern Ireland; *Griffiths Valuation:* County of Louth, Barony of Dundalk, Lower Parish of Ballyboys, Bellurgan, 138–140.

4. "Tithe Applotment 1828," Moyneard, Parish of Moyne, Thurles Library; Ratebook, A Rate for the Relief of the Poor of the Thurles Union in the County of Tipperary, Moyneard, January 1842, October 1845, October 1847, 1850 [no month listed], October 1852, March 1856.

5. My experience at Worcester Polytechnic Institute was wonderful and I do not remember any troubles with "Yankees," or any sense of ethnic or racial tension at the school.

6. Paul Bew, *Ireland: The Politics of Enmity* (Oxford: Oxford University Press, 2009), 466–467; J. J. Lee, *Ireland, 1912–1985: Politics and Society* (Cambridge: Cambridge University Press, 1989), 219–221.

7. Garry Wills, *Bare Ruined Choirs* (New York: Dell Publishing, 1974), 15.

8. Unions never gained much traction in Worcester, in large part because of the power of religious and ethnic loyalties, thus hiding, stifling, and/or deflecting class conflict into ethnic or religious resentments: see Bruce Cohen's fine articles on labor in Massachusetts in the *Historical Journal of Massachusetts*, 1988, 1992, and 2001. David Doyle, "Unestablished Irishmen," in *American Labor and Immigration History, 1877 to the 1920s: Recent European Research*, ed. Dirk Hoerder (Urbana: University of Illinois Press, 1983), 194–198.

9. Eric Arnesson, "Whiteness and the Historian's Imagination," *International Labor and Working Class History* 60 (2001): 13.

10. John McGreevey, *Parish Boundaries: The Catholic Encounter with Race in the Twentieth Century Urban North* (Chicago: University of Chicago Press, 1998); David Roediger, *Working towards Whiteness: How America's Immigrants Became White* (New York: Basic Books, 2005). For another view of Irish Catholic racial liberalism in the 1950s, see Paul Blanshard, *The Irish and Catholic Power: An American Interpretation* (Boston: Beacon Press, 1953), 289.

11. Leslie Woodcock Tentler, *Catholics and Contraception: An American History* (Ithaca, N.Y.: Cornell University Press, 2004); Andrew Greeley and Peter Rossi, *The Education of Catholic Americans* (New York: Doubleday, 1968).

12. Marcus Lee Hansen had a theory of why ethnic identities survived, but he argued that the third generation, the grandchildren of the immigrants, my parents for example, and not the second generation, were the keys to ethnicity's survival. Hansen claimed that second-generation ethnics, ashamed of their foreign past, wanted to forget their past, but the third, more secure in their Americanism, were eager to recall and celebrate it. Yet it did not seem that my second-generation grandparents were allowed to forget by an often hostile society. Moreover, my parents' ethnicity, particularly my father's, as I have said, seemed central to him and rooted in ongoing ethnic competition, not a psychologically needy rediscovery of roots as in Hansen's third generation. See Marcus Lee Hansen, "The Problem of the Third Generation Immigrant," *Commentary* 14, no. 5 (November 1952): 492–500. For a book that had an influence on me early on, see Oscar Handlin, *Children of the Uprooted* (New York: Grosset and Dunlap, 1968).

8

In Our Own Words

Reclaiming Chinese American Women's History

JUDY YUNG

The fifth daughter of Chinese immigrants, I grew up in the 1950s knowing very little about my own family history, let alone the history of the Chinese in America. Like most people in San Francisco Chinatown, my family went by two different surnames. Among our relatives and friends we were known as the Tom family, but at school and on our birth certificates we were known as the Yung family. We always knew that if ever questioned by any *fan gwai* (foreign devils), we were not to divulge our real Chinese surname; otherwise, the family would be in big trouble. As an illegal immigrant, my father was forced to live in the shadows of society for the rest of his life, always fearful of detection and deportation. Consequently, his children were denied any information about our family background and immigration history.

Twenty years later, while doing research about the Chinese experience at the Angel Island Immigration Station in San Francisco Bay, I learned that my father, Tom Yip Jing, had come to America in 1921 posed as Yung Hin Sen, the nineteen-year-old "paper son" of a Chinese merchant in Stockton, California. Like thousands of other peasants from the Pearl River Delta of Guangdong Province, he took this "crooked path" to circumvent the Chinese Exclusion Act of 1882, which barred the immigration of Chinese laborers to this country.[1] To better enforce the Chinese exclusion laws, a new immigration station modeled after Ellis Island was built on Angel Island in 1910. Upon arrival, my father was detained on Angel Island for more than a month until he could pass the medical examination and immigration interrogation verifying his identity and eligibility to enter the country. For the next ten years, he labored as a houseboy, a cook, and, later, as a gardener in the San Francisco Bay area to repay two uncles who had financed his passage to America.[2]

When my father turned thirty-three, he decided it was time to get married and start a family. He returned to China and was introduced by a matchmaker to Jew Law Ying, the granddaughter of Chin Lung, who had made his fortune growing potatoes in the Sacramento-Stockton delta. My mother was studying to be a midwife at the time, but she agreed to give up her education and marry Tom Yip Jing because she had always dreamed of going to Gaam San (Gold Mountain), the Cantonese name for California. However, the Chinese exclusion laws prohibited my father, as a laborer, from bringing his wife to America. He returned to San Francisco alone. It would take him four years to save enough money to buy a few nominal shares in an import-export company, which in turn enabled him to establish merchant status and send for his wife and daughter, Bick Heung, who had been born in Macao. Mother and daughter finally arrived in San Francisco on board the *President Coolidge* in 1941.[3] The family settled in Chinatown, where my mother worked as a seamstress in a garment sweatshop while my father found a union job as a janitor at the ritzy Mark Hopkins Hotel. They had four more daughters before the son that they had long yearned for was born. Then they stopped having any more children.

My father always said that I was born at the right time. As the fifth daughter, I was considered the lucky one to have "led" my brother into this world. But he also meant to say that I was lucky to be born after World War II, when increased educational and economic opportunities for Chinese Americans allowed me to make more of my life than he or my mother ever could. Considering that I would not have been born at all if my brother had preceded me, and that I eventually found my calling as a Chinese American historian, I know he was right.

I did not grow up wanting to become a historian but was led to it by fortuitous circumstances. My first eight years of life were spent in the insular and racially segregated neighborhood of Chinatown, a twelve-block area bordered by the financial district on the south, North Beach and Italians on the north, and posh Nob Hill on the west. My family lived in very crowded conditions, eight people packed into two rooms in a three-story tenement on Stockton Street. Everything we needed was within walking distance—the elementary school, Chinese language school, and Presbyterian church that we attended regularly; the public library, Chinese Playground, and movie houses that we frequented on weekends; and numerous bakeries, grocery and produce stores, delicatessens, and meat and fish markets where we did our shopping. There was even a Chinese Hospital around the corner from where we lived.[4] So fearful were our parents of the larger society that we were seldom allowed to venture outside Chinatown except for family excursions to the zoo, the beach, or Golden Gate Park in the summer when my father had two weeks of vacation time.

Even before the U.S. Supreme Court mandated bilingual education in the San Francisco public schools in 1974, I was lucky enough to receive a bilingual

FIGURE 6. The author with her parents, Tom Yip Jing and Jew Law Ying, at the dedication ceremony on Angel Island in San Francisco Bay in 1979. The Chinese couplet on the granite monument reads, "Leaving their homes and villages, they crossed the ocean only to endure confinement in these barracks. Conquering frontiers and barriers, they pioneered a new life by the Golden Gate." Photo by Harry Jew.

and bicultural education at home and by attending American (public) school during the day and Cantonese-language school at night. I learned to read and write in English and Chinese as well as to appreciate the glorious history of the United States and China. I came to feel proud of my Chinese cultural heritage, but I could not identify with being an American for the longest time, as we were taught a very Eurocentric version of U.S. history in American school. Our history textbooks did not include people of color, or women for that matter, while Chinese school emphasized Confucian values and loyalty to the Nationalist government in Taiwan. When Chinese people were depicted in the mass media at all, it was usually in the demeaning roles of Hop Sing (the cook in the TV show *Bonanza*) or Suzie Wong (the seductive prostitute in the film *The World of Suzie Wong*). None of my teachers inspired me to pursue history or higher education. As far as my parents were concerned, they expected their daughters to finish high school, get an office job, and help support the family until it was time for us to marry a rich Chinese man and start our own family.

I really thought this was my destiny until I discovered Jade Snow Wong's autobiography, *Fifth Chinese Daughter*, in the Chinatown Branch Library one day.[5] Here was a story of a second-generation Chinese American daughter like myself who when confronted with cultural and generational conflicts at home and racial and gender discrimination in the larger society dared to defy her traditional parents' wishes as well as challenge the White male establishment. Jade Snow Wong found a way to develop as a person in her own right, dating and marrying whomever she chose, pursuing a college education, and becoming a successful ceramicist. By the end of the book, she had returned home to San Francisco Chinatown, where she found a comfortable niche for her pottery and craft, a newfound appreciation for her bicultural heritage, and, most important, respect and recognition from her parents for her many achievements. Why couldn't I do as much?

By the time I finished high school, my family had moved into a five-room flat in the North Beach district and was financially better off. Like Jade Snow Wong, I was permitted to go on to college as long as I could pay my own way, which I did by attending a low-cost state college while working part-time at the public library. Young women like myself were then being career-tracked into teaching, social work, or nursing. I initially enrolled at San Francisco State College, planning to become an elementary school teacher. But after my disastrous experience as a counselor and instructor at a Chinese-language summer camp, where I had difficulties managing a wild bunch of American teenagers living away from home. I decided to switch to librarianship. My parents were quite proud of me when I received my master's degree in library science from the University of California at Berkeley, landed a civil service job with the San Francisco Public Library, and married a dependable Chinese American man who was well educated and a devout Christian. Then I got caught up in the social movements of the 1970s and, to my parents' dismay, my life took a dramatic political turn.

In 1968, a year after I had graduated from college, students of color at San Francisco State College, inspired by the civil rights movement, went on strike for five months and succeeded in shutting down the campus and winning concessions from the university administration to establish the first Ethnic Studies Department in the country. In the process, Asian American studies as a new field of inquiry was born, and so began our efforts to call attention to the racist underpinnings of the Vietnam War, to protest stereotypes of Asian Americans in the mass media, and to correct the Eurocentric bias of public schooling and history books with new research and curriculum. College-age Asian Americans like myself were inspired to return to our ethnic communities to work for social change.

My community activism began in the early 1970s when I was assigned to head the Chinatown Branch Library and improve library services for the disadvantaged and underserved population, namely low-income immigrants and senior citizens. It was a godsend assignment that dovetailed nicely with my bilingual and bicultural background as well as my newfound commitment to "serve the people." I immediately started to order Chinese reading materials and develop a Chinese American–interest collection. To encourage library usage, I did outreach in the community and organized cultural and film programs in the library. Wanting to further immerse myself in community work, I volunteered as a reporter for the *East/West* weekly, a bilingual newspaper that covered community events and issues of concern to Chinese Americans across the country. I started out writing an innocent column, "The Chi-Am Corner," about what it meant to be a Chinese American, and gradually moved on to covering social and political issues in the community—labor disputes, substandard housing, school desegregation, mental health needs, youth gangs, and "Communist" China. I had lived in Chinatown all my life, but I was just getting to know the neighborhood, warts and all. So exhilarating did I find community journalism that I gave up my secure job as a librarian to work full-time as associate editor at *East/West* for a pittance. By then, my marriage had fallen apart and I was seeking an alternative lifestyle by hanging out with political radicals and hippies. I am sure my parents were aghast. I had first embarrassed them by moving out before getting married, and now I was divorced and working for a "Communist" newspaper. "What will become of our fifth daughter?"

Then, against their wishes, I joined a group of Chinatown journalists in 1974 to attend China's October 1st celebration of the establishment of the People's Republic of China in 1949. This was five years before the normalization of diplomatic relations between China and the United States. We were given a red-carpet tour of China's cultural and historic landmarks as well as its model communes, factories, and schools. Along with 150 other overseas Chinese from many countries, we had a private audience with Vice-Premier Deng Xiaoping in Beijing. He spoke for more than an hour about China's industrial development and socialist policies and answered our questions about Taiwan and dual citizenship. It was an important occasion for us, demonstrating China's recognition of the help and support it has always received from its overseas compatriots.

I remember being struck by the clean, calm, and orderly lifestyle I witnessed during our one-month tour of China. Everywhere we went we saw luscious green fields and tree-lined streets. There was no smog, traffic congestion (except for the zillions of bicycles), litter, or fear of crime, nor any signs of beggars and prostitutes. We were told, and could see for ourselves, that people's basic needs—food, clothing, shelter, health care, jobs, education—had all been met, and that ethnic minorities and women were treated with greater respect and equality than before. True, people worked longer hours and for lower wages than we did in America, but they worked at a leisurely pace and enjoyed a lower cost of living. We were in China during the tail end of the Cultural Revolution, and there must have been political dissent or dissatisfaction among the intellectual and bourgeoisie classes, but we were not aware of it at the time. However, my relatives in Canton gave me more than a mouthful of complaints about their hard lives under the yoke of Communism. I was disappointed that they would rather rely on overseas remittances than practice self-reliance and sacrifice for the sake of their country. Like my parents before, they dreamed of some day immigrating to Gold Mountain.

The trip to China changed my outlook toward life and my ethnic identity as a Chinese American woman. For the first time in my life, I was in a totally Chinese environment, but I did not feel at home. Although I looked like them, I knew I was not Chinese like them. "As an American of Chinese extraction," I remember writing in *East/West*, "my home is America, where I was born and where I grew up. And no matter how badly I feel about how wrong things are in America, I would not by choice give up the ship. My commitment is to the struggle at home."[6] I must admit I also felt a great sense of relief and gratitude toward my parents for choosing to immigrate to America when they did.

Upon my return home, I was laid off from my job with *East/West*, supposedly because of financial difficulties. Soon after, I was hired by the Oakland Public Library to build a new Asian Community Library with a generous Library Services Construction Act grant. It was another godsend assignment I took on with enthusiasm. I devoted the next six years of my life to developing the first Asian multilingual and Asian American-interest collection in a public library. I could have stayed in that job for the rest of my working life except that Him Mark Lai, a mechanical engineer by vocation and a passionate historian in his spare time, made me an offer I could not resist. I had met Him Mark while working at *East/West*. A truly bilingual and biliterate scholar, Him Mark devoted his life to collecting, researching, and writing articles and books in Chinese and English about Chinese Americans. Through his prodigious scholarship, he not only rescued Chinese American history from oblivion, but he also made it an integral part of both U.S. history and the history of modern China.[7]

It was Him Mark Lai who first told me about the Chinese poems that a park ranger had found carved into the barrack walls of the Angel Island Immigration Station. I remember being moved to tears when I first visited the immigration site and saw the poems for myself. Touching the carved calligraphy that was covered by a thin layer of chipped paint, I thought I could hear the voices of immigrants bemoaning their fate imprisoned on this lonely island. "Grief and bitterness entwined are heaven sent," wrote one poet. "Sadness kills the person in the wooden building," wrote another. And I wondered why my father had never talked about it before. Afterward, I eagerly accepted Him Mark's invitation to join him and writer Genny Lim in their effort to translate the poems and document the story of Chinese detention at Angel Island. Nothing had been written about this dark chapter of U.S. history and nobody in the Chinese community really wanted to talk about it. For the next five years, during our time off from our full-time jobs, we collected and translated as many poems as we could find and conducted oral history interviews with any former detainee willing to talk to us. Many of the poems on the walls had been partially obliterated by layers of paint and natural deterioration. We were lucky to find two immigrants, Smiley Jann and Tet Yee, who had meticulously copied down close to one hundred poems in their notebooks while detained on Angel Island in the early 1930s.

Convincing people to talk about their memories of Angel Island proved to be more difficult. Many had come on fraudulent papers and no one wanted to recall the harsh treatment accorded them while detained on Angel Island for weeks and months because of the Chinese exclusion laws. We started with our own families and branched out to relatives of close friends in the Chinese American community. That was the first time I ever heard my father talk about the hardships he suffered immigrating to this country. I remember feeling both sad and angry for him. Only by promising anonymity were we allowed to tape record thirty-nine interviews and publish these stories along with the English translations of 135 Chinese poems.

We were turned down by a number of publishers who at the time felt there was no market for books about Chinese Americans. Undeterred, we self-published *Island: Poetry and History of Chinese Immigrants on Angel Island, 1910–1940* with grants from the Zellerbach Family Fund and the Wallace A. Gerbode Foundation. A decade later, the University of Washington Press, one of the earliest to publish books on Asian Americans, reprinted it.[8] Since then, *Island* has become a literary classic and required reading in many U.S. immigration and Asian American studies classes, and it remains in print today. Over the years, this collection of poems and oral histories has stood as a testament to the hardships experienced by, and to the perseverance of, Chinese immigrants to endure and establish new lives in America. By calling attention to the injustices they suffered on Angel Island, we have helped to restore a sense of dignity among paper sons like my father as well as to foster healing and reconciliation in the Chinese American community. Ultimately, *Island* serves as a cautionary tale of the real impact of flawed immigration policies on immigrant lives and our values as a nation of immigrants.

Among the people we interviewed for *Island* were eight Chinese women who told us their tearful tales of woe while detained on Angel Island. At the invitation of *Frontiers: A Journal of Women's Studies*, I shared their stories in my first article to be published in an academic journal, "'A Bowlful of Tears': Chinese Women Immigrants on Angel Island."[9] Sparked by an interest in our own backgrounds as Chinese American women, Genny Lim and I decided to work on recovering the rest of their "herstory." By then, the women's liberation movement was going strong and there was a crying need for materials on women's history to be included in the school curriculum. Genny and I teamed up with historian Vincente Tang and successfully applied for a two-year grant from the Department of Education's Women's Educational Equity Act program to mount the first traveling exhibit and write the first book about Chinese American women. Our goal was to give voice and visibility to their lives, struggles, and accomplishments; dispel stereotypes of Chinese women as the subservient China Doll or diabolical Dragon Lady; and provide young women with Chinese American role models. In order to devote full time to the project, I quit my job as head librarian at the Asian Community Library in Oakland. By then, I had run out of steam, having built that library from scratch and moved it twice to larger quarters. I was ready for a new challenge.

Influenced by the methodological practices of public history, social history, and women's history, we conducted primary research in the absence of any publications or secondary sources on the subject. (Remember: this was before the invention of the personal computer, Internet searching, and the webcam.) We had to travel all over the country looking for photographs, documents, and women's writings in libraries, archives, community organizations, and homes, and interviewing close to three hundred Chinese women of diverse backgrounds about their lives in America. By piecing together bits and pieces of archival research with the oral histories, writings, and photographs we collected, we were able to trace the history of Chinese women from 1834, when Afong Moy first appeared in Barnum's Chinese Museum in New York City, to contemporary times. The exhibit traveled to ten cities with the largest Chinese American populations and was well received by thousands of viewers in museums, historical societies, libraries, and community centers. My second book, *Chinese Women of America: A Pictorial History*, was published by the University of Washington Press in 1986.

My passion for researching and writing Chinese American women's history was ignited. Rather than return to librarianship, I decided to go back to graduate school in an effort to retool myself as a historian and to pursue an academic career. It seemed like the right choice at the time—to be paid to do research and write full-time to my heart's content. In 1984 I was fortunate enough to be accepted into the first class of the newly minted PhD program in Ethnic Studies at UC Berkeley. I knew before I applied that my dissertation topic would be an in-depth study of social change for Chinese women in San Francisco from the turn of the twentieth century through World War II. I wanted to continue reclaiming my history as a Chinese American woman and setting the historical record straight.

Reentering graduate school after an absence from college of sixteen years and transitioning from majoring in English literature as an undergraduate to ethnic studies at the graduate level proved to be more difficult than I had expected. Compared to my younger classmates, I lacked grounding in U.S. history and critical race theory. I had a difficult time understanding the assigned readings on internal colonialism and postmodernism, participating in theoretical discussions in class, and writing to prove or disprove a theory. Often I felt like "a fish out of water" or like "an old cow trying to learn new tricks." But I was determined to finish.

The best thing that happened to me in graduate school was to study and work with Ronald Takaki—a great thinker, teacher, writer, and mentor to me. From taking graduate courses to working closely with him as his research assistant on *Strangers from a Different Shore: A History of Asian Americans*,[10] I learned how to analyze race, class, and gender inequities and to write in the narrative style of a social historian—based on grounded theory, and employing the voices of ordinary people "from the bottom up" to tell the larger history of multicultural America. I spent many hours in public and private archives looking for Asian American voices and stories for his publications. I had the foresight to make copies of all the documents I found for my own use later on.

I somehow passed the worst part of graduate school—the comprehensive oral exam, and was advanced to candidacy in my third year. With financial support from the UC president's affirmative action program and the American Association of University Women, I was able to devote my full time to finishing my dissertation, which was later revised and published as *Unbound Feet: A Social History of Chinese Women in San Francisco*.[11] Aside from documenting the lives and perspectives of two generations of Chinese women during a period of great social ferment in China as well as in the United States, I wanted to show how race, class, and gender discrimination had shaped their work, family, and political lives in America. I drew heavily from the work of sociologist Evelyn Nakano Glenn, who at the time was the only scholar including Asian American women in her analysis of the triple oppression faced by women of color in the labor force.[12] I also owe a great debt to historian Peggy Pascoe, who taught me how to do women-centered history. She generously shared research materials with me on the rescue work of missionary women and showed me how the Chinese prostitutes and slave girls they rescued were not passive victims but active agents in the making of their own history.[13] And I continued to be influenced by the work of Him Mark Lai in his use of Chinese-language sources and transnational approach to researching and understanding Chinese American history, politics, and culture. I spent hundreds of hours poring through microfilms of old Chinese newspapers and I traveled to China to interview Gold Mountain wives (left behind by Chinese emigrants) about their overseas Chinese connections. The ten years of learning that I had spent at Chinese school finally paid off!

As there were few written records to begin with, and what material existed on Chinese American women was full of inaccuracies and distortions, I had to draw from a variety of primary sources to reconstruct their history: immigration records and census data, the archives of Christian and Chinese women's organizations, Chinese- and English-language newspapers, oral history interviews, personal memoirs and writings, scrapbooks and photographs from public archives and private collections. To lend symbolic significance to the study, I decided to organize the chapters around the theme of foot binding as a symbol of women's subjugation and subordination, even though the Chinese custom was not widely practiced in America. How did "bound feet" and other social restrictions circumscribe women's lives in China and America in the mid-nineteenth century? How were immigrant women able to "unbind their feet" and bound lives, and how were their daughters able to take the "first steps" toward challenging traditional gender roles at home and racial discrimination in the larger society in the early twentieth century? How did the two generations of Chinese women make "long strides" during the Great Depression and end up falling "in step" with the rest of the Chinese community and mainstream society during World War II? These were the questions I wanted to answer in *Unbound Feet*.

My father died of cancer in 1988 and did not make it to my graduation at UC Berkeley. But before he died, he told me how proud he was of my accomplishments: "I never dreamed that one of my daughters would become the first in my village to earn a doctorate degree." My mother, beaming with happiness and pride, broke out in religious song at my graduation party (and repeated her performance at every one of my book launches). She was even happier when I landed a tenure-track position in the American Studies Department at UC Santa Cruz, a research institution eighty-five miles away from home.

I had been hired specifically to teach and develop Asian American studies at the only UC campus without a major or department in ethnic studies or Asian American studies. The position proved to be a good fit for me, as it was in an interdisciplinary program with liberal colleagues who were committed to promoting faculty, student, and curriculum diversity. I spent the next fourteen years helping to build the university library's Asian American collection, coordinating and teaching classes in Asian American studies across the campus, introducing multicultural perspectives into the other American Studies classes I taught (America and Americans, Race and Ethnicity in America, and Oral History), and fighting the anti-immigrant and anti–affirmative action backlash in California.

UC Santa Cruz was very much a White campus in the 1990s. As one of the few Asian Americans on the faculty, I found myself constantly in demand as a speaker, committee member, advisor, and mentor. I found it difficult to say no to any reasonable request from student, faculty, and community organizations in need of my support or services. My most difficult years were spent as department chair of American Studies, when I had to learn how to deal with personnel problems and campus politics. Somehow, I still found the time and energy to continue writing and publishing articles and books on Chinese American women. It helped that I was only required to teach four courses a year, that I had teaching assistants to help grade papers and exams, and that the university generously provided me with research fellowships and leave time for my various book projects. More important, I remained passionate about reclaiming my history as a Chinese American woman. I did not need the pressure of publish or perish in the academic world to keep me going.

My strong urge to let Chinese American women tell their own stories in their own words led me to compile and write *Unbound Voices: A Documentary History of Chinese Women in San Francisco*. By the time I finished *Unbound Feet*, I had accumulated a vast amount of primary materials on Chinese American women, crammed into sixteen vertical file drawers in my study. Although I had quoted extensively from these sources in my publications, I felt that my selective use of them had not done them justice and that the full range of the women's voices and lives deserved to be heard. I had originally wanted to include some of the writings and oral histories in the appendix of *Unbound Feet*, but Ramón Gutiérrez, who was on the editorial board of the University of California Press at the time, advised me to save it for a second book. Thus, *Unbound Voices* is an annotated collection of primary sources—letters, essays, poems, folk songs, autobiographies, speeches, testimonials, editorials, and oral histories—cited in *Unbound Feet*, revealing the complicated lives of Chinese women as they struggled to make a home for themselves and their families in America.

Without interruption, we hear their testimonies as they were interrogated by immigration officials at Angel Island; their laments at being abandoned in China by Gold Mountain husbands; their sorrow over being duped into prostitution; their struggles and accomplishments as wives, mothers, and second-generation daughters; the myriad ways they coped with the Great Depression; and their contributions to the causes of women's emancipation, Chinese nationalism, workers' rights, and victory in World War II. I intended *Unbound*

Voices to be used and read as a collection of primary sources, as an educational tool for researching and reclaiming women's history, and as a feminist lesson on how certain Chinese women were able to overcome the legacy of bound feet and bound lives in America. My mother passed away peacefully in her sleep before the book was published, no doubt comforted by the knowledge that her story of trials and tribulations would receive top billing in the book.[14]

For the same purpose of correcting the glaring omission from and misunderstanding of Chinese Americans in the U.S. historical record, I next teamed up with Gordon Chang, professor of history at Stanford University, and Him Mark Lai to compile and edit a collection of primary documents, *Chinese American Voices: From the Gold Rush to the Present.*[15] By then, all three of us had devoted most of our lives to researching, writing, and teaching Chinese American history. Having each developed extensive research collections through the years, we began by going through our own libraries for Chinese American voices in published sources (magazines and newspapers, pamphlets and newsletters, autobiographical accounts, and government documents) as well as unpublished materials (business records, speeches, testimonials, oral histories, and correspondence). We looked for documents that would cover a broad spectrum of experiences, hoping to reveal the diversity of socioeconomic status, gender, generation, geographic affiliation, political perspective, and cultural lifestyle in the Chinese American community across 150 years of history. In some instances we had to conduct additional oral history interviews, pore through Chinese newspapers on microfilm, surf the Internet for recent voices, and dig in public and private archives for additional stories to fill certain gaps.

Contrary to popular and scholarly opinion, our findings showed that the Chinese had left written records behind about their experiences in America; only much of it was in Chinese. We collected more than three hundred documents, from which we selected and annotated some sixty for inclusion. We wanted each document to shed light on an important moment or turning point in Chinese American history, whether it be the Chinese Exclusion Act of 1882, World War II, or the civil rights movement. Some of the voices, such as the memorials from the Chinese Six Companies and speeches by the Chinese American Citizens' Alliance protesting racial discrimination, were selected because they challenged the stereotypes of Chinese Americans as silent sojourners and perpetual foreigners. Especially important and unique were our inclusion of translations of Chinese voices and writings, such as the folk songs of Gold Mountain wives and the editorials of journalist Gilbert Woo on two important historical events—the repeal of the Chinese exclusion laws in 1943 and the normalization of diplomatic relations between China and the United States in 1979. As the only book to present primary documents generated exclusively by Chinese Americans, *Chinese American Voices* helps to correct America's historical amnesia and provide a deeper understanding of Chinese American life from the perspective of the historical actors themselves.

It was in the process of working on *Chinese American Voices* that I first met Eddie Fung, the subject of my next book. We needed a World War II story for the anthology, preferably one told from the perspective of a Chinese American at the front. I was introduced to him by Colonel Bill Strobridge, a military historian who told me that Eddie had the dubious distinction of being the only Chinese American soldier to be captured by the Japanese and put to work on the Burma-Siam railroad made famous by the film *Bridge on the River Kwai*. What intrigued me even more was that Eddie had run away from home when he was sixteen to become a cowboy in Texas. He turned out to be an oral historian's dream come true. A solidly built man of short stature—5 feet 3 inches and 120 pounds to be exact—he was a natural storyteller with a fantastic memory for details, a precise way of expressing himself, a wonderful sense of humor, and a strong determination to tell the story right. Until then, my research and writing had mainly focused on Chinese American women. I never thought that I would be working on a book about a man's life, but the opportunity was too good to pass up. I remember thinking that this had to be how Theodore Rosengarten must have felt when he happened upon Nate Shaw, an illiterate Black sharecropper in Alabama with a story to tell, or how Alex Haley felt when he was asked to write Malcolm X's autobiography.[16] I had found my whopper of a Chinese American story!

What started out to be a five-hour interview and short story for *Chinese American Voices* evolved into a seventy-five-hour oral history project and autobiography, *The Adventures of Eddie Fung: Chinatown Kid, Texas Cowboy, Prisoner of War*.[17] Along the way, the unthinkable happened. Eddie proposed to me sometime during our fifth session of taping, which presented me with a dilemma. I did not want to jeopardize or compromise our professional relationship and the book that was materializing so well. And there was the age difference—he was old enough to be my father. But I was also attracted to him because he reminded me of my father. Despite being a generation apart, we came from a similar background and shared the same values. Fifty more hours of interviews later, we decided to give in to Cupid's arrow and got married on April Fool's Day, 2003. I recorded another twenty hours of interviews with him as his wife and confidante; edited one thousand pages of typed transcript while making sure I remained faithful to his actual words and style of speaking; and gave him every chapter to review and correct as I wrote it. Ultimately, *The Adventures of Eddie Fung* is very much a collaborative life history project and a labor of love. At one level, the book chronicles a rambunctious Chinatown boy's journey to manhood and how he came to terms with his ethnic identity. At another level, it offers valuable lessons and insights into Chinatown family life during the Great Depression, cowboy culture and race relations in Texas, and the survival tactics of a POW under Japanese brutality—all told from the unique perspective and exact words of a second-generation Chinese American who was exceptional for his time.

Soon after I finished writing Eddie's memoirs, I was approached by the Angel Island Immigration Station Foundation (AIISF) to write a comprehensive history of the Angel Island immigration site that would encompass the diverse stories of immigrants beyond the Chinese. Thanks to the financial support of my husband, I had just taken early retirement from my position at UC Santa Cruz and was looking for a meaningful book project to sink my teeth into. Fortunately for me, Erika Lee, a history professor at the University of Minnesota who had done extensive research on Chinese immigration during the exclusion era, agreed to coauthor the book.[18] Our goal was to finish the book by January 21, 2010, in time for the immigration station's centennial celebration.

Even with two of us working continuously on the book for five years, it proved to be a daunting undertaking. Luckily, we had full access to all the feasibility studies on the site's immigration history, historic structures, wall inscriptions, and cultural landscape that had been commissioned by AIISF to guide the restoration of the immigration station. We also had access to seventy thousand Angel Island immigration case files at the National Archives in San Bruno, California. But incomplete statistics and lost records made it difficult for us to even determine the exact numbers and ethnic backgrounds of all the immigrants who had been processed through Angel Island between 1910 and 1940. Moreover, there had been very little written about the experiences of immigrants other than the Chinese, and by now most of the former detainees had passed away or were difficult to locate, making oral history interviews nearly impossible. Nevertheless, we felt strongly that it was time to tell their stories as well as the stories of Angel Island's gatekeepers, preferably in their own words and interpreted within the larger context of pacific migration and U.S. immigration policies. Who were these immigrants? How and why were their experiences at Angel Island so different? What impact did immigration policies and decisions have on their lives, their families, and their communities? And what does Angel Island tell us about America and its complicated and contentious relationship to immigration then and now?

Drawing on extensive new research, including immigration records, ethnic newspapers, oral histories, and published autobiographical accounts, we were able to uncover Angel Island poems in Japanese, Korean, and Russian and to produce a sweeping yet personal history of Chinese paper sons, Japanese picture brides, Korean refugee students, South Asian political activists, Russian and Jewish refugees, Mexican families, Filipino repatriates, and many others from around the world. We learned that European and Japanese immigrants were usually admitted into the country within a day or two; South Asians had the highest rejection rate; and Chinese had the longest detention while they awaited decisions on their legal appeals. Regardless of their race or ethnicity, immigrants with wealth and education were usually landed right off the ship while women were asked intrusive questions about their sexual histories and routinely excluded on the grounds that they were "likely to become public charges." How the various immigrant groups came to Angel Island and how they fared once there were determined by a range of influential factors, including international relations, histories of colonialism, and U.S. immigration policies that treated individuals differently according to race, class, gender, and nationality.

We concluded that although the immigration station at Angel Island was popularly called the Ellis Island of the West, it was in fact very different from its counterpart in New York. Ellis Island enforced American immigration laws that restricted but did not exclude European immigrants. Angel Island, on the other hand, was the chief port of entry for Chinese and other immigrants from Asia and, as such, enforced immigration policies that singled out Asians for long detention and exclusion. Contrary to the celebratory story of Ellis Island, which has become synonymous with America's immigrant heritage and national identity, the Angel Island story represents both the best and worst of American immigration history. It is the story of men, women, and children who crossed the Pacific Ocean and traveled north from Latin America to establish new lives in the United States. But it is also the story of harsh discriminatory immigration laws and of immigrant perseverance. Remembering both sides of this complex history helps us to recognize what is still great about the United States and what remains to be done to fulfill America's promise as a nation of immigrants.

Thanks to the great teamwork and the expeditious research and writing skills of my coauthor Erika Lee, *Angel Island* was published in time for the centennial celebration of the immigration site.[19] The immediate impact of the book was tremendous in calling attention to the personal stories and great diversity of immigrant experiences at Angel Island, in cementing Angel Island's important place in U.S. immigration history, and in sparking discussion on current immigration issues and the need for comprehensive immigration reform. *Angel Island* is being used as the authoritative guidebook by docents and visitors to the Angel Island immigration site, as the "roots" book for Americans who can trace their immigration story to Angel Island, and as required reading for classes interested in a more inclusive and accurate history of the United States as a nation of immigrants. My effort to reach a larger and broader audience with the Angel Island story did not end with the publication of the book. I continue to work closely with AIISF in giving lectures, book talks, and interviews; writing up immigrant profiles for their website and multimedia exhibits; providing research assistance on restoring the rest of the immigration site; and serving as a consultant to other researchers, filmmakers, and the news media. And my next book project will be a major revision and update of my first book, *Island: Poetry and History of Chinese Immigrants on Angel Island, 1910–1940*, which was published in 1980.

Completing *Angel Island* has brought me full circle back to where I had started researching and writing about Chinese immigration history. After spending the last few years burning the midnight oil to meet a publication deadline, I could easily slip into full retirement and rest on the laurels of this last book, but already I feel the spirits of my parents, Him Mark Lai, and Ronald Takaki (who died in 2009) reminding me that there are still miles to go, many more stories to tell, and pages to write before I sleep.

Notes

1. Passed by Congress at the height of the anti-Chinese movement, the Chinese Exclusion Act of 1882 was the first time in U.S. history that a group of people was barred entry to the United States solely based on their race. To circumvent the Chinese exclusion laws, which were in effect from 1882 to 1943, many Chinese immigrants assumed false identities and came with fraudulent documents claiming to be members or family members of the exempt classes (merchants, teachers, students, diplomats, and tourists) or U.S. citizens. Because they were who they claimed to be on paper only, they were known as "paper sons" and "paper daughters."

2. My father's immigration papers and travel expenses amounted to $2,000 in 1921. His immigration story is based on oral history interviews that I conducted with him on April 17, 1977, November 20, 1986, and November 16, 1987, and on Yung Hin Sen, file 20288/3–8, Chinese Departure Case Files, San Francisco District Office, Immigration and Naturalization Service, Record Group 85, National Archives, San Bruno, California.

3. For the full story of my mother's immigration history, see "Lessons from My Mother's Past: Researching Chinese Women's Immigration History," in Judy Yung, *Unbound Voices: A Documentary History of Chinese Women in San Francisco* (Berkeley: University of California Press, 1999), 9–98.

4. For a pictorial history of San Francisco Chinatown showing these local landmarks, see Judy Yung and the Chinese Historical Society of America, *San Francisco's Chinatown* (Charleston, S.C.: Arcadia Publishing, 2006).

5. Jade Snow Wong, *Fifth Chinese Daughter* (New York: Harper, 1950).

6. Judy Yung, "Journey to the Motherland," part 12, *East/West*, February 19, 1975, 3.

7. Him Mark Lai passed away in 2009 at the age of eighty-four, after completing ten books and over one hundred articles about Chinese American life and history. He did not have enough time to finish his autobiography, which I and two other close colleagues promised to complete for him. *Him Mark Lai: Autobiography of a Chinese American Historian*, edited by Judy Yung, Ruthanne Lum McCunn, and Russell C. Leong, was published posthumously by the UCLA Asian American Studies Center and the Chinese Historical Society of America in 2011.

8. Him Mark Lai, Genny Lim, and Judy Yung, *Island: Poetry and History of Chinese Immigrants on Angel Island, 1910–1940* (San Francisco: HOC-DOI, 1980; Seattle: University of Washington Press, 1991). The book received the American Book Award from the Before Columbus Foundation in 1982.

9. Judy Yung, "'A Bowlful of Tears': Chinese Women Immigrants on Angel Island," *Frontiers: A Journal of Women Studies* 2, no. 2 (Summer 1977): 52–55. This article was later revised and published as "'A Bowlful of Tears' Revisited: The Full Story of Lee Puey You's Immigration Experience at Angel Island," *Frontiers: A Journal of Women Studies* 25, no. 1 (2004): 1–22.

10. Ronald Takaki, *Strangers from a Different Shore: A History of Asian Americans* (Boston: Little, Brown, 1989).

11. Judy Yung, *Unbound Feet: A Social History of Chinese Women in San Francisco* (Berkeley: University of California Press, 1990). The book won four book prizes, including the Robert G. Athearn Award from the Western History Association and the National Book Award for History from the Association of Asian American Studies.

12. See Evelyn Nakano Glenn, "Racial Ethnic Women's Labor: The Intersection of Race, Gender, and Class Oppression," *Review of Radical Political Economics* 17, no. 3 (1985): 86–108; "Split Household, Small Producer, and Dual Wage Earner: An Analysis of Chinese-American Family Strategies," *Journal of Marriage and Family* 45, no. 1 (February 1983): 35–48; and *Issei, Nisei, Warbride: Three Generations of Japanese American Women in Domestic Service* (Philadelphia: Temple University Press, 1986).

13. See Peggy Pascoe, *Relations of Rescue: The Search for Female Moral Authority in the American West, 1874–1939* (New York: Oxford University Press, 1990).

14. See "Lessons from My Mother's Past," in Judy Yung, *Unbound Voices*, 9–98.

15. Judy Yung, Gordon H. Chang, and Him Mark Lai, *Chinese American Voices: From the Gold Rush to the Present* (Berkeley: University of California Press, 2006).

16. Theodore Rosengarten, *All God's Dangers: The Life of Nate Shaw* (New York: Alfred A. Knopf, 1974), and Alex Haley, *The Autobiography of Malcolm X* (New York: Ballantine Books, 1973).

17. *The Adventures of Eddie Fung: Chinatown Kid, Texas Cowboy, Prisoner of War*, ed. Judy Yung (Seattle: University of Washington Press, 2007).

18. A granddaughter of Angel Island immigrants, Erika Lee is the author of *At America's Gates: Chinese Immigration during the Exclusion Era, 1882–1943* (Chapel Hill: University of North Carolina Press, 2003).

19. Erika Lee and Judy Yung, *Angel Island: Immigrant Gateway to America* (New York: Oxford University Press, 2010). The book won the Caughey Western History Association Prize for the most distinguished book on the American West and the Adult Non-Fiction Award for Literature from the Asian/Pacific American Librarians Association.

9

Ordinary People

EILEEN H. TAMURA

My research has highlighted issues of identity, marginality, and social justice as they impact the lives of ordinary people. I have been drawn to themes
of power and resistance, oppression and dominance, competing interests and
worldviews, and the oft-stated ideal of creating a more open society.[1]

At the same time, as a Japanese American in Hawai'i, I have occasionally
found myself in the unwelcome position of being a member of an ethnic group
that has at times been accused of closing the door to others seeking better
opportunities. These experiences have brought home to me the sobering realization that people can easily forget the discrimination that their own forebears
faced. In this essay I reflect on my experiences, interests, and choices as they
relate to my profession and my research.

I am a Sansei—third-generation Japanese American. I grew up in the late
1940s through the 1950s in Wailuku, a small town on the island of Maui, one
of the seven major islands in the Hawaiian Island chain. Then, as now, the
population in Hawai'i was ethnically diverse, with Nikkei—ethnic Japanese—
constituting the largest group. In 1950, for example, population percentages
were as follows: Japanese, 37 percent; Caucasians, 23 percent; Native Hawaiians,
17 percent; Filipinos, 12 percent; Chinese, 7 percent; Puerto Ricans, 2 percent;
and Koreans, 1 percent. In this essay, the terms *Japanese, Filipino, Chinese,* and
Korean refer to their ethnicity and not their national origins, and thus include
immigrants as well as U.S. citizens. As for the term *Caucasian,* the 1950 census
combined two groups within that category: those who descended from northwestern Europeans, who were the islands' economic and social elite, and those
who were Portuguese, recruited in the early twentieth century to work as sugar
plantation field supervisors.[2]

I grew up as the youngest of four children in a lower-middle-class family in the 1950s. My father, who was a dentist, died unexpectedly when I was four years old, leaving no life insurance to help my mother raise her children. With only an eighth-grade education, she was forced to turn suddenly from housewife to breadwinner. She worked in a small flower shop, eventually becoming part owner.

My family lived a comfortable and simple life without material frills. On two occasions, however, my mother was able to provide for adventures that allowed my sister and me to experience life away from the confines of our neighborhood. The adventures were trips to visit relatives in the city of Honolulu. For our family, these excursions were costly, since they entailed flying from Maui to the island of Oahu.

I lived in an ethnically diverse neighborhood in which the Nikkei predominated. The public schools I attended were also ethnically diverse, but again the Nikkei were most numerous. Most of my classmates and all of my friends were Japanese. I did very well in school, but in class I did not speak out, and neither did most of my classmates. Yet, I was more timid than most. Essentially, I was afraid of strangers, especially adults. On one occasion when I was about twelve years old, I was in my mother's flower shop helping to pluck carnations for floral *lei*. An adult female customer entered the shop, greeted my mother, saw me, and began to speak to me in a friendly manner. Too frightened to speak to a stranger, tears filled my eyes as I turned my head away from her. As an adult many decades later, it is difficult, even for me, to understand my timidity. But there it was.

Despite my interpersonal timidity, I had large dreams. In 1962, when I was a high school senior, I read an article in *Seventeen* magazine about the Peace Corps, which had begun a year earlier. Inspired, I said to myself, "This is what I am going to do." Why? I was idealistic, I wanted to make a contribution, and I wanted to live in a place different and distant from Hawai'i and the rest of the United States. Knowing that my mother would not want me to do this, I told no one about it. I decided that I would join right after graduating from college.

I knew that I would attend college because my older siblings—a brother and two sisters—had done so. Although I had wanted to attend a mainland liberal arts college, and was encouraged to do so by the school counselor, my family could not afford it. Reluctantly, I attended the University of Hawai'i. My disappointment was short-lived, however, since my university experience proved to be intellectually stimulating. I majored in psychology, with a particular interest in social psychology. I enjoyed my liberal arts courses; moreover, I regularly attended campus-wide symposia that featured nationally known speakers from across the country. These opportunities opened my thinking to new ideas and different worldviews.

While growing intellectually, I nevertheless remained shy and introverted. I was to learn that my reticence could be a liability as a university student. In my freshman world history honors seminar, for example, the talkative students, either from Honolulu or the mainland, dominated class discussions. There were a few other quiet students like me. Although I read and digested the assigned readings, I barely spoke up in class. Besides being reticent, my first language was Hawai'i Creole, a language that was created by the children of plantation workers and used by later generations as an everyday, common language. Although I could write in standard English, I had difficulty speaking it spontaneously. Before expressing my thoughts, I had to translate them from Hawai'i Creole to Standard English. Often, by the time I was ready to speak, someone else had said what I had intended to say.

In my second semester of this two-semester course, the professor assigned a history research paper. Students were to select a topic from a given list. I chose Fabian socialism because socialism was something that interested me. Because I had barely spoken in class, I decided to produce the best paper I could in order to prove to myself and to the professor that I was just as capable intellectually as the talkative students. With this in mind, I spent considerable time and effort doing the research and writing for my project. What happened next, however, stunned me. After turning in my paper, I was asked to meet with the professor. He said that it was an excellent paper, that he wanted a copy of it, but that he did not think that I had written it. Shaken, I told him firmly that I had done all of the research and writing myself. His response was that because I spoke little in class, I gave no indication that I was capable of such work. He gave me an A for the paper and a B for the course.

The professor's comments were instructive. It was obvious that, having relocated from the mainland, he did not understand the upbringing of local, neighbor-island youths like me. This experience burned itself into my mind and has remained with me to this day. Decades later, as a professor, I make it a point not to assume that quiet students are less intelligent than talkative ones. In larger classes I have students discuss ideas in pairs or small groups before having the whole class discuss the topic. Although I allow students to volunteer comments in whole-class discussions, I also call on quiet ones to contribute, consciously providing time for them to gather their thoughts before they speak. In seminars, which are more conducive to whole-class discussions, I make it a point to encourage quiet students to speak and not to let a few dominate the discussion.

As an undergraduate during the late 1960s, I was drawn to the ideas of New Left activists, particularly their civil rights advocacy and their opposition to the Vietnam War. As a firm opponent of the war, I joined like-minded faculty and students in standing in silent vigil on campus to protest for peace. I also attended Quaker meetings and gatherings of college students in coffeehouses. I did this on my own because none of my dormitory friends, who were

Japanese and from the neighbor islands, were interested in the issue. My activities involved superficial encounters with other protesters, most of whom were European Americans, and I did not form any friendships with them. Although I agreed with them politically, I felt awkward near them and therefore avoided them socially.

In my senior year at the university, I applied to the Peace Corps. In my application, I stated that I was not interested in living in countries in Asia and the Pacific. I believed that they would be too similar to what I knew in Hawai'i. Upon graduation and acceptance as a Peace Corps volunteer, I left the islands for Miami, the training ground for volunteers bound for Senegal, West Africa. By then I had informed my mother that I was leaving. Knowing that she could not stop me, she gave me her blessing. Because I had stated in my application that I hoped to become a social worker, I was placed with other similarly intentioned college graduates. We volunteers were paired and then placed with families living in housing projects, which proved to be an effective testing ground to see whether we were able to live comfortably with people unlike us. In the intensity of this Peace Corps training, I was able for the first time to have an intimate understanding of Caucasians. I came to appreciate the diversity among them, and developed friendships that have continued to this day.

In Senegal, I was paired with a gregarious and enthusiastic young Caucasian woman from a northeastern, upper-class family. She skied, sailed, sang, and played the guitar. No one could have been more different than I was in background and personality. In addition, her ability to speak French and Wolof—the two dominant languages in Senegal—far exceeded mine. Although I had preferred being paired with someone more like myself, I decided to take up the challenge of living and working with her. This proved to be a wise decision. In the ensuing two years, we worked with nurses and community leaders on issues of sanitation and hygiene in the small town of Kaffrine, situated in the interior of the country. My introspection and keen observation served to balance and complement her extroversion and positive disposition. In our numerous interactions with people all over town, I slowly and often painfully emerged from my shell, shed my fear of meeting strangers, and gained confidence in my ability to enjoy people from all walks of life. At that time, I knew that I was changing, but only later did I realize how transformational my Peace Corps experience had been. I also later realized that this experience further cultivated my interest in understanding people, which dovetailed with my undergraduate interest in social psychology. My Peace Corps experience also nurtured my self-confidence, which continued to grow after I left Senegal, and later helped me when I encountered a problem with my PhD advisor, which I discuss later in this narrative. It also helped me in my subsequent work with faculty colleagues and in my role as department chair.

FIGURE 7. The author with fellow Peace Corps volunteer Judith Whitcomb and a Senegalese man in Kaffrine, Senegal, 1969. Courtesy Peace Corps.

When my Peace Corps experience ended, I received transportation fare from Senegal to Hawai'i. I thought that it would be a waste of resources to use that money to fly through the continental United States. Instead, it would be so much more interesting to travel eastward and visit a place for several weeks or months before reaching Hawai'i. Having lived for two years in Senegal with an extrovert, I wanted to experience life on my own in a place outside the United States. I was interested in Egypt and China, but was told that both places were closed to U.S. citizens. Disappointed, I settled on Japan. I was not especially eager to visit the country of my ancestors, since there were so many Nikkei in Hawai'i, but I knew that I would probably be able to get a long-term visa because I had an aunt who lived there. As a young girl, she had been adopted by her aunt and uncle in Hawai'i, and at the age of seventeen had left the islands to accompany her adoptive parents, who were returning to Japan. My aunt therefore knew some English and some Hawai'i Creole. Upon receiving a letter from me, my aunt, with my uncle's consent, graciously agreed to be my sponsor, and with that support I decided to make Japan my destination.

In the fall of 1969, at age twenty-three, I purchased a second-class ticket on a French passenger liner. I boarded the ship in Dakar, Senegal, joining the liner's first-, second-, and third-class passengers, who had begun their journey from Marseille, France. The ship was bound for Yokohama, Japan; on its way, it stopped at the ports of Durban, Mogadishu, Mumbai (then Bombay), Colombo, Bangkok, Hong Kong, and finally Yokohama. To say the least, it was a noteworthy trip, affording me the opportunity to meet fellow passengers from all walks of life, and visit places I would not have otherwise visited.

Fortunately for me, my aunt and cousin met my ship at Yokohama. Having seen the *ukiyo-e* prints by such masters as Utagawa Hiroshige and Katsushika Hokusai, I had had terribly naïve visions of Japan as a rural country, where I could wander around, meet people, and visit places of interest. Instead, I was confronted immediately by a dense metropolis, with high rises and heavy traffic. Moreover, I had not planned for the language barrier that would prevent me from negotiating the train system on my own. Although I knew some words in Japanese, I could not converse with native speakers. I could not have been more ill prepared for life on my own in Japan.

My aunt took me to her home in Hiroshima, where I lived with her family for the next seven months. I gradually learned some basic Japanese, which enabled me to travel by bus and taxi on my own within the city. I took lessons in brush calligraphy, taught English, and gained increasing confidence in myself as I met people and formed friendships.

As a youth in Hawai'i, I had had a strong identity as an American. In Senegal, that feeling was reinforced whenever I informed the Senegalese that, no, I was not Chinoise, but American. In Japan my identity as an American confronted me daily, as I observed the cultural differences between Japanese and Americans. There were small differences—for example, the way one sat and the way one laughed—that I could adapt to easily. But there were larger differences that I found unacceptable, such as the subordination of women and the surface homogeneity of the population that emphasized conformity and made the Burakumin—ethnic Japanese who historically filled low-caste jobs as butchers and leather workers—de facto outcasts. Yet I enjoyed my seven months there, and considered staying longer were it not for the fact that my brother was getting married and asked that I attend the wedding.

Before returning to Hawai'i, I was accepted at the Antioch Graduate School of Education, which actively recruited ex–Peace Corps volunteers for a master's degree program in Philadelphia. Although I had not thought seriously about teaching earlier, teaching in what was then called the "inner city" attracted me because of my interest in marginalized populations. My visit to Hawai'i thus lasted only a few months before I departed once again for a life away from home.

Philadelphia was as different for me as Senegal and Japan had been, and it took some time to acclimate myself to life there. Teaching at elementary schools in the city and in a White working-class area just outside the city gave me a close-up view of some of the issues and struggles facing those outside the mainstream of middle-class life. Also, after a couple of years, I realized that although Philadelphia was much larger than Honolulu, and people there had the opportunity to travel to other states more easily than people in Hawai'i, there were many residents who had never left the confines of their neighborhood and had no desire to do so. And while some had traveled to other cities and states, they were no more cosmopolitan than the people in Hawai'i. I came to realize that my earlier assumption—that Hawai'i's residents were more narrow-minded than people living in urban areas of the United States—had been ill founded. After five years in Philadelphia, I decided to return to Hawai'i.

Once in Honolulu, I found part-time teaching jobs, followed by a full-time position in a federally funded, K–12 multicultural curriculum project located at the University of Hawai'i. I worked there for several years, and when the funds dried up, I was hired to teach K–12 social studies and continue developing and writing curriculum materials. In my spare time, I volunteered with and later was elected chair of the local chapter of Common Cause, the national nongovernmental organization that, among other things, has sought ways to diminish the role of big money in politics.

Eventually, I found myself feeling like I was losing interest in my work, and I began to consider the idea of continuing my schooling. Although I had previously done well in school, I did not grow up in an intellectual environment; my family did not discuss ideas from books or current events, nor did I have a family role model in academia. Thus, it was only as an adult, almost two decades after graduating from college, that I considered pursuing a PhD. By then I realized that intellectual stimulation would enrich my life and open it to new possibilities. Because I had a full-time job and had no desire to leave the islands after having recently returned, I decided to explore the possibility of pursuing my degree at the University of Hawai'i's flagship campus, where I worked.

I decided to begin by taking a course in American history, certainly not because I had enjoyed any of my high school and undergraduate courses in history. In fact, I had disliked them because of their emphasis on remembering names, dates, and other specific information that had little meaning for me. Despite these previous experiences, however, my turn to U.S. history at this juncture in my life was a way for me to understand myself as an American. Although I never doubted my identity as an American, my Japanese ancestral background and life in Hawai'i made me very interested in understanding what an American was and how American the islands were. I wanted to learn more about the country's history so that I could situate myself in it. With this in mind, I began to take graduate courses in U.S. history as an unclassified student, to see whether I would be interested in pursuing a PhD in history. This time I found the courses stimulating because they focused on interpretation and not memorization.

My first course, in particular, demonstrated to me that I had an inherent interest in history that could be separated from the particular teaching effectiveness of the professor. In this course, which was on labor history, the professor invariably put his students to sleep with his long monologues that droned on incessantly. What saved the course for me was the required research paper. I decided to learn about the origins and early years of the Industrial Workers of the World. As I read about their ideas and actions, I became fascinated by their efforts to increase the power of working people. My experience in this course encouraged me to take other graduate courses in history, and ultimately I became convinced that I should pursue a doctorate in history.

In retrospect, I realize that through the discipline of history I have been able to satisfy my desire to learn and write about three fundamental areas of interest—the struggles of ordinary people at the margins of power, people's identity as Americans, and economic and social justice. These interests are reflected in choices I had made earlier: my research into Fabian socialism, my opposition to the Vietnam War, my decision to join the Peace Corps, my attraction to the thinking of New Left advocates, my interest in social psychology and social work, my decision to teach in the inner city, and my activism in Common Cause.

Although I understood what my interests were, I did not approach my doctoral program with the idea of focusing on a particular historical topic. Therefore, like my decision to pursue a doctorate, my choice of dissertation topic came late, after I had reached all-but-dissertation status. Furthermore, it was only serendipitously that I stumbled onto a research subject that was, ironically, at my front door.

But before I could settle on a research topic, I had to find an advisor with whom I could work. At that time the history department required its graduate students to select an advisor soon after entering the program, so I selected a professor from whom I had taken a course. We had a cordial relationship until I was ready to select a dissertation topic, at which time he announced to me that there were two subjects worthy of research. Each focused on the life history of an elite, White male. Although surprised and dismayed at his definitive stance, I decided to explore the possibility of following his suggestions. I spent some hours attempting to read the existing literature, but my lack of interest literally put me to sleep. At this point I knew that this was not going to work, that I needed to find a topic that would engage me for long hours of research and writing, and that I needed to find a new advisor. Even though the department did not encourage its students to change advisors, nor speak to the process of doing so, I decided that I would do what I thought was best for my growth as a historian. I thanked the professor for what he had done for me thus far, and told him that I had asked another professor to take me on as his advisee.

This was another lesson from my student days, which I have carried into my current role as professor. In my department, we have a policy that I strongly support. It is this: the graduate chair asks faculty to advise entering graduate students on an interim basis with the idea that students will select their thesis or dissertation advisors after they have taken enough courses to have a good idea of whom they can work with on their research. Often students decide to continue with their interim advisors; at other times they select other faculty members.

In my case, I did not select my dissertation advisor, Idus Newby, because of his research interest, which was on Southern history.[3] I selected him because I knew that he would take the time to give me thoughtful and candid advice about my research and writing. Although I had not yet found a research topic when I asked him to serve as my advisor, I knew that I would examine a facet of Hawai'i's history because I wanted to see how American the islands were during the first half of the twentieth century, when Hawai'i was a territory of the United States. In the 1980s, when I was a graduate student, Hawai'i was considered to be peripheral to American history, and as a result no professor in the department specialized in Hawai'i's history. Because I had taken a course from Newby, however, I was confident that he would help me think through possible topics without telling me what the topic should be.

Although I knew that he would be unfamiliar with my eventual topic, I was confident enough about my own research abilities to know that I could find the secondary and primary sources on my own, and use his expertise—as a historian and as a researcher of social-cultural issues—to help me evaluate my research, analysis, and writing. My decision to change advisors was one of the best choices that I made in my PhD program.

Although I knew that I would focus my research on Hawai'i, I had come to the conclusion that the islands' Nisei—second-generation Japanese Americans—who by the 1980s had become part of the state's political and economic establishment, were too politically conservative to be of any interest to me. Furthermore, I recalled being disturbed at racist remarks I heard as a youth, made by my Nisei relatives about other minority groups.

I decided that my research would focus on the lives of ordinary people who were on the periphery of power. With this in mind, I delved into the literature on early twentieth-century Hawai'i. It did not take me long to realize that

I would not be able to study all of the many ethnic groups that had immigrated to the islands since the mid-nineteenth century. At the same time, my interest in ordinary people led me to the Nikkei, who at the time were the largest ethnic group living in the territory. In 1920, for example, they constituted almost half (43 percent) of the islands' population. By this time I had read enough to become increasingly interested in learning about the lives of the Nisei, who were growing up as children of working-class immigrants during a period of widespread anti-Japanese hostility. Moreover, reading about the Americanization movement on the continental United States led me to wonder about the extent to which this crusade had penetrated the islands. The result was a study that was later published as *Americanization, Acculturation, and Ethnic Identity: The Nisei Generation in Hawaii.*[4]

I learned that the Nisei, like children of other immigrant families who struggled to make ends meet, sought to make a place for themselves as Americans. But Japan's growing military strength raised suspicions toward them and their parents. With the outbreak of World War I, the Americanization crusade that swept the continent also engulfed Hawai'i. Americanizers on the mainland targeted German and other non-English language schools while those in Hawai'i and California targeted Japanese language schools.[5] Even though a U.S. Supreme Court decision prevented nativists from eliminating the schools, they succeeded in pressuring Congress to pass the 1924 immigration act, which effectively closed the doors to migrants from Japan. Previously, the doors had effectively been closed to other Asians.[6]

It was in this context that the Nisei in Hawai'i, born largely between 1900 and 1930, grew up. Many eschewed the backbreaking work that their parents endured on sugar plantations. Many agreed with their parents that persistence in schooling would enable them to enter the middle class. Even those who did not attend high school sought jobs that would give them a better life than plantation work did. In some ways the Nikkei experience was the common story of immigrants and their children striving—amid hardship and setbacks—for a better life in the larger society. In other ways, the contours of Nikkei history in Hawai'i were unique. Investigating the commonalities and uniqueness of their experiences during the decades before World War II became important aspects of my study.

After the war, Nisei veterans, like other veterans, responded to the benefits afforded by the G.I. Bill. Many attended college and returned to the islands ready to enter professions and fight for economic and political opportunities formerly closed to them. By the 1970s, they could claim satisfaction in having achieved middle-class status. Having moved from the margins to the center, and constituting a relatively large proportion of the islands' population, which made them particularly visible, they had become objects of both admiration and resentment. Although the proportion of Nikkei in the population had decreased to 28 percent, it continued to be considerably more than other Asian American groups. The numerical size of the Nisei made them noticeable as schoolteachers and principals, state and city administrators, and politicians. As a result, the Nisei and their descendants came to be seen as part of the establishment. At the same time, some books, but primarily newspaper articles and television newscasts, glorified the Nisei soldiers' feats of heroism during World War II. This media saturation produced a backlash, a feeling of antipathy among veterans of other ethnic groups, and growing hostility among other minorities toward a group that had come to be seen as part of the islands' power structure.[7]

My research on the decades before World War II had given me an understanding of the difficulties Nikkei faced during the first half of the twentieth century, when anti-Japanese sentiments were widespread nationally and locally. As a result, I had softened my earlier criticism of them. At the same time, I was aware of incidents that had emerged during the latter decades of the twentieth century that turned the status of the Nikkei from being subjects of discrimination to being accused of perpetuating intolerance.

One such instance occurred in the 1970s as a result of an influx of new immigrants entering the state, about half of whom were from the Philippines. Their arrival showed that class, race, ethnicity, and culture continued to be contentious issues in Hawai'i.[8] To appreciate the irony of the dispute of the 1970s, one needs to turn to the past to understand the social-political climate of the islands during the first half of the twentieth century. Especially during the first three decades, island life reflected a highly stratified society. At the top were Euro-Americans, who constituted less than 8 percent of the population, and who nevertheless controlled the economic, governmental, and political life of the territory. Under this elite was a small—primarily Euro-American—middle class, of teachers, craftsmen, and small-business people. At the bottom were the immigrants, mostly Asians, most of whom were laborers who had been recruited to work on the sugar plantations. The Nikkei were by far the most numerous of the ethnic groups.[9]

By the 1920s, their large numbers had become a threat to the status quo. There was a subtle undercurrent of fear, born from anxiety over the question of the future control of the territory. Euro-Americans worried that the Japanese held on to their customs and language, and their large numbers meant that they and their children might well dominate island society in future decades.[10] It was in this context that the children of plantation workers attended school. Many female youths saw their teachers as role models, and many aspired to become teachers themselves. As on the continental United States, teaching in Hawai'i was a means of upward mobility for daughters of immigrants.[11]

Although teaching was not the first choice of Japanese American males, many, in the end, chose teaching because it was the profession most accessible to them. Although not as severe as on the West Coast, discrimination served to thwart them from entering law, big business, engineering, and higher levels of government. Teaching, on the other hand, was relatively accessible. The Hawai'i public school system needed teachers for its burgeoning student population, and, unlike its counterparts on the West Coast, it was willing to employ children of Asian immigrants. Additionally, a standard salary schedule in Hawai'i meant that Asian American and European American teachers received the same pay.[12]

However, the accessibility of teaching as a career did not translate to a society of inclusion and tolerance. White Americans spoke derisively of the hiring of public school teachers who were of Japanese and Chinese ancestry. Agnes Weaver, of the College Club—an organization of White, female college graduates—pointed accusingly at public school teachers of Asian ancestry. "Notice how largely they are drawn from a social group the least American in blood and bringing up," she noted in 1916. That year Whites constituted most of the teachers, while children of immigrants made up only 15 percent. At the same time, immigrant children constituted 72 percent of public school students. Similar anti-immigrant sentiments were expressed by Frank F. Bunker, sent by the U.S. Bureau of Education commissioner Philander P. Claxton to investigate schooling in Hawai'i. Bunker interviewed government and school leaders, all Euro-Americans, before he wrote Claxton that Hawai'i's teachers were the result of "the spell of a desire for numbers," repeating "the vicious circle" of "the blind attempt[ing] to lead the blind."[13]

Despite these sentiments, Japanese Americans entered teaching as well as other occupations during the 1930s, '40s, and '50s. With Congress passing the 1952 McCarran-Walter Act, which allowed Asian immigrants to become naturalized U.S. citizens, and with the coming of age of their citizen children, the Nikkei formed a formidable voting bloc that revitalized the Democratic Party and "dislodged the Republican plantation oligarchy."[14] By the 1960s, because of their large numerical proportion, Japanese Americans and other Asian Americans in Hawai'i experienced greater opportunities than Asian Americans in the continental United States, enabling them "to weave themselves and their cultures into the very fabric" of island life.[15]

Some Asian Americans, however, were not so fortunate. After Congress passed the Immigration and Nationality Act of 1965, a new source of friction developed as large numbers of immigrants arrived from the Philippines. The previous Filipino migrants who had been recruited for the sugar plantations had been largely from the economically depressed Ilocos region. Because family reunification was emphasized in the 1965 law, the post-1965 migrants to Hawai'i reflected the lower socioeconomic levels of their sponsors.[16] Nevertheless, although only a small percentage of the total number of Filipino immigrants to Hawai'i in the 1970s were college-educated before their arrival, there were enough of them—hundreds—that they created a visible demand for employ-ment in occupations such as teaching.[17]

At the same time, the post-1965 immigration law changed the ethnic com-position of Hawai'i's public schools. By 1978, of the over fifteen thousand stu-dents with limited English proficiency (now called English Language Learners), 35 percent were Filipino. Among all public school students, 20 percent were of Filipino descent, while less than 3 percent of all teachers were ethnically Fili-pino. In contrast, about 60 percent of all teachers were of Japanese descent, and 75 percent of new hires were of Japanese or Caucasian ancestry, while only 5 percent of new hires were of Filipino ancestry.[18]

Among the students who were of Filipino ancestry, there was a divide between those who were born in Hawai'i and were therefore American citizens, and those who were newly arrived immigrants. Fights broke out in schools, par-ticularly in 1974 and 1975, some so violent that students were killed.[19] It was in this context that activists, disturbed by the dearth of ethnic Filipino teachers, called for hiring teachers who would be able to reach out to students more effectively to help quell the violence. With no response from the Hawai'i State Department of Education, the activists submitted a petition to the U.S. Department of Health, Education and Welfare, listing seven civil rights violations, "from the denial of employment to the lack of equal access to quality education," and insisted that a thousand teachers of Filipino ancestry be hired within three years.[20]

At this point, thirty years after having been the outsiders wanting in, Japanese Americans—who by the mid-1970s had filled the teaching ranks and attained positions of power and influence as public school administra-tors—found themselves as insiders holding on to the status quo. In response to the push to hire more Filipino teachers, one Japanese American state offi-cial defended his position. "No doubt about it, many (civil servants)are [ethnic] Japanese," he said. "During the years of World War II, it was difficult to get federal and private employment. The Civil Service had the lowest paying jobs—in fact, the only jobs you could get (were the low paying ones). They got these jobs, and they worked their way up. That ought to be taken into consideration."[21] Although his explanation had some validity, he failed to acknowledge the structural barriers that impeded newly arrived, college-educated immigrants in the 1970s. For one thing, it was not until 1986 that the state rescinded its earlier requirement that only citizens could be hired as teachers. The state's rescission came after the 1986 federal Immigration Reform and Control Act forbade discrimination based on citizenship. Yet even after Congress passed the 1986 law, some school officials in Hawai'i continued to ask whether the applicant was a citizen.[22]

Another barrier was Hawai'i's three-year residency requirement, estab-lished in 1935, for most state and local government jobs.[23] As a result, the only public school jobs readily available to Filipino teacher-immigrants were temporary, part-time work with youths in Students with Limited English Proficiency (SLEP) classrooms, and these jobs offered no fringe benefits.

Reflecting on the controversy, I found myself as a member of an ethnic group that seemed to have forgotten that their own parents and grandparents had been immigrants who had themselves struggled to overcome discrimination and poverty. The irony of the situation dismayed me. Power had changed the social imagination of a group who had moved to the center, but who had once lived on the margins of society and who—in those earlier years—had sought opportunities to achieve their dreams, only to deny them later to others. The result was a failed promise of Asian American solidarity, and a turning away from new possibilities of diversity in knowledge and ideas.[24]

While my reflections on the Nikkei and their relationship with other groups in Hawai'i continued, I sought to learn more about their history on the continental United States. I had read a fair amount of Nikkei history on the decades before World War II, but had only superficial knowledge of the World War II incarceration of Japanese Americans. Like other Sansei who were born after the war, I was ignorant in my youth of the incarceration episode.

My ignorance, however, resulted from a set of circumstances that differed from that of Sansei living on the U.S. mainland. Sansei there grew up ignorant of the subject because their parents refused to discuss it. Most of the Nisei who were living on the West Coast at the outbreak of World War II, and who had been sent to U.S. concentration camps, did not discuss their experiences with their Sansei children. Many of those who had been incarcerated saw it as a shameful experience. It was only after the late 1960s that the situation began to change, when Sansei on college campuses, inspired by the civil rights and Black Power movements, and further activated by protests against the Vietnam War, joined other Asian Americans to call for courses on their own history. As the Sansei learned about the incarceration episode and spoke openly about it, and as Japanese American newspapers published articles on it, an increasing number of Nisei began to discuss their experiences.[25]

Unlike Sansei on the continent, my ignorance was not because my parents refused to discuss the incarceration. My parents and grandparents—living in Hawai'i during the war—were not incarcerated. Ironically, despite the surprise attack on Pearl Harbor and the intentions of the Roosevelt administration to remove and confine Hawai'i's Nikkei to an isolated island in the territory, only a small minority, 3,200 of the 158,000 Nikkei in Hawai'i, were incarcerated. This contrasted with the forced removal of 120,000 Nikkei living on the U.S. West Coast, including men, women, and children. The different situation of Nikkei in Hawai'i placed me at an emotional distance from what was a traumatic and humiliating experience for those who were expelled from their homes and livelihoods, and imprisoned because of their ancestry.[26]

Because the incarceration was a definitive chapter in the history of Nikkei in the United States, my ignorance of its complexities meant that I lacked knowledge and understanding of a major part of the social and cultural heritage of Japanese America. Reading a few books and articles on the subject left me dissatisfied. The only way for me to gain the type of intimate understanding I wanted was to absorb myself in a research project on some aspect of the incarceration.

Such a project emerged naturally from my earlier research, when I had come across an excerpt from an unpublished autobiography written by a Nisei, Joseph Y. Kurihara. I was instantly drawn to his narrative style because of its boldness and directness. Written with obvious passion, it contrasted with what I understood to be the communication style of Nisei men. My own observations and what I had read about them indicated characteristics of self-restraint, control of emotions, reticence, nonverbal communication cues, and composure in the face of hardship. This did not mean that Nisei men lacked feelings. Rather, it meant that they avoided public displays of their emotions. Although I recognized that this was a broad generalization, its validity was strong enough to cause scholars who have studied the Nisei to remark on it.[27]

Kurihara's seemingly European American interpersonal style of verbal assertiveness, confrontation, bluntness, and spontaneity, and his use of dramatic emphasis, led me to wonder, "Who was this man?" I later realized that my question dovetailed well with my interest in engaging in research on the World War II incarceration of the Nisei, since Kurihara had been at the center of a revolt in Manzanar, one of ten camps created in 1942 by the U.S. War Relocation Authority. I decided to examine Kurihara's role in the revolt, which had ended with the death of two innocent young men, who were killed by gunfire from Manzanar guards. I knew that in order to understand the uprising and Kurihara's place in it, I had to know about more than the incident itself. It did not take me long to find myself immersed in the twists and turns of his multilayered experiences.

By focusing on Kurihara, I was able to explore issues of identity and social justice. Moreover, in examining his life, I was able to learn about facets of the American experience during the first half of the twentieth century: immigrant lives in the Territory of Hawaii, agricultural field labor in the Sacramento region, Catholic schooling in San Francisco, boot camp during World War I, soldiering in France, working-class lives in Los Angeles, tuna fishing in the high seas south of California, life and conflict in the War Relocation Authority camps of Manzanar, Moab, Leupp, and Tule Lake, and Nisei expatriate lives in Japan in the early months and years after the war, all of which were part of Kurihara's experiences. The result was a book, *In Defense of Justice: Joseph Kurihara and the Japanese American Struggle for Equality*.

My study of Kurihara, like my earlier studies, enabled me to grapple with issues of oppression, dominance, power, resistance, and competing worldviews, all of which have been central to American history. Along the way, in my own lifetime I have witnessed the recurring tensions that have arisen as ethnic groups struggle to achieve a place in mainstream society.

Decades ago, in his introduction to *The Uprooted*, Oscar Handlin stated, "Once I thought to write a history of the immigrants in America. Then I discovered that the immigrants were American history." His statement crystallizes for me the essence of my own scholarly experience, which has demonstrated for me the centrality in American history of immigration and its attendant issues of ethnic identity, marginality, and power.[28]

Notes

1. Examples of my work include *In Defense of Justice: Joseph Kurihara and the Japanese American Struggle for Equality* (Urbana: University of Illinois Press, 2013); an edited work, *The History of Discrimination in U.S. Education: Marginality, Agency, and Power* (New York: Palgrave Macmillan, 2008); *Americanization, Acculturation, and Ethnic Identity: The Nisei Generation in Hawai'i* (Urbana: University of Illinois Press, 1994); "African American Vernacular English & Hawai'i Creole English: A Comparison of Two School Board Controversies," *Journal of Negro Education* 71, no. 1 (2002): 1–14; "Power, Status, and Hawai'i Creole English: An Example of Linguistic Intolerance in American History," *Pacific Historical Review* 65, no. 3 (1996): 431–454; "Using the Past to Inform the Future: An Historiography of Hawaii's Asian and Pacific Islander Americans," *AmerasiaJournal* 26, no. 1 (2000): 55–85.
2. Andrew W. Lind, *Hawaii's People*, 3rd ed. (Honolulu: University of Hawaii Press, 1967), 28.
3. I. A. Newby, *Black Carolinians: A History of Blacks in South Carolina from 1895 to 1968* (Columbia: University of South Carolina Press, 1973); Newby, *The South: A History* (New York: Holt, Rinehart and Winston, 1978); Newby, *Plain Folk in the New South: Social Change and Cultural Persistence, 1880–1915* (Baton Rouge: Louisiana State University Press, 1989).
4. Tamura, *Americanization*, 28.
5. Ibid., 146–151.
6. Yuji Ichioka, *The Issei: The World of the First Generation Japanese Immigrants, 1885–1924* (New York: Free Press, 1988), 176–254; Roger Daniels, *Asian America: Chinese and Japanese in the United States since 1850* (Seattle: University of Washington Press, 1988), 149.
7. Lind, *Hawaii's People*, 28.
8. Eleanor Nordyke, *The Peopling of Hawai'i*, 2nd ed. (Honolulu: University of Hawaii Press, 1989), 80.
9. Lind, *Hawaii's People*, 28; Lawrence H. Fuchs, *Hawaii Pono: A Social History* (New York: Harcourt, 1961), 37.
10. Daniel E. Weinberg, "The Movement to Americanize the Japanese Community in Hawaii: An Analysis of One Hundred Percent Americanization Activity in the Territory as Expressed in the Caucasian Press, 1919–1923" (master's thesis, University of Hawaii, 1967), 29–35.
11. Geraldine J. Clifford, "'Marry, Stitch, Die, or Do Worse': Educating Women for Work," in *Work, Youth, and Schooling: Historical Perspectives on Vocationalism in American Education*, ed. Harvey Kantor and David B. Tyack (Stanford, Calif.: Stanford University Press, 1982), 253.

12. George K. Yamamoto, "Political Participation among Orientals in Hawaii," *Sociology and Social Research* 43 (May–June 1959): 360.

13. College Club, "Letter to the Governor of the Territory of Hawaii, Superintendent of Public Instruction, and Commission of Public Instruction," copy sent to Claxton, November 15, 1996, quoted in Noriko Asato, "Mandating Americanization: Japanese Language Schools and the Federal Survey of Education in Hawaiʻi, 1916–1920," *History of Education Quarterly* 43, no. 1 (Spring 2003): 18; Bunker to Claxton, October 13, 1919, quoted in Asato, "Mandating Americanization," 23.

14. Dean Itsuji Saranillio, "Colliding Histories: Hawaiʻi Statehood at the Intersection of Asians 'Ineligible to Citizenship' and Hawaiians 'Unfit for Self-Government,'" *Journal of Asian American Studies* 13, no. 3 (October 2010): 295.

15. Ronald Takaki, *Strangers from a Different Shore* (New York: Basic Books, 1998), 176. See also George Cooper and Gavan Daws, *Land and Power in Hawaii: The Democratic Years* (Honolulu: Benchmark Books, 1985).

16. Sister Mary Dorita, "Filipino Immigration to Hawaii" (master's thesis, University of Hawaii, 1954), 17–18, 100–107, 124–129; John M. Liu, Paul M. Ong, and Carolyn Rosenstein, "Dual Chain Migration: Post-1965 Filipino Immigration to the United States," *International Migration Review* 25, no. 3 (Autumn 1991): 492–493; Nordyke, *The Peopling of Hawaiʻi*, 80; F. Caces, "Immigrant Recruitment into the Labor Force: Social Networks among Filipinos in Hawaii," *Amerasia Journal* 13, no. 1 (1986–1987): 22–38.

17. Liu, Ong, and Rosenstein, "Dual Chain Migration," 492–493, 499, 505. In one year, 1973, for example, 118 college-educated, English-speaking Filipinos immigrated to Hawaiʻi.

18. Jeff Chang, "Lessons of Tolerance: Americanism and the Filipino Affirmative Action Movement in Hawaiʻi," *Social Process in Hawaiʻi* 37 (1996): 116, 127.

19. Ibid., 117.

20. Ibid., 119.

21. Tom Coffman, "State Defends Its Hiring Practices," *Honolulu Star-Bulletin*, December 22, 1971, A2.

22. Chang, "Lessons of Tolerance," 122, 141n7.

23. Ibid., 115.

24. "Failed promise of Asian American solidarity" is adapted from the title of Neil Foley's book, *Quest for Equality: The Failed Promise of Black-Brown Solidarity* (Cambridge, Mass.: Harvard University Press, 2010).

25. Mitchell T. Maki, Harry H. L. Kitano, and S. Megan Berthold, *Achieving the Impossible Dream: How Japanese Americans Obtained Redress* (Urbana: University of Illinois Press, 1999), 57–59; Sachiko Takita, "The Tule Lake Pilgrimage and Japanese American Internment: Collective Memory, Solidarity, and Division in an Ethnic Community" (PhD diss., University of California, Los Angeles, 2007), 62.

26. Greg Robinson, *A Tragedy of Democracy: Japanese Confinement in North America* (New York: Columbia University Press, 2009), 113–121; Lind, *Hawaii's People*, 28. Of the 158,000 Nikkei living in the islands, 1,500 Nikkei, most of whom were Issei men, were incarcerated in the territory, while 1,700 were sent to mainland camps.

27. S. Frank Miyamoto, "Problems of Interpersonal Style among the Nisei," *Amerasia Journal* 13, no. 2 (1986–1987): 29–45; Stanford Lyman, "Generation and Character: The Case of Japanese-Americans," in *East across the Pacific*, ed. Hilary Conroy and T. Scott Miyakawa, 279–314 (Santa Barbara, Calif.: ABC-Clio Press, 1972); William Caudill, "Japanese-American Personality and Acculturation," *Genetic-Psychology Monographs* 45 (1952): 3–102.

28. Oscar Handlin, *The Uprooted: The Epic Story of the Great Migrations That Made the American People* (Boston: Little, Brown and Company, 1951), 3.

10

Americana

MARÍA CRISTINA GARCÍA

*A*mericana, the Spanish translation of the word *American*, positions one both within and beyond the nation-state. To say "yo soy Americana" can mean that I am a citizen of a specific country—the United States—or a citizen of a region or hemisphere—the Americas. I remember the first time I identified myself as Americana in a Latin American country, my host hesitated, smiled, and gently responded in Spanish "But, of course, dear. We are *all* American." People from the Caribbean, Central America, and the southern cone have long claimed this term. The fact that today most people around the world associate the term solely with the United States speaks to the economic, political, and cultural influence this country has exerted on its neighbors to the south and north for generations.

In the course of my life, I have encountered multiple meanings of the term American—some personal, some national, and some hemispheric—and I have tried to understand what relevance each one has for me. This quest has deeply informed my work as a historian, but it began much earlier in my life, during my childhood in a refugee family.

Act One

My family emigrated from Cuba a few years after Fidel Castro's triumphant march into Havana. Although my parents welcomed the end of Fulgencio Batista's dictatorship, they became disillusioned by the Castro government's failure to enact the promised democratic reforms. Many elements of the new authoritarian state troubled them: the neighborhood watch committees that monitored their every move; the censorship and eventual shutdown of the independent press; the suspension of free elections; the deportation of the clergy. My father, a lawyer (and Fidel's law school classmate), was especially disturbed by the lack of due process, the mass trials and public executions of those considered enemies of the state. A student of history, he knew that it was only a matter of time before the revolutionary government turned on its initial supporters; already neighbors were turning against neighbors. For months my parents debated whether to leave their home and homeland, and in the end chose to do so because they wanted their children to have choices: the choice to read and study what they wanted; the choice to express themselves freely without looking over their shoulders to see who was listening; the choice to be religious or not. The family drove to José Martí International Airport with one suitcase per person and a few U.S. dollars—the maximum allowed by the state. The plane ride to the United States took approximately forty-five minutes. They arrived in Miami essentially penniless, without any idea of where to go or what to do next. It was May 18, 1961. By 1975, they had been joined by close to half a million of their compatriots, and hundreds of thousands more would follow in the decades to come.

My parents left Cuba with their two children, my brother José Ramón and me, who were both under the age of five, and my maternal grandmother. Aunts, uncles, and cousins followed over the coming months. The family never imagined that the move would be permanent. Cubans have migrated back and forth across the Florida Straits for generations as tourists, students, merchants, and political exiles, and they thought they were part of that migratory tradition. Given the United States' long history of intervention in Cuban and Latin American affairs, they, like most Cubans who left during the 1960s, thought they would eventually return to their homeland. The United States, they argued, would never tolerate a communist government so close to its shores. At midnight each New Year's Eve, with the local Spanish-language radio station, WQBA, playing the Cuban national anthem in the background, we ate the traditional twelve grapes, drank Spanish *cidra*, and toasted "Next year in Havana!" Within a decade we had abandoned that toast.

Because my father found employment as legal counsel for a well-known U.S. corporation, we lived in different cities around the Caribbean—Nassau, San Juan, Miami—but the United States is the country we came to call home and whose citizenship we claim. My childhood memories are most attached to south Florida, where my siblings and I spent most of our formative years. My brother José Ramón and I—as well as our U.S.-born sister, Victoria—attended a Catholic parochial elementary school in Coral Gables, Florida, run by the Sisters of St. Joseph, many of whom were from Dublin, Ireland. Half of our classmates were Cuban refugees like ourselves, and many of our parents knew one another from Havana. The Sisters took their pupils' academic and spiritual formation seriously and, like most Catholic educators, were known for their rigor and discipline. Ironically, these Irish nuns from Dublin became our agents of Americanization, socializing us not only to be good Catholics but also good Americans. They taught us our U.S. history, geography, and civics. But this Americanization had an Irish tone: we studied the geography of Ireland as well as of the United States; our English vocabulary included many Irish words like shillelagh, brough, and hooligan; and we dressed as leprechauns and danced the jig and reel for our Cuban parents at the annual Saint Patrick's Day festival. Those of us with Spanish names too unfamiliar to pronounce found ourselves renamed in school as Maggie, Paddy, or in the case of my brother and me, Joseph and Marie. For these nuns, a good American meant a good *Irish* American.

I encountered a different type of American education in other parts of the city, as I accompanied my grandmother on trips to the supermarket, *el ten-cent* (the five-and-dime store), and other public places in south Florida. In the 1960s south Florida residents were not tolerant or forgiving of the Cuban refugees who were rapidly growing in number, at the rate of one thousand to fifteen hundred per week. They resisted the cultural transformation of their city and often lashed out angrily, and so I found Americans more than a little scary. I remember the employees at our local Woolworth's as particularly ugly, hissing at my grandmother whenever they heard her heavily accented English: "Why don't you go back to where you belong?" "Speak American!" As a child, I seethed with indignation to see my beloved grandmother so publicly attacked, but my grandmother never lost her poise and elegance in the face of that ugliness. As we walked out the door, she held my hand tightly and reminded me to be proud of who I was and where I came from. "We are exiles," she told me. "Never allow ignorant people to make you feel inferior."

The implied distinction between exiles and immigrants puzzled me. Cubans were exiles, and recognized as refugees by the United States, but the challenges they faced accommodating to life in the United States did not seem all that different from the challenges faced by my immigrant classmates from other parts of the world. However, for that first generation of Cuban refugees—those who arrived in the 1960s and 1970s—the exile discourse was their raison d'être; and a central feature of that Cuban exile discourse was that our experience was, indeed, different from that of other people who cross national borders. Immigrants migrated for economic reasons, the Cuban émigré discourse went; refugees migrated for political reasons. Going into exile was not an act of economic desperation but of political defiance, and that political stance, the discourse posited, distinguished refugees from all others regardless of social class.

The symbols of day-to-day life reinforced that discourse. The principal institutions of Cuban society were reestablished a few hundred miles away in south Florida, linking past and present, and offering a sense of stability and continuation. The U.S. government passed special legislation to facilitate the Cubans' naturalization, and created one of the most generous relief packages in immigration history to help them retool for success in the American economy. By the 1970s, periodicals such as *Time, Newsweek,* and *Fortune* celebrated the Cuban success story, the rapid economic transformation of Miami, and the Cubans' growing political clout. Over time, I came to realize that the distinctions between immigrant and refugee and between economic and political motivations were arbitrary. *Migration is always a political act.* But as a young child, I did not question the message that the Cuban experience was different and special. To some extent, that discourse empowered me and countless others in our community. It assisted our adaptation to the United States by infusing our experience with meaning.

My Cuban-born classmates received similar messages from their parents and grandparents. We were taught to be proud of our heritage, and proud of the community we had re-created in south Florida. On the individual level we may have all had insecurities and anxieties about our self-worth, but on the collective level we never questioned our worth as Cubans. If a non-Cuban classmate ever used a derogatory slur, we generally laughed it off, certain that his comments had to be motivated by jealousy. It wasn't until many years later, when I moved to Austin, Texas, to attend graduate school and heard the experiences of some of my Chicano/a classmates that I more fully realized how fortunate Cuban refugee children of my generation had been. We were never forced to attend segregated schools, or tracked into vocational training programs, or punished for speaking Spanish. No members of our family had ever been denied access to professions, membership in organizations, or medical care because of our national origin or ethnicity. No family members had ever been lynched.

If the Cuban Americans who arrived during the 1960s and 1970s were one of the more successful migrations in U.S. history, that success was due as much to the U.S. government's investment in our futures as to the entrepreneurial values attributed to our compatriots. Cubans may have been caught up in and displaced by Cold War intrigues, but on some level we also became its beneficiaries. Millions of people were politically or economically displaced throughout the region over the span of the Cold War, but I know of no other group that received as generous a response from a host society. On the local level we may have been resented and despised by our south Florida neighbors who were debilitated by fear of change, but at the macro level we had the U.S. government stamp of approval and that carried us far.

In retrospect, I think the admonitions to *be American!* shaped my future academic pursuits. Our American neighbors were very insistent that we shed the traits that identified us as Cuban and become American as quickly as possible, but they offered contradictory models of what American might look like. Many years later, in college, I realized that my preoccupations with defining and understanding *the American* were not new. J. Hector St. John de Crevecoeur,

Alexis de Tocqueville, Israel Zangwill, and Randolph Bourne, among many others, had tried to define what it meant to be American with unsatisfying results; and the boom in ethnic literature suggested that my preoccupations with adaptation were shared by millions of my contemporaries. But growing up in the Miami of the 1960s, I was frustrated that I was offered no blueprints. U.S. society made many demands of its immigrants (some unreasonable) and expected us to figure everything out.

Fortunately, I had the advantage of youth. It is easier to immigrate as a child than as an adult. Like most immigrant children, I learned what my parents expected of me at home, and I somehow learned what American society expected of me in the classroom, on the playground, and through popular culture. I picked up the idioms of American English at a young enough age that I now speak without an identifiable accent. I also became cognizant of the fact that I had certain cultural advantages that facilitated my acceptance. My parents were of European ancestry, had educations that transferred across borders, and were well remunerated for their skills, and this meant that I had access to social circles and to institutions that are closed to many first-generation immigrants. My "segmented assimilation," to quote the sociologists, was a privileged one. By my teen years I came to understand that *ser americana*, or "to be American," meant simply to adopt and exhibit the traits that allowed people to feel comfortable around you.

As I learned to navigate and claim a space in American society, the members of my nuclear and extended family insisted that I remain familiar to them, which meant also retaining the traits of *cubanidad*. My elders had left one revolutionary society only to enter another society in flux. They found the 1960s counterculture bewildering and they feared for their children. At baptisms and weddings, my relatives jokingly referred to my siblings and cousins as *los americanitos*, but they could barely disguise their unease. Would these children run wild, disrespect their parents, heritage, and culture, and adopt behaviors they negatively stereotyped as "American"? Would they become so Americanized that Cuba would lose sight of us?

When, in the second grade, I told my grandmother that George Washington was the father of my country, she corrected me (once she regained her composure) pointing out that José Martí was the father of Cuba. From that day on, my grandmother regaled me with stories of Cuba as I helped her prepare each evening's meal, anchoring me to a country I couldn't remember. Language was central to her efforts. My grandmother and I established a daily ritual: she read my schoolbooks out loud to practice her English, and I read to her in Spanish from local newspapers. My grandmother, like other elders in our extended family, hoped that by retaining Spanish and claiming a Cuban cultural identity, her grandchildren would easily fit back into Cuba when we returned; but as returning became less likely, her goal was simply to ensure that her grandchildren would remain connected to family, community, and heritage.

Act Two

As a student, I made new discoveries about American-ness. Whatever apprehensions my parents may have had about American culture, they encouraged us children to immerse ourselves in the study of the United States and claim the United States as our own. We became U.S. citizens as soon as immigration law permitted, and my parents learned English quickly, even though age prevented them from speaking without an accent. Every summer, my parents loaded their children in the car (with grandmother once again in tow) and drove off to explore our new country. Over the years, we covered thousands of miles and got into all sorts of trouble. We got stuck in the Mojave Desert with an overheated radiator, drove through tornadoes, hurricanes, and hailstorms, and got flagged down by dozens of state troopers who searched our car looking (they said) for illegal produce. We visited St. Augustine, Colonial Williamsburg, Philadelphia, the Grand Canyon, San Francisco, Disneyland, Niagara Falls, among many other places. These yearly trips piqued my interest in U.S. history, though I suspected even then that the historical narratives packaged for tourist consumption told only part of the story. On one particularly fateful visit to Washington, D.C., I saw the beautiful spires of Georgetown University across the Potomac and I fell in love with it. I announced to my parents right then that I would study at Georgetown. They looked at each other startled, not because I wanted to go to college—my parents had college degrees and expected their children to have them as well—but because young Cuban girls of my generation were expected to live at home even while attending college, and until marriage. To my parents' credit (especially my mother, who was my strongest advocate), they ignored the considerable resistance they encountered from Cuban family and friends, and permitted me to be the first of my female cousins to attend college away from home.

I majored in—big surprise—American Studies. I studied Americana: all things related to the United States. At Georgetown, the American Studies major provided an interdisciplinary education in what was then considered the canon: primary sources and literary readings that included Cotton Mather, Jonathan Edwards, Benjamin Franklin, Alexis de Tocqueville, Thomas Jefferson, Ralph Waldo Emerson, Walt Whitman, Henry David Thoreau, Ernest Hemingway, John Dos Passos, F. Scott Fitzgerald; and recent historical works by Bernard Bailyn, Gordon S. Wood, Richard Hofstadter, William Leuchtenburg, and Michael Kammen, among others. Our readings had a largely White, elite, male, and east-of-the-Mississippi bias; however, the program did grant us the opportunity to design the occasional independent study in topics that interested us. It was one such independent study with Emmett Curran, who taught immigration history, that turned my personal interest in immigrants, refugees, and exiles into a broader intellectual interest in displaced persons and people who move across national borders.

Professor Curran introduced me to the works of Oscar Handlin, John Higham, John Bodnar, and Nathan Glazer, among other important specialists in U.S. immigration history. And, much to his credit, he introduced me to readings in comparative immigration and the newly emerging interdisciplinary fields of Chicano studies and Puerto Rican studies. When it came time to write my senior thesis, I chose to write about the migration from Cuba and examine it in light of this larger U.S. narrative of migration. The persistent detective work required to track down elusive sources was exciting, and I soon abandoned my plans for law school and instead applied to graduate programs in American Studies (then called American Civilization).

Immediately after my graduation from Georgetown University in 1982, I began my graduate studies at the University of Texas at Austin to expand the geographic and conceptual boundaries of American Studies as I then knew it. The graduate program at U.T. was rigorous but eclectic for its time, and challenged the narrative of American exceptionalism that was the foundation of Cold War American Studies programs. Topical courses in women's literature, the American West, American photography, folklore, and architecture—none of which I had studied at Georgetown—complemented the more traditional courses in nineteenth- and twentieth-century intellectual and cultural history. We were encouraged to read widely and across disciplines. I became certain that a career in academia made sense, even though my parents would have preferred more practical training in law, accounting, engineering, or medicine (the traditional course of study of students from developing countries). I wanted to spend my professional life around students and scholars who thought, debated, and wrestled with ideas, who researched and wrote, and who contributed to our understanding of various topics.

It was my contact with students and faculty at the Center for Mexican American Studies (CMAS) that helped me identify my own particular niche within my discipline and within the academy. Founded in 1970 by Américo Paredes, the scholars associated with CMAS had committed their professional lives to recovering the histories of those who had been erased from the U.S. national narrative. During my graduate school years, CMAS was one of a dozen or so Chicano/ Mexican American Studies programs in the United States, which, together with the small number of Puerto Rican Studies programs, became sites for important intellectual work and for advocacy on behalf of Latino students who were woefully underrepresented in U.S. colleges and universities. The number of Latino graduate students, especially women, was even smaller; by the time I received my doctorate in 1990, for example, there were fewer than a dozen Chicanas in the United States with doctorates in history.

The first graduate course I took in Chicano Studies introduced me to the intellectual origins of the field. We read some of the foundational work of scholars like Carlos Eduardo Castañeda and Américo Paredes, who were among the first to document the history and folklore of people of Mexican ancestry in Texas, as well as some of the newer scholarship by Rodolfo Acuña, Mario Barrera, Alberto Camarillo, Richard Griswold del Castillo, and Robert Rosenbaum, among others. It was an exciting and dynamic field with a strong sense of mission, committed not only to inserting Mexican Americans into the scholarship of the United States but also reframing and reconceptualizing what we know and teach as U.S. history. The intellectual excitement was palpable and I wanted to be part of it. The fact that many of my graduate school classmates in Texas—a state that had once been a part of Mexico—had never read any work by or about Mexican Americans for their candidacy exams (or any other underrepresented minority, for that matter) suggested that we needed to reconsider what constituted core knowledge in American history. Sadly, the recent debates over curricular reform in Texas and Arizona suggest that not much has changed in the past twenty years.[1]

During my final years in graduate school, I had the chance to assist in curricular reform at a very modest level. I was hired to work as a staff writer and researcher for the Texas State Historical Association's *New Handbook of Texas*. The *Handbook*, a two-volume encyclopedia of Texas history first published in 1952, contained only a handful of entries on people of Mexican ancestry, most of them nineteenth-century figures such as Juan Seguín and Lorenzo de Zavala, who were central to the history of the Texas Republic. Women and racial and ethnic minorities were almost totally absent, and the *New Handbook* sought to address this oversight.

The revised encyclopedia, now six volumes (and also available online), included more than twenty thousand articles, hundreds of which focus on individuals, organizations, and events central to the histories of underrepresented peoples, and is routinely consulted by teachers across the country. At one annual meeting of the Texas State Historical Association, I overheard a group of historians of Texas derisively call our efforts revisionist history, which in the 1980s and 1990s was a euphemism for a history designed to appease certain constituencies but not worthy of serious intellectual engagement. For those of us working to make U.S. history inclusive, however, revisionism meant recovering and broadening what we consider American. As Gary Okihiro wrote a decade later, the core values of the United States emanate from peoples on the margins of U.S. society because it is their struggles for inclusion, legal and otherwise, that reaffirm the ideals of the founders and ultimately make the United States a more democratic nation.[2] Latino history *is* U.S. history.

When it came time to choose a dissertation topic, I knew that I wanted to contribute to the scholarship on Hispanics/Latinos in the United States while developing my interests in immigration and foreign policy. I redirected my attention once again to the post-1959 Cuban migration. During the 1980s, Cuban studies was booming. The Castro revolution had inspired hundreds of scholarly works, and much of the scholarship understandably focused on U.S.-Cuba relations during the Castro era; but comparatively little had been written about Cuban migration as an aspect and consequence of foreign relations. Dozens of social scientists had written excellent studies on the Cubans' economic and political accommodation in the United States, but historians had largely neglected the post-1959 Cuban migration.[3] I decided to write a history of the post-1959 Cuban migration that might appeal to scholars of both immigration and foreign policy, and this dissertation later inspired my book *Havana USA*.[4] In this book, I chronicled the history of this migration up to 1994 and explained how the Cubans became a powerful economic and political presence in the United States, influenced foreign policy and electoral outcomes, reshaped the cultural landscape of the South, and ultimately reinterpreted what it means to assimilate in U.S. society. I am honored that the book has been cited so frequently in other works on refugee history and the Cuban American experience. I wish I could say that the elders in my family have all read the book that I dedicated to them. Although I know they are proud of my work, their copies of the book are buried deep in bookshelves, collecting dust. It is a history they would rather not relive.

As I wrote my dissertation in Austin, Texas, during the late 1980s, a different migration story was unfolding south of the U.S.-Mexico border. Tens of thousands of Salvadorans, Guatemalans, and Nicaraguans were fleeing the wars in Central America, crossing national borders in search of refuge. Their stories attracted a considerable amount of attention. In the United States, churches became part of growing nationwide "sanctuary" movement that tried to call attention to the wars in Central America and the people caught in its crossfire. Though advocates popularly referred to the Central Americans as refugees, officials of the Reagan and Bush administrations claimed that this migration was driven by economics; consequently, fewer than 5 percent of asylum applicants were successful in their petitions for protection in the 1980s. Once again, the arbitrary distinctions between immigrant and refugee, and between political and economic motivations for migration, became obvious.

As I finished my dissertation on the Cubans, a group so privileged by comparison, I committed myself to beginning a new project that would focus on this Central American migration. I decided to examine this migration in a broader comparative context, for this migration had affected a number of countries in the region, not just the United States. This project ultimately became my second book, *Seeking Refuge*,[5] a study of the individuals, groups, and organizations that responded to the Central American refugee crisis of the 1980s and 1990s, and helped shape refugee policies throughout North America. Collectively, these domestic and transnational advocacy networks collected testimonies, documented the abuses of states, reframed national debates about immigration, pressured for changes in policy, and ultimately provided a voice for the displaced and the excluded.

If *Havana USA* is a study of a particular refugee community, *Seeking Refuge* is a study of how refugee policy is constructed by state and nonstate actors. My forthcoming book project is the natural outgrowth of these two studies: I am now examining how the end of the Cold War altered the ideological lens that for half a century shaped definitions of—and policies toward—refugees and asylum seekers. It is a study of the changing definition of refugee in the United States.

In a 1999 study, the Cuban-born sociologist Rubén Rumbaut reported on the pronounced tendency of nativity and identity to influence an individual's choice of immigration studies as a field. The fact that I have chosen to write about immigration, while not predictable, is not surprising either. However, I do not identify as an *ethnic historian*. Although I recognize that my personal history as an immigrant has shaped my intellectual interests, the term ethnic historian narrowly places me solely within a U.S. framework. When I study the movement of peoples across national borders, I am as much interested in the countries of origin as in the receiving societies. (Im)migrants and refugees move *between* countries and localities, within or across regions. They highlight global interdependencies. Their stories are not just a part of the history of the United States; they are also part of other histories, national and regional. The study of migration makes those linkages and interdependencies evident. The study of immigration to the United States, more specifically, can sustain a national or ethnic identity while encouraging a more cosmopolitan sense of being an American.[6]

Act Three

My scholarly work on migration from Latin America has benefited from my association with Latino Studies programs. Even though I don't claim the label of ethnic historian because it is too limiting, I do have a strong commitment to the field of Latino/a studies because of what it seeks to accomplish in the academy, namely, a recognition and inclusion of people and events who have been erased from U.S. history. I am gratified to see how this field has evolved since I began my graduate studies more than twenty years ago. During the 1990s, a generational shift occurred: Many of the students and scholars of the new Latino Studies were now the children of the post-1965 migration and they brought a new perspective to the field. Latino Studies programs are concerned less with asserting a cultural nationalism, as ethnic studies programs of the 1960s sometimes were, and more with the transnational relationship of Latino immigrants to multiple societies. Latino Studies is also framed by, and in dialogue with, the theoretical insights developed by studies of feminism, postcoloniality, sexuality, and race. Latino/a studies scholars speak as readily to scholars in diplomatic/foreign relations history (what some now call "U.S. in the World") as to those in critical race studies and immigration history.

For budgetary reasons, Latino Studies programs are often subsumed into either Latin American Studies (which symbolically positions Latinos as *outside* the United States) or American Studies (which symbolically positions them as one of the many ethnic peoples on the periphery of the state). Neither option sits well with me. If Latino history is U.S. history, it's also Latin American history. It links the two. In my ideal world, universities would have *Americas Studies*: a program, department, or center dedicated to the study of the hemisphere, of which the United States is just one of many interrelated parts. In this conception, the study of migration is given as much attention as the study of foreign relations, commercial trade and development, and cultural exchange.

It is easy to assume that studying immigrants and ethnic groups forces one to look too inward and become parochial, to gaze at the particulars of one little piece of a more complicated whole. However, the study of immigrants and ethnics has had just the opposite effect: It has forced me to look outward, beyond the nation, to consider interdependencies, and overlapping histories and cultural geographies. Localities are always connected to the broader world, whether we choose to acknowledge these connections or not; and immigrants are characters on international as well as local and national stages. Latino immigrants may be "new Americans" in a particular U.S. context, but they have always been *Americanos*.

Act Four

I write these final sentences on a charter flight from Miami to Havana. I occasionally travel to Cuba for scholarly presentations or research, when U.S. and Cuban travel policies permit. (At the time of this writing, in 2012, the trade embargo remains in place and diplomatic relations are limited to small "interest sections" in both countries.) Fifty-plus years after the Castro revolution, the decision to travel to Cuba is still fraught with emotion and controversy in the Cuban exile community where I grew up; many of my parents' generation consider it a betrayal, a validation of the government that displaced them and caused so much pain. As a teacher and scholar of Cuban history, I do not have the option of ignoring Cuba. In the 1960s, some airline magazines erased Cuba from their maps, as if the lack of political recognition from the United States meant that the country had ceased to exist. I cannot erase Cuba. I envy other immigrant scholars who can travel to their countries of heritage with less emotional baggage. As I look out the window at the blue ocean below, I try to imagine what my parents felt on that fateful day in May 1961, when they left their home and homeland, to face an uncertain future in the United States. It's a very long ninety miles between Cuba and the United States. I've tried to shorten that distance through my teaching and scholarship.

Because I was born in Cuba, the Cuban government does not recognize my U.S. citizenship and I must travel on a special visa that identifies me as both a part of the Cuban nation and outside of it. The visa captures, for me, the intersecting political and cultural worlds in which I have traveled all these years. My identity is complicated. I am American *and* Cuban. I am a citizen of the United States *and* a national of Cuba *and* a resident of the Americas. I am refugee *and* immigrant *and* citizen. I am *Americana*: a simple word that captures multiple realities. I wouldn't have it any other way.

Notes

1. Erik W. Robelen, "Rewriting of States' Standards on Social Studies Stirs Debate," *Education Week* 29, no. 27 (March 31, 2010): 1–19; Ed Wetschler, "After 50 Years, Ethnic Studies Still Controversial," *District Administration* 47, no. 7 (July 2011): 46–53.
2. Gary Y. Okihiro, *Margins and Mainstreams: Asians in American History and Culture* (Seattle: University of Washington Press, 1994). See also his *Common Ground: Reimagining American History* (Princeton: Princeton University Press, 2001.)
3. As I was completing my dissertation on Cuban migration to the United States, Felix Roberto Masud-Piloto published his book, *With Open Arms: Cuban Migration to the United States* (Totowa, N.J.: Rowman & Littlefield, 1988). This important work was later revised and published as *From Welcomed Exiles to Illegal Immigrants: Cuban Migration to the U.S., 1959–1995* (Lanham, Md.: Rowman & Littlefield, 1996).
4. María Cristina García, *Havana USA: Cuban Exiles and Cuban Americans in South Florida, 1959–1994* (Berkeley: University of California Press, 1996).
5. María Cristina García, *Seeking Refuge: Central American Migration to Mexico, the United States, and Canada* (Berkeley: University of California Press, 2006).
6. I wish to highlight Thomas Bender's *A Nation among Nations: America's Place in World History* (New York: Hill and Wang, 2006), which affirms the many reasons why U.S. history (including migration) is best studied in a hemispheric or global context. This is indispensable reading for the student of American history.

11

Meddling in the American Dilemma

Race, Migrations, and Identities from an Africana Transnational Perspective

VIOLET M. SHOWERS JOHNSON

One day in my first year of full-time teaching in the United States, the class discussion got very heated over an assessment of the legendary early twentieth-century conflict between African American activist W.E.B. Du Bois and Jamaican immigrant Black nationalist Marcus Garvey. I attempted to steer the different factions away from arguments shaped solely by their personal, emotionally charged sentiments to interpretations grounded in clearly substantiated scholarly work. Responding to my efforts, one of the students remarked: "It is easy for you because you are not an American." From the reactions of her classmates, it was clear that there was a consensus that although I was the instructor responsible for designing and teaching the course, I had come into it as an outsider. For a moment I felt an overwhelming sense of alienation, as an intruder in the American saga of race and race relations. I regained my poise, emboldened by my quick recollection that as far back as the nation's infancy, the outsider assessment of American pluralism has been fundamental in American historiography. From French J. Hector St. John de Crevecoeur's *Letters from an American Farmer* to Swedish Gunnar Myrdal's *An American Dilemma*,[1] some of the most definitive statements on the history of race and ethnicity in America have been made by foreign-born writers, underscoring the viability of the outsider perspective.

This essay revisits and analyzes locations, episodes, interpretations, and scholarly endeavors in an academic journey that started in Nigeria, West Africa; brought me to a classroom in the American South as a recently graduated international student; progressed with my experiences as a resident alien; and continues in my current status as naturalized American. The voyage started in 1967. As a ten-year-old, I was growing up in Kaduna, a complex emerging postcolonial society in northern Nigeria, which was defined by glaring ethnic and religious diversity and challenged by the Hausa-Igbo conflict that contributed tremendously to the Nigerian/Biafra Civil War of 1967–1970.[2] My life was being shaped as much by the fast-moving developments in the larger Hausa/Nigerian community as the social and cultural dictates of the subculture of my parents' ethnic enclave. Although my four brothers and I were born in Nigeria, we were firmly grounded in the Sierra Leonean immigrant community. Known as Saros, the Sierra Leoneans in Nigeria during that period, mostly of the Krio ethnic group, initially came under British auspices, as expatriate workers in the colonial West African regional administrative complex.[3] I crisscrossed linguistic, religious, and other cultural boundaries between the larger Nigerian society and my parents' Saro community, which fostered and projected strong physical and cultural ties with its homeland origins in another West African country. This early in my life, I did not yet grasp the important fact that this was my first practical existence in a transnational community, one that would prove insightful in understanding the ones I would later study as a scholar of U.S. immigration history.

American history found me in Kaduna via the Peace Corps. By 1966, Peace Corps volunteers were adding to the diversity of my universe. One of them actually rented a self-contained room in our family house on Abuja Road. He stood out like a rescue beacon. Never ever learning his name, the neighborhood children all simply called him "Peace Corps." We were fascinated by Peace Corps and his handful of fellow volunteers who hung out at the house on Abuja Road: They let us play with their motorbike helmets; shared with us candies and other goodies from home; let us look at pictures in those glossy American publications, including *Ebony*; cracked us up by their attempts to speak Hausa and join us in popular folk songs and games; finally, and most pertinently for this essay, Peace Corps told us stories of his homeland. We always looked forward to the yarns of this *Baturé griot* (*Baturé* is Hausa for White person; a *griot* is a traditional professional storyteller/historian in African communities). In the two or so years that Peace Corp lived among us, he told us numerous stories. One of them made a lasting impression and stands as the threshold to my foray into American history. The story, the way Peace Corps told it in 1967, started with two men but clearly expanded into vast and complicated ramifications. He showed us pictures of Malcolm X and Martin Luther King Jr. Explaining how these two historical figures fought for justice, he also broke the shocking news that his country, which had sent him to be friends with us and to do so much good, had not always dealt fairly with people who looked like us. Still, Peace Corps ended the story on an upbeat note, convinced that the men's struggle would yield the desired results and emphasizing that his country (in spite of what he had just revealed) was the greatest nation on earth, where dreams came true. That story, told by Peace Corps in the simplest of terms, was profound. It hit on many crucial aspects of American history—the American promise, the paradox, and the salience of race. Although I did not fully recognize these themes at the time, I concluded that the United States was an enigma that I was determined to unravel, if given the chance.

The opportunity to formally study U.S. history came a little over a decade later in Sierra Leone, where my family had moved to in 1971. My final year in college, I took the American history survey (the only American history course in the curriculum) as part of the requirements of the honors in history program. This single course was a catalyst. It inspired me to launch that quest to unravel the enigma. Therefore, when I finally landed on American soil in 1985 on a Fulbright scholarship to pursue a PhD, it was to be a specialist in the story Peace Corps had introduced to me decades before. I not only wanted to hear the intriguing story, I was also determined to be able to tell it as a scholar.

Peace Corps' story, my introductory study of American history in my undergraduate program in Africa, and eighteen months of graduate work in Canada had already persuaded me of the magnitude of race and ethnicity in American history. Only a few weeks in Boston convinced me even further that these categories are prominent driving forces in American history: The Coolidge Corner area, not too far from where I found an apartment in Brookline, was a "Jewish neighborhood"; the North End was "Italian"; Roxbury was "Black"; South Boston was "Irish"; and, even Boston College, in which I had just enrolled, was, among other things, "Irish Catholic."[4] These and other neighborhoods and institutions in my new place of residence underscored the significance of immigration as a lens into the dynamics of race, ethnicity, and identities in American society. Therefore, immigration history would be my path to studying, understanding, explaining, and teaching the enigma that is the United States.

American immigration history is huge but not amorphous. Stories of immigration waves from a wide range of geographic regions, nationalities, ethnicities, and epochs do intersect and, in both sharply distinct and nuanced ways, illustrate intricate phenomena in American life and society. Studies on specific groups in various eras have provided useful case studies that contribute to the whole story. Still thinking of Peace Corps' categorization of "people who looked like us," I decided I was going to contribute to the broader immigration narrative by focusing on those immigrants "who looked like me"—immigrants of African descent. I started with a basic question: Where are immigrants of African descent in the historiography of American immigration? I quickly found out that they were marginalized in the broader narrative. While, by the 1980s, the literature on immigration and ethnicity in the United States was quite robust, it was heavily weighted with a variety of case studies of European immigrants. General studies, which mostly only alluded to immigrants of African descent, were even more indicative of the peripheral scholarly positioning of Black immigrants. From Oscar Handlin's *The Uprooted* (1952) to Maldwyn Jones's *American Immigration* (1960), John Bodnar's *The Transplanted* (1980), and Roger Daniels's *Coming* to America (1990), such general histories focused overwhelmingly on European immigrants.[5] By the mid-1980s, when I entered the field as a graduate student, this marginalization had already become a scholarly concern that was being addressed. One of the most notable challenges came from sociologist Simon Bryce-Laporte who, in a landmark article in 1973, lamented: "no place has really been given to Black immigrants, and precious little to Blacks in that interpretation of American history which describes successive waves of immigrants entering this country in search of new opportunities and contributing by their presence and participation to its cultural richness, its political complexity, its material-technological advance."[6] Criticizing the flawed telling of the American immigration story, Bryce-Laporte admonished scholars, including historians, to draw more attention to the Black immigrant experience. And, indeed, in the 1980s and 1990s a revision was under way. My work on Black immigrants has been inspired and shaped by the revisionist trends to which it also contributes. Specifically, for a start, I joined the efforts to revisit and more properly illuminate the Afro-Caribbean presence in America.

Immigrants from the Caribbean, commonly referred to as West Indians, had for a long time been the face of foreign Blacks, even though significant waves of voluntary migration of Cape Verdeans from West Africa predated the Caribbean influx.[7] As a 1985 annotated bibliography confirmed, the relatively scanty research on foreign Blacks that existed at the time was overwhelmingly on immigrants from the Caribbean, especially those from English-speaking countries, notably, Jamaica, Barbados, Trinidad and Tobago, the Virgin Islands, Guyana, and Montserrat.[8] Scholarly work on Anglophone West Indians started as early as the 1920s. However, research conducted from that time to the 1970s was skewed by its excessive concentration on the rivalry between West Indians and American-born Blacks and its almost exclusive focus on New York City. West Indians were only attractive as research subjects in downplaying the salience of race in socioeconomic mobility in the United States. For decades, these immigrants were used to show that, given the right group characteristics, Blacks did extremely well in America.[9] Researchers and casual commentators concluded that West Indians outperformed native Blacks in every sphere: they were more educated, more occupationally successful, more hardworking, more frugal, and more politically agile. This approach of studying West Indians only in relation to their success vis-à-vis that of African Americans gained a foothold very early in the twentieth century. The main architects of this trend were West Indian political activists and intellectuals living in New York who were anxious to establish their legitimacy as brokers of Black advancement. Ironically, in their quest for this goal the small West Indian elite became embroiled in various political rivalries with their American-born counterparts and fought hard to vindicate their leadership roles.[10] What better way to do this than to amplify the positive group characteristics? This consideration did not encourage a great deal of scholarly objectivity. At the forefront of the West Indian propaganda was Wilfred A. Domingo, a prominent Jamaican activist and one of the first commentators to expound on the role of historical-cultural premigration values in the successful adaptation of West Indian immigrants. In his discourse, appropriately titled "Gift of the Tropics," he attempted to explain how the homeland society helped cultivate persistence, ambition, frugality, and other traits found in West Indian immigrants.[11] Using sources such as Domingo, pre-1970s scholars constructed a body of literature that examined West Indians in the United States in light of their success and overall superiority over American-born Blacks. The most noted classic in this tradition is sociologist Ira De Augustine Reid's *The Negro Immigrant*.[12]

Consequently, although the literature on English-speaking West Indians was impressive in terms of volume, especially when compared to that of other Black immigrant groups, there were some serious shortcomings. First, most of the literature was narrowly focused on a comparative study of two Black groups. Second, most of the conclusions were derived from biased, impressionistic accounts and not from well-grounded empirical investigation. Third, while most of the studies talked about "West Indians in the United States," their focus was often entirely on those who lived in New York City.

As the twentieth century came to a close, a flurry of new studies began to address the shortcomings. Sociologist Milton Vickerman's *Crosscurrents* studied how ideas about and experiences with race, color, and class in the home society converged with unique characteristics of race and racism in America to influence and shape West Indian identity and adaptation in America. Although historian Irma Watkins-Owen's *Blood Relations* is about the much-researched New York West Indian community, unlike previous studies it emphasizes the complex dynamics of work, ethnicity, gender, and class. Similarly, economist Ransford Palmer's *Pilgrims from the Sun* moves away from the myopic theme of the West Indian–African American rivalry to put the immigrants' experiences within a wider context of work, political economy, and social mobility. However, its focus is almost exclusively on New York. Historian Winston James's *Holding Aloft the Banner of Ethiopia* tackles some of the pivotal questions on the West Indian contribution to Black radicalism in the United States. Importantly, James searched for answers beyond New York by looking at the Afro-Hispanic Caribbean radical tradition in Florida. Sociologist Mary C. Waters also made her mark on the new scholarship on the West Indian American experience. Interestingly, her 1999 work, *Black Identities: West Indian Immigrant Dreams and American Realities*, revisits familiar terrain—New York and the ubiquitous subject of West Indian success. But she breaks new ground in the way she analyzes familiar themes. She demonstrates that the West Indian success story is not a simple one. Giving an unprecedented amount of attention to the second generation, she discusses how different levels of Americanization determined the socioeconomic achievements of the immigrants and their American-born children. Stressing her resolve not to follow the path of previous conservative writers who criticized African American culture and praised West Indian culture, Waters looks instead at the ways that racist structures and behaviors deny equal opportunities to people identified as Black in American society, whether they are native- or foreign-born.[13] Sociologist Suzanne Model pursued a similar critical inquiry in her article, aptly titled "Caribbean Immigrants: A Black Success Story?"[14]

The revisionist trends continue in the twenty-first century. In *The West Indian Americans*, political scientist Holger Henke, looking at post-1965 Caribbean immigrants, forges a significant path. For the first time, clear distinctions are made between the diverse peoples of African descent, East Indian, and mixed ancestry that make up what has been traditionally simply dubbed "West Indian." But New York is still Henke's focus. Perhaps more pathbreaking is Rachel Buff's *Immigration and the Political Economy of Home: West Indian Brooklyn and American Indian Minneapolis*. For the first time in a substantial study, West Indians are compared with Native Americans, a refreshing departure from the West Indian–African American preoccupation. Finally, sociologist Percy Hintzen moved far away from New York to the West Coast to study post-1965 West Indians in California. In his book *West Indians in the West*, he demonstrates how Caribbean immigrants have used performance, rituals, and symbols to define and represent their collective presence.[15]

Prima facie, the foregoing detailed review of West Indian American historiography might seem interruptive in this autobiographical account. However, it is crucial for the light it sheds on the evolution of the arena within which I "meddle in the American dilemma." Much of my work has been shaped by developments in the study of Caribbean immigrants in the United States. Therefore, as I recount my personal experiences and contributions, it is useful to provide instructive details about landmark studies that informed and charted my own intellectual trajectories. This overview of West Indian American historiography depicts a burgeoning arena of scholarship. However, it is still a space that is dominated by sociologists and political scientists. Therefore, my work adds to the much-needed historical perspectives. My first major contribution was to address the historiographical imbalance by shifting the focus from New York to Boston, another major northeastern city. Black radicalism and the phenomenal cultural production of the Harlem Renaissance brought a certain distinctiveness to New York, an appeal that lured researchers to study the West Indians of that city. I recognized that the West Indians of Boston could evoke a similar appeal for the light they shed in analyzing that city's own traditions. From its inception, Boston was supposed to be like no other city. As two of Boston's foremost historians explain: "The history of Boston is unique because of the remarkable persistence of a theme first articulated in 1630 by its Puritan founders. Boston was intended to be a 'City on a Hill,' a shining example of how men and women motivated by a commitment to hard work and to personal, religious, and civic reform might change the course of history."[16] By the nineteenth century, Bostonians were celebrating the attainment of the founders' goals by pointing to Boston's lead in education, its cultured, genteel class of Brahmins, and its abolitionist history, all qualities that made it the "Athens of America," "Freedom's Birthplace," and, more expansively, the "Hub of the Cosmos."

The fascination with Boston's special place in the foundation of America guaranteed constant scholarly interest in that city. Therefore, perhaps not surprisingly, most early historians were drawn to the story of the elite, dubbed Brahmins, who had been credited with building the city and planting its laudable traditions.[17] By the 1970s, there was no doubt that Boston was an attractive case study of an American community. But historian Stephan Thernstrom pioneered a revised approach to community history that emphasized the worth of marginalized groups. *The Other Bostonians* is the classic work that emerged from Thernstrom's resolve to write a local history that clearly focused on the "common Bostonians, the masses of anonymous Americans rather than the 'proper' Bostonians."[18] As a critical, quantitatively substantiated assessment of socioeconomic mobility, this work dissected the experiences of diverse groups of Europeans who were not of the original Puritan stock, probing their advancement in the society. Instructively, Thernstrom paid focused attention to Blacks in a special chapter that demonstrated, as he put it, "the burden of being Black men in a White society."[19] Thernstrom's primary focus was not foreign Blacks. He stated clearly that he was concerned with the socioeconomic mobility of Blacks from the rural South, especially in relation to the collective success of other (European) newcomers. Similarly, native-born Blacks were the focus of case studies that specifically examined Black Boston, notably James and Lois Horton's *Black Bostonians*.[20] Although John Daniels's *In Freedom's Birthplace* gave tangential attention to the handful of foreign Blacks in Boston in the late nineteenth century and early twentieth century,[21] by the 1980s a comprehensive history of Black immigrants in that city was yet to be written. My study of West Indians came to be that much-needed story of the "other Black Bostonians," who, like the Jews, Italians, and American-born Blacks examined by Thernstrom, also shed light on how newcomers fared in that American exemplary city.

In Boston's history, I saw clearly the American promise that Peace Corps told us about many years before in Kaduna. West Indian immigrants, whose history in America was being better illuminated by scholars, were a perfect research subject to study this American phenomenon. As Peace Corps had revealed, America had not always been fair to people who looked like me. The

overwhelming majority of the West Indians looked like me, their ancestors having been brought to the Caribbean from Africa in the Atlantic slave trade. In the
first half of the twentieth century, how did this group fare in Boston, one of the
first places where the awe of the American promise was crafted and articulated?
On the surface, the West Indians were extremely well suited for Boston: Unlike
the Irish, they were mostly Protestants, Anglicans of the Church of England; they
embraced values that echoed the Puritan work ethic and civic responsibility;
and, unlike many of the city's Jewish, Polish, and Italian immigrants, as British
subjects they spoke and wrote English. But against these advantages there was
one big mitigating fact. In the socially constructed categorization of race, they
were Black. Thus, blackness is a pivotal element in the migration story of this
group. Scholars long before me had recognized this. But like my fellow revi-
sionists of the post-1970s scholarship on Black immigrants, I recognized that
understanding race in the Black immigrant experience went beyond a tumultuous relationship with American-born Blacks. In America, the immigrants' blackness, whether they accepted, downplayed, or ignored it, was paramount. But it
did not develop in isolation.

   Black immigrant histories in America must be understood within the
diverse contexts of the African Diaspora. My experiences as a child of the diaspora have proved to be extremely valuable in helping me recognize, conceptu-
alize, describe, and analyze dynamics of identities, community, and activism
among African American and foreign Black groups. Before I go on to explain the
centrality of transnational and diasporic forces in the Black immigrant experience in America, I must first elaborate on my own identity as a child of the
diaspora. My diasporic identity begins with my premigration ethnicity. My family in West Africa identifies as Krio (Creole). The Krios of Sierra Leone are truly
an illustration of the complex outcomes of the global dispersal of people of
African descent. This group emerged in Freetown, the capital of present-day
Sierra Leone, in the middle of the nineteenth century as a result of the interactions among five distinct groups: (1) Descendants of the *Black Poor*, a group
of Blacks relocated from England to Sierra Leone in 1787 through the advocacy
and sponsorship of Quakers and abolitionist members of the British Parliament.
(2) The *Nova Scotians*, former slaves in the thirteen American colonies, who, as
Black Loyalists during the American Revolution, fought for the British and were
promised their freedom. After the war, they had been resettled in Nova Scotia
and New Brunswick, Canada. Disgruntled with the inclement climate and continuing racism of the White Loyalists, they petitioned the British government
to resettle them in Africa. Repatriated to Sierra Leone in 1792, they are credited
with establishing Freetown. (3) The *Maroons*, a group of rebel slaves in Jamaica
who had formed free communities in the mountains, and whom the British
could not effectively subdue. Therefore, after a truce, a large part of the Maroons

were resettled in Freetown in 1800. (4) *Liberated Africans* or *Recaptives*, who were slaves recaptured from ships violating the British Abolition Act of 1807. Instead of returning the freed slaves to their various origins in West Africa, the British released and resettled them in Freetown, which had been designated as a depot for the implementation of the abolition of the slave trade. (5) *Indigenous Africans*, made up mostly of the *Temnes*, the original inhabitants of the Sierra Leone peninsula, where Freetown is located.

By the 1860s, commercial and cultural interactions, including high rates of intermarriage, had blurred the distinctions and a single hybrid ethnicity had emerged. Known as Creoles/Krios, this group, while evolving as a legitimate African ethnicity, continued to carry visible cultural traits of its partial provenance in the diaspora in Europe and North America. These markers included their English/American names; the preponderance of Christianity; the traditional dress known as *print*, made from fabric that always had as a motif a variety of the crops of their plantation past; and the Krio music and dance, which includes the instrument called *gumbé*, Jamaican patois for saw, one of the main implements for the harvest of sugar cane but also used to produce music in the cane fields of the Caribbean.

The British, who were crucial in the formation of this new African ethnic group, were more than eager to use its members as instruments of colonial administration across Africa. The deployment of Krio men as missionaries and civil servants served as a catalyst for a Krio diaspora in Africa. Although it was not uncommon for these men to start families with the indigenous women in their work destinations, most of them either moved with their families or returned to Sierra Leone to marry Krio women with whom they established families in Nigeria and other British African colonies. My mother and father, just like their parents, went to work and live in Nigeria. Numerous facets of my identity have been fashioned by this Krio diaspora. Moving from Nigeria to Sierra Leone at the age of fourteen complicated my identity. While my parents were return migrants, initially, in spite of my grounding in Krio culture, I felt like a complete foreigner, a Nigerian in Sierra Leone.

When I arrived in the United States at age twenty-eight, some of my most profound diasporic experiences began. For the first time, I could see firsthand the complexity of Africana, a myriad of African peoples, cultures, and societies, beyond African nations and ethnicities. In America, in fact in only one city, Boston, were various Black groups, many of which I had never encountered in my life: African Americans from Boston, but also from other parts of the country; diverse Anglophone, Francophone, and Hispanic Caribbean people; and a small but growing and diverse African population. I had already been seasoned in "living migration." But for the first time I was confronted by an extremely powerful all-pervasive force—race, or more specifically, my blackness. My diasporic identity evolved in more complicated and fascinating ways as my stay in America increased and I moved from Boston to Atlanta in the Deep South and changed my legal immigration status from student to permanent resident alien. By the time I became naturalized, the United States had become the place where I had lived the longest. Yet the influences of the other locations in Nigeria and Sierra Leone continued to shape my personal and professional life. By the 1990s England had become another important site in my diasporic universe. With three brothers and my mother living there permanently, that European country became the central point for family reunions. The realities of our transnational existence are often played out in my mom's tiny London flat where her children, their spouses, and their children from Sierra Leone, England, and the United States converge to socialize in ways that illustrate a marked mixture of Sierra Leonean, English, and American accents and mannerisms. This small space in South London is always a potent reminder that our extended family lives in what Paul Gilroy famously called the Black Atlantic.[22]

The immigrant communities that I study are parts of this Black Atlantic. Therefore, their members' individual and collective experiences are influenced and shaped by the many points in this diasporic complex, including the United States. Identity, community, and activism, the three main areas of focus in my studies, bear this out.

Issues of identity are vital in adaptation. For immigrants of African descent, blackness is at the center of their identity, but it is not the only facet. To get at the complexity of their racial and ethnic identities, I address questions like the following: What homeland identities do they come with? How do they attempt to nurture and project these identities? How do they grapple with the imposed identity of Black in America? When and how do they become race conscious? What are the complex relationships between these immigrants, not just with American-born Blacks but with their counterpart foreign Black groups and other racial and ethnic groups as well? What are the experiences of the 1.5 generations (those who came here as young children) and second generations?[23]

English-speaking West Indians in Boston in the first half of the twentieth century, the first group I studied, exhibited many of the patterns I would later see in other Black immigrant communities. From the moment they disembarked from the fruit company steamers, the immigrants' racialization process started with reference to them in the U.S. Immigration Passenger Lists as British Negro. Consequently, effectively, they became, as my 2006 book title indicates, the other Black Bostonians.[24] Individually and collectively, they resisted this arbitrary identification. Community institutions and cultural production were mainstays in the negotiation of evolving identities in their new home. In *The Other Black Bostonians* I describe and explain how institutions such as the family, church, island associations, sports and other recreational organizations were used to develop and sustain transnational communities that reflected the immigrants' continuing affiliations with the homeland and their changing identities in America. By the 1920s associations such as the Jamaica Associates, Barbados Union, and the Montserratian Progressive League were sponsoring activities designed as much for recreation as for assertion of their nonracial, foreign, West Indian, and British identities. With tea parties, formal ballroom events, and parades, they celebrated such non-American holidays as Emancipation (of slaves in the Caribbean) Day, Empire Day, and Coronation Day. Cricket was one of the main indices of the immigrants' foreign identity. A non-American sport, it not only underscored their identity as foreigners but also, importantly, affirmed their British affiliation. A British identity was very important to them. As a European marker, they saw it as a badge of equality in a predominantly White American society. In addition to the Boston-based activities, the associations maintained concrete links with institutions in the Caribbean and created agendas that included activities to support homeland projects. I explain this feature in my article on the transnational orientation of the associations.[25] Also, recently, I wrote an article discussing how women in particular and specifically as mothers helped to develop and sustain a transnational community.[26]

The Boston West Indian community bore many similarities to the Saro subculture in which I grew up. As I collected and analyzed materials for my study, I recalled vividly the vibrant recreational and cultural activities that set my family and other Saros apart from the Hausa, Yoruba, and Igbo people among whom we lived. Christmas and Easter were celebrated with foods, music, and dances of the homeland and the annual highlight event of the community was the huge Sierra Leone Independence Day celebration during the weekend closest to the April 27 independence day.

Attempts to differentiate the Saro enclave from the host Nigerian communities were aimed at national and ethnic exclusiveness. In Boston, the situation of my research subjects was further complicated by the compelling issue of race. Managing the inescapable identity of Black was a salient feature of the West Indian community, a responsibility that was absent in my Saro Nigerian experience before I emigrated to the United States. No matter how hard they tried, the British West Indians could not overcome the rigidity and power of blackness as a designation for all people of African descent in the United States. Sociologist Everett Hughes describes this futility: "Membership in the Negro race, as defined in American mores and/or law, may be called a master status-determining trait. It tends to overpower, in most crucial situations, any other characteristics which might run counter to it."[27] In a 2008 article I discuss and assess the encounters of several Black immigrant groups with this master status-determining trait. I illustrate how Afro-Caribbean groups and the more recent immigrants from Africa use cultural production to simultaneously

negotiate their imposed designation as Blacks in America while projecting foreign national and ethnic identities.[28]

Growing up in Nigeria, I lived an in-between life. On the one hand, my
parents insisted that I was a Sierra Leonean Krio and, on the other hand, I was
a Nigerian-born girl whose first language was Hausa and who was immersed in
several aspects of Nigerian culture transmitted through school (especially my
boarding school), and daily, intense interactions with neighborhood children
who were, to use my parents' term, 100 percent Nigerian. Propelled by this personal background, I am always on the lookout for the stories of young people
in the immigrant communities that I study. I have been able to uncover similar
in-between experiences. Like my Saro community, the West Indians in Boston
in the first half of the twentieth century eagerly involved their children in the
churches, associations, and transnational activities of the community. But as
they participated in the activities of the Sons and Daughters of the Associates
(a youth offshoot of the Jamaica Associates), and attended cricket matches—
experiences that defined their West Indian identity—they also attended public
school and interacted with the other children in their predominantly African
American neighborhoods, experiences that defined their American, Black
American identity. In an essay titled "Navigating a Past Not Lived," I analyze the
dilemma of the children of Boston's West Indian immigrants who are compelled
to function in a subculture heavily defined by their parents' premigration past.[29]
My research revealed numerous instances of frustration similar to what I felt
when I tried to convey to my parents the reality of my experiences and my strong
sense of being Nigerian.

Of course, in my Boston study, race, which was absent in my African experience, was always a factor. From the oral histories I collected, the following quo-
tation is one of my favorite illustrations of the dilemma of the young members
of the community: "My son, a well-brought-up boy, came home from school
looking very rough. Some Irish kids had angered him by calling him a good-for-
nothing nigger. This was not the first time, but this time it really got out of hand.
I was furious with him. I said, 'Why don't you just make it clear to these kids that
you are not a Negro? You are Bajan [from Barbados], a West Indian, a British.'
With tears running down his cheeks he replied: 'But Ma, I am not completely
those things. I am an American, a Black American. And you too, Ma, when most
people around here see you, they see a *Negro*'" (my emphasis).[30]

This mother further explained that this was the moment she became Black.
Indeed, race consciousness is a salient theme in Black immigrant histories.
When and how do immigrants of African descent in the United States become
Black, and what do they do with their blackness after that discovery? In *The
Other Black Bostonians* and journal articles and book chapters, I have discussed
the complex and sometimes controversial ways that these immigrants recognize

their status as Blacks in America. A more personal observation, years ago, fascinated me and helped me understand and write about race consciousness. A year after I arrived in the United States, my sixty-year-old mother brought my fourteen-month-old son from Sierra Leone to join me. This was her first trip out of Africa. Only days after she arrived, she started asking questions about what she considered America's obsession with race. She said she was confident about who she was—a Sierra Leonean of Krio ethnicity. About four months after she arrived, we were in a small restaurant when, after looking around for a while, she blurted out that she was uneasy because it seemed like we were the only Black people there. Later that evening, she conceded that without really seeing it happen, she had become Black, she had acquired some race and minority consciousness. In "becoming Black," my mother had discovered what had already been a key element in my own American experience and in shaping my consciousness.

The consequences of race consciousness are a crucial subject of the Black immigrant experience. The evidence demonstrates that race consciousness generates a desire to learn about the plight of Blacks in America and to support Black activism, from merely understanding why protest is necessary to being involved directly and actively in the Black struggle. It was in this sphere that early twentieth-century Afro-Caribbean migrants made their mark as feisty Black activists. Who talks of the Black struggle in America in the 1920s and 1930s without mentioning Jamaican Claude McKay and his radicalism in the Harlem Renaissance? Or fiery stepladder/soap box agitators, Virgin Islander Hubert Harrison, Barbadian Richard B. Moore, and Jamaican Grace Campbell? Of course, absolutely impossible to ignore is Jamaican Marcus Garvey, who formed the Universal Negro Improvement Association, the first mass Black movement in the United States, which at its height had more than two million members.

Although the contributions to the American struggle by prominent West Indian activists cannot be denied, their race consciousness and activism went beyond America and the Black struggle. My research emphasizes that the immigrant agitators were involved in both the colonial struggle in the Caribbean and Black protest in the United States. Contrary to earlier portrayals, their activism was not static and narrowly focused on the Black struggle in America, an arena in which they collided with American-born Blacks. Instead it was fluid, and the activists altered their focus and strategies according to changing eras and situations in the United States, the Caribbean, other parts of the diaspora, and Africa. In one of my studies I examine the West Indian newspaper, the *Boston Chronicle*, as a forum for activism geared toward change in America, the Caribbean, and Africa in the period from 1930 to 1950, during which people in the British Caribbean struggled for freedom from colonial rule." Titled "Pan-Africanism in Print," this piece concludes that the publishers and readers in the Boston West Indian

community kept abreast of developments in a wider Black theater and envisioned a fight against a collective oppression that linked the Black struggle in
Boston and America to the anticolonial struggles in the Caribbean and Africa.[31]
Often, their vigorous advocacy for political and social changes was directed
equally at the racial status quo in America and the colonial repression in their
former homes, in which they still had relatives and to which they were still
emotionally connected. It was this dualism that I sought to analyze in my essay,
"Relentless Ex-Colonials and Militant Immigrants."[32] I observed a similar dualism in the Kaduna Saro community. My parents and others in their generation
always paid attention to unfolding political developments (the rise and fall of
political parties, elections, riots, and military coups) in Sierra Leone and Nigeria. My father was very active in his printers' union, which agitated for workers'
rights in Kaduna. At the same time, I recall that the Sierra Leonean Organization
of Kaduna constantly discussed and submitted petitions to Freetown about a
host of issues, the real nature of which I did not grasp at the time.

I have recently expanded my focus on the evolution of Black immigrant
communities in the United States to place them within larger diasporic or Africana contexts. In addition to studying the long-established Afro-Caribbean
presence, I am now also looking at the phenomenally increasing African presence. The growth of the African population in the United States has been colos-
sal. Between 1960 and 2007 the number of African immigrants grew from 35,355
to 1.4 million, with 75 percent of the increase taking place since 1990.[33] By the
beginning of the twenty-first century this demographic development was being
discussed beyond academic circles. The mass media, including print, television,
and Internet publications, reported on the profound implications of the growing African presence, as noted by a much-talked-about *New York Times* article
that revealed that for the first time Africans were now entering the United States
in far greater numbers than during the period of slavery.[34]

African communities, especially West African immigrant groups, are much
closer to home for me. I have lived strikingly similar transnational experiences
to those that define the emerging African immigrant communities. My insider
(as an African-born) and outsider (as a prying scholar) positions are yielding
fascinating and productive results, even if sometimes I felt ambivalent about
them. My first study on the current history of Africans in America focused on
the experiences of Sierra Leonean refugee women who fled the horrendous civil
war of 1991–2000. As an active member of the vibrant Sierra Leonean community in metro Atlanta, I had valuable insights into the evolution of the community and recognized areas, themes, and issues that needed to be studied. It
was in this insider privileged position that I saw the fascinating transnational
networks that refugee women had created and were using to transplant social
and cultural resources for their new lives in America. These women grappled

with challenges not just from the larger American society but also from the stratified Sierra Leonean immigrant enclave that put most recent arrivals, especially refugees, at the bottom. Capitalizing on my fluency in Krio, and my transnational connections, I was able to conduct research in Atlanta, London, and Sierra Leone. The article that resulted from my research, "Recreating Sustainable Communities in Exile," is a good example of the transnational, diasporic characteristics that define late twentieth-century and early twenty-first century Black immigrant communities in America.[35]

Now, almost two decades after that encounter in my classroom, in which an African American student questioned my "Americanness," how do I see myself as a historian of American ethnic and immigration history? More than ever, I realize the inextricable connections between American immigration history and other histories. Studying immigrants of African descent in America is an enterprise that should be anchored in African American history, African history, and the history of the African Diaspora. My own personal experiences are steeped in these histories. Therefore, instead of alienating me from my research, my foreign-born origins and affiliations, which prima facie might seem to distance me from American history, are in reality advantages that help me contribute in meaningful ways to an understanding of the complex dynamics of race, ethnicity, and immigration in American history. Taking into consideration the forced migration story of African Americans and the many waves of voluntary migrations from Africa and the Caribbean since the nineteenth century, the African Diaspora should be seen as a legitimately important facet of American immigration history. Today, if confronted again with the dilemma of facilitating a heated classroom discussion in American history on the life and work of two iconic leaders who were products of the African Diaspora, I will not feel like an outsider. And it is not because I now possess a certificate that verifies that I am an American. It is because of what has been always true: I am a child of the African Diaspora and this important facet of American history is also my story.

Notes

1. J. Hector St. John de Crevecoeur, *Letters from an American Farmer* (London, 1782); Gunnar Myrdal, *An American Dilemma: The Negro Problem and Modern Democracy* (New York: Harper & Row, 1944).
2. For a comprehensive account of the Nigerian Civil War of 1967–1970, see Eghosa Osaghae, Ebere Onwudiwe, and Rotimi Suberu, *The Nigerian Civil War and Its Aftermath* (Ibadan, Nigeria: John Archers, 2002).
3. For more on the Krios of Sierra Leone, see Akintola Wyse, *The Krio of Sierra Leone: An Interpretive History* (Washington, D.C.: Howard University Press, 1991). A concise, illuminating case study of Sierra Leoneans in Nigeria is Mac Dixon-Fyle, *The Saro Community in the Niger Delta, 1912–1984* (Rochester, N.Y.: Rochester University Press, 1999).

4. For more on the racial and ethnic history of Boston, see Andrew Buni and Alan Rogers, *Boston: City on the Hill* (Boston: Windsor Publications, 1984); Thomas O'Connor, *Bible, Brahmins, and Bosses: A Short History of Boston* (Boston: Boston Public Library, 1984).

5. Maldwyn Jones, *American Immigration* (Chicago: University of Chicago Press, 1960); Oscar Handlin, *The Uprooted: The Epic Story of the Great Migrations That Made the American People* (Cambridge, Mass.: Harvard University Press, 1952); Roger Daniels, *Coming to America: A History of Immigration and Ethnicity in America* (New York: Harper Collins, 1990); John Bodnar, *The Transplanted: A History of Immigrants in Urban America* (Bloomington: Indiana University Press, 1985). By the 1990s, there were more calls for the inclusion of non-European immigrants in the general narrative about the making of America. Some of the updated editions to these general histories demonstrate the positive responses to this call. Historian David Reimers made conscious efforts to illuminate the experiences of previously marginalized immigrants in his book *Other Immigrants: The Global Origins of the American People* (New York: New York University Press, 2005). In a chapter on Black immigrants, he effectively demonstrates the rich history and diversity of immigrants of African descent from the Caribbean, Africa, and South America.

6. Roy Simon Bryce-Laporte, "Black Immigrants: The Experience of Invisibility and Inequality," *Journal of Black Studies* 3 (September 1972): 29–56, at 35.

7. See Marilyn Halter, *Between Race and Ethnicity: Cape Verdean American Immigrants, 1860–1965* (Urbana: University of Illinois Press, 1993).

8. Center for Afroamerican and African Studies, University of Michigan, *Black Immigration and Ethnicity in the United States: An Annotated Bibliography* (Westport, Conn.: Greenwood Press, 1985).

9. In the 1970s and 1980s, the most prominent proponent of this interpretation was African American economist Thomas Sowell. See Thomas Sowell, *Race and Economics* (New York: David MacKay, 1975); and Sowell, "Three Black Histories," in *Essays and Data on American Ethnic Groups*, ed. Thomas Sowell (Washington, D.C.: Urban Institute, 1975), 7–64.

10. The rivalry between W.E.B. Du Bois and Marcus Garvey, mentioned in the beginning of this essay, is representative of this rivalry. For more on the political rivalry between African Americans and Afro-Caribbeans in the early twentieth century, see David J. Hellwig, "Black Meets Black: Afro-American Reactions to West Indian Immigrants in the 1920s," *South Atlantic Quarterly* 77 (Spring 1978): 373–385; and Keith Henry, "The Black Political Tradition in New York: A Conjunction of Political Cultures," *Journal of Black Studies* 7 (June 1997): 455–484.

11. Wilfredo A. Domingo, "Gift of the Tropics," in *The New Negro*, ed. Alain Locke (New York: Charles Boni, 1925; reprint, New York: Arno Press, 1968), 341–349.

12. Ira De A. Reid, *The Negro Immigrant: His Background, Characteristics and Social Adjustment, 1899–1937* (New York: Columbia University Press, 1939).

13. Milton Vickerman, *Crosscurrents: West Indian Immigrants and Race* (New York: Oxford University Press, 1999); Irma Watkins-Owens, *Blood Relations: Caribbean Immigrants and the Harlem Community, 1900–1930* (Bloomington: Indiana University Press, 1996); Ransford Palmer, *Pilgrims from the Sun: West Indian Migrations to America* (New York: Twayne Publishers, 1995); Winston James, *Holding Aloft the Banner of Ethiopia: Caribbean Radicalism in Early Twentieth Century America* (London: Verso, 1998); and Mary Waters, *Black Identities: West Indian Immigrant Dreams and American Realities* (New York: Russell Sage Foundation, 1999).

14. Suzanne Model, "Caribbean Immigrants: A Black Success Story?" *International Migration Review* 25 (Summer 1991): 248–276.

15. Holger Henke, *The West Indian Americans* (Westport, Conn.: Greenwood Press, 2001); Rachel Buff, *Immigration and the Political Economy of Home: West Indian Brooklyn and American Indian Minneapolis, 1945–1992* (Berkeley: University of California Press, 2001); Percy Hintzen, *West Indian in the West: Self Representation in an Immigrant Community* (New York: New York University Press, 2001).

16. Buni and Rogers, *Boston: City on a Hill*, 6.

17. See for example, Cleveland Amory, *The Proper Bostonians* (New York: Dutton, 1947); Bernard Bailyn, *The New England Merchants in the Seventeenth Century* (Cambridge, Mass.: Harvard University Press, 1955); and Darrett Ruttman, *Portrait of a Puritan Town* (Chapel Hill: University of North Carolina Press, 1965).

18. Stephan Thernstrom, *The Other Bostonians: Poverty and Progress in an American Metropolis, 1880–1970* (Cambridge, Mass.: Harvard University Press, 1973), 1.

19. Ibid., 176.

20. James Oliver Horton and Lois E. Horton, *Black Bostonians: Family Life and Community Struggle in the Antebellum North* (New York: Holmes and Meier Publishers, 1979).

21. John Daniels, *In Freedom's Birthplace: A Study of the Boston Negroes* (Boston: Houghton Mifflin, 1914).

22. Paul Gilroy, *The Black Atlantic: Modernity and Double Consciousness* (Cambridge, Mass.: Harvard University Press, 1993).

23. The term 1.5 generation was introduced by sociologists, notably Mary Waters and Phillip Kasinitz, to describe children not born in the United States but arrived when they were very young, from infancy to early teenage years.

24. Violet Showers Johnson, *The Other Black Bostonians: West Indians in Boston, 1900–1950* (Bloomington: Indiana University Press, 2006).

25. Violet Johnson, "The Transnational Orientation of West Indian Associations in Boston," in *Colloquium Papers in Celebration of Black History Month* (Chestnut Hill, Mass.: Boston College Press, 1994), 13–20.

26. Violet Showers Johnson, "Fostering or Surrogate Mothering as an Immigration Tool: The Making of Transnational West Indian American Families," *Journal of the Motherhood Initiative for Research and Community Involvement* 2 (2011): 197–208.

27. Everett Hughes, "Dilemmas and Contradictions of Status," *American Journal of Sociology* 50 (1945): 353–359.

28. Violet Showers Johnson, "'What, Then, Is the African American?' African and Afro-Caribbean Identities in Black America," *Journal of American Ethnic History* 28 (2008): 77–103.

29. Violet Showers Johnson, "Navigating a Past Not Lived: Children of West Indian Immigrants in the United States and the 'Back Home' Factor" (paper presented at the Conference of the Society for Caribbean Studies, University of Newcastle, England, June 14, 2005).

30. Yvonne Mason, personal interview, Roxbury, Mass., February 2, 1988. Ms. Mason was born in Bridgetown, Barbados, in 1920, came to New Bedford, Massachusetts, in 1939, and moved to Boston in 1942.

31. Violet Johnson, "Pan-Africanism in Print: The *Boston Chronicle* and the Struggle for Black Liberation and Advancement, 1930–1950," in *Print Culture in a Diverse America*, ed. James Danky and Wayne Wiegand (Chicago: University of Illinois Press, 1998), 13–20.

32. Violet Showers Johnson, "Relentless Ex-Colonials and Militant Immigrants: Protest Strategies of Boston's West Indian Immigrants, 1910–1950," in *The Civil Rights Movement Revisited: Critical Perspectives on the Struggle for Racial Equality in the United States*, ed. Patrick B. Miller, Therese Frey Steffen, and Elisabeth Schafer-Wunsche (Piscataway, N.J.: Lit Verlag/Transaction Publishers, 2001), 9–20.

33. Aaron Terrazas, "African Immigrants in the United States," report of the Migration Policy Institute, February 2009, http://www.migration.org/usfocus/.

34. Sam Roberts, "More Africans Enter the U.S. Than in Days of Slavery," *New York Times*, February 21, 2005.

35. Violet Showers Johnson, "Recreating Sustainable Communities in Exile: Leadership Roles of Sierra Leonean Refugee and Internally Displaced Women in Freetown, London, and Atlanta," *International Journal of Environmental, Cultural, Economic, and Social Sustainability* 5 (2009): 287–300.

12

From Uncle Mustafa to Auntie Rana

Journeys to Mexico, the United States, and Lebanon

THERESA ALFARO-VELCAMP

My family history has led me to question national narratives and to uncover discrepancies between the content of historical records and that of oral traditions. This has taken me to U.S. archives to understand how Mexico governed immigration, and conversely to work in Mexican archives to understand how the U.S. governed immigration as an adjacent nation-state.[1] The invitation by the editors has enabled me to ask how immigrant and national myths fuse and get translated into family histories. And most importantly, what do our family histories tell us about our national and larger transnational histories? In the case of my family history, there was not a discursive space to talk about Arab immigrants in the Mexican metanarrative, and where my family fits into Mexican history. I would like to think this is changing in Mexican historiography, thanks in large part to scholarly work on ethnicity in Mexico. Moreover, Arab family research histories are reaching mainstream media with such documentaries as *Beirut Buenos Aires Beirut* that traces an Argentine woman's journey to understand her great-grandfather's migration from southern Lebanon.[2] My story is similar to hers, but mine begins in Mexico.

On my maternal side, I am the great-granddaughter of a Lebanese Shi'a Muslim who migrated to Mexico, and I am the granddaughter of a Mexican *bracero* worker who migrated to the United States around 1942. The Bracero Program was an initiative by both the United States and Mexican governments between 1942 and 1964 to bring Mexican workers to the United States to help with labor shortages. Initially, it was conceived to help with the loss of labor caused by American soldiers going to war, but with the end of World War II the need for workers in the agricultural sector continued, and the program was extended.[3] My grandfather came to the United States to first work in the coal mines in Pennsylvania and then found work unloading the bodies of dead American soldiers in the New York City area. He later became a truck driver. (The duration of each job during World War II and afterward remains unclear.) When I read about the history of the Bracero Program or think about its legacy including issues related to the North American Free Trade Agreement (NAFTA)—such as whether to license Mexican commercial trucks in the United States—the image of my grandfather and his truck comes to mind.

The inclusion of family history in my scholarship has created an entry for others who want to learn more about their Arab past. For instance, in a popular U.S. newspaper column called "¡Ask a Mexican!," a reader wrote the following to columnist Gustavo Arellano in April 2009:

> Dear Mexican: First of all, don't think that I'm a self-loathing Mexican. . . . For some strange reason, I have developed an intense fascination with—you might say love for—Arab culture, language, cuisine, etc. especially Lebanese, Syrian, Jordanian, Palestinian and Iraqi, and I don't even have a drop of Arab blood in me. . . . Do you think I could be of Lebanese ancestry and not know it? . . . Would a DNA test tell me what my ancestry is, and could it turn up libaneses in my family tree? Let me know. [Signed] Wannabe Arab, a.k.a. El Libanés

Gustavo Arellano responded:

> Dear Wab [Wannabe Arab]: Your chances that the *sangre* [blood] of the Levant courses through your veins are more likely than *gabachos* [literally French person, White person] may think. As you noted, Lebanese migrated to Mexico throughout the twentieth century and contributed to the *patria* [homeland] in ways both positive (tacos al pastor, Salma Hayek) and negative (billionaire Carlos Slim Helú).[4]

Although this curiosity about Arabs and Mexicans has been articulated at a popular culture level, the issue of incorporating family or one's explicitly ethnic history into larger national or transnational histories is still a delicate subject within Latin American history, and particularly in Mexican academic historiographies.

In the following essay, I begin by contextualizing my identity and then explain my journey to understand my family and how that journey has informed my thinking and analyses of immigration. My family story highlights the larger issue of how to write about histories that cross nation-state boundaries in the context of changing geopolitics, and it sheds light on elements of family history that are often easily dismissed. By listening to family histories and what is said (and not said), we can interrogate social history, uncovering hidden transcripts. As James Scott theorizes, the hidden transcript refers to the discourse that takes place offstage, beyond the direct observation by power holders, and in places such as private homes and among families.[5]

Self-Identifications

In 2008, at the American University of Beirut, I was asked to give a lecture about my book, *So Far from Allah, So Close to Mexico: Middle Eastern Immigrants in Modern Mexico* (2007), with a class lecture the following day on Arabs in the Americas. Although I had prepared a PowerPoint lecture and research on a new project, the Lebanese and a couple of Syrian students immediately interrupted me and asked, "How do you identify yourself? As an American? As a Mexican? As Lebanese? As Muslim? Catholic?" I knew that people often wondered about my self-identification, but few had asked so pointedly; so I told the students, "It depends on who is asking and where I am. For me, it is all depends on the context."[6]

This answer did not satisfy the audience of young students reeling from Lebanese sectarian politics. Three years earlier, in 2005, then President Rafik Hariri (a Sunni Muslim) had been killed in a car bomb explosion along with twenty-two others.[7] Many believed the Syrian government was behind the attack, with a 2010 United Nations report suggesting that both high-level Syrian officials and Hizbullah (the Shiʻa Muslim group and political party based in Lebanon) had been involved.[8] Rafik Hariri's death unleashed the Cedar Revolution, during which thousands of Lebanese demonstrated for Syrian withdrawal from Lebanon, and a new period of peace was negotiated between the various sects in Lebanon. For these Lebanese students, who witnessed the Cedar Revolution in February 2005 followed by Israeli airstrikes from November 2005 to September 2006, my self-identification with both Muslims and Christians made no sense. These recent events (among many others) have shaped how Lebanese see themselves and, in turn, how they respond to others. Moreover, by having Lebanese ancestry, they could not understand that alternative identifications were possible for me. As I argue in my work, categories of personhood complicate and confuse scholars and the general public alike, and identity, in my opinion, is contextual.

How to categorize people who came from the Middle East to Mexico, especially those from the contemporary nation-states of Lebanon, Syria, Israel, Jordan, Egypt, Iran, Iraq, and Turkey, as well as regions that had yet to develop into nation-states from the Arabian Peninsula and the West Bank, depends in part on when the immigrants migrated. Many of the immigrants left as subjects of the Ottoman Empire during the late nineteenth and early twentieth centuries, and were therefore called *turcos* (Turks), whereas others left during the French and British occupations and had French or British passports. After World War II, the changing geopolitics of the Middle East, especially in the Levant area and the new nation-states of Syria, Lebanon, and Israel, complicated how the immigrants self-identified and were labeled by others. These categories of personhood have remained fluid, dynamic categories of process and are difficult to capture in writing history.

For my book, I used the term Middle Eastern immigrants to diffuse the politically sensitive term *árabes* (Arabs), but for this essay I will call those migrating
from the Middle East *Arabs*, based on the broad commonality of Arabic language. For consistency in family history, my great-grandfather self-identified as
Arab on his Mexican immigration card. He did so as part of the first wave of
Arab immigrants to Mexico, subjects of the Ottoman Empire, who left a region
known as the Province of Greater Syria, which encompassed present-day Syria,
Lebanon, Jordan, Israel, and the West Bank. Although he entered Mexico in
1907, his immigrant registration card was completed in 1932. I learned those
dates by piecing family history and archival research together.

Historians and Their Ethnic History in the Mexican Case

Historians are trained to look at old documents—whether the documents are
formal government records in established archives or personal diaries and
letters by individuals—to provide insights on a past that has been previously
overlooked or needs to be revised. Oral historians have certainly expanded this
approach. Latin American historian William Taylor writes, "I think of historical
study as a restless kind of discipline of context."[9] From this perspective, family
records and histories would seem to offer a natural line of inquiry for historians
and one for which the need to contextualize is ongoing.[10]

Specifically, in the case of historians located in the United States and writing about their family histories, Friedrich Katz wrote about his father, Leo Katz,
a writer, who had participated in the Spanish Civil War and was denied a permanent visa by the U.S. government. The Katz family was granted political refugee
status in Mexico by the Lázaro Cárdenas administration (1934–1940) while in a
refugee camp in France.[11] Katz also wrote introductory chapters and commentaries on refugees and exiles in Mexico,[12] and encouraged Jürgen Buchenau to
write about his German family, the Bokers, in *Tools of Progress* (2005). Buchenau
notes in his introduction, "Because of the pitfalls of oral history, especially in a
case where the interviewer had a previous personal relationship with many of
his interviewees, I have used it primarily as a source of anecdotal evidence."[13]
He provides a detailed economic and cultural history of his family's merchant
business from 1865 through the present, concluding that the later generations
tend to assimilate in Mexican society. Katz and Buchenau are only two examples
of how ethnic histories from Mexico have reached academic institutions in the
United States.

Other Mexican historians, anthropologists, and sociologists have also written about their ethnic histories and are making strides to bring these histories
into mainstream Mexican historiography.[14] That said, it appears that a familial
historical line of inquiry has not been fully explored among historians of Mexico

located in the United States. For example, Latin American historian Allen Wells, inspired by his father's migration to the United States, recently wrote about the Jewish Sosúa community in the Dominican Republic; yet, it is not until the epilogue that Wells clearly identifies his father and his father's place in Sosúa.[15]

That choice raises questions familiar to my experience: Are family histories and social histories inherently linked? Do academic approaches legitimate family history or do personal interests detract from scholarship? And how much information can we share about family histories when family members are still alive? A certain distance from the communities may be analytically helpful, yet being deemed part of the communities under study (both being Latina and of Arab ancestry in my case) may grant some legitimacy and access. It can also spark skepticism. Why, for example, would a woman from the United States be interested in the Arab migration to Mexico?

As historians William Taylor and Prasenjit Duara suggest, history and identity are fluid, flexible, and subject to change with regard to context. I have argued that immigrants in Mexico have participated in the Mexican discourse by adopting *mestizo*—that is, a mixture of Spanish/European and indigenous identities. This illustrates the fungibility of *mexicanidad*. This fungibility denotes the relational and contextual use of identity as theorized by Duara.[16] I argue that ethnic groups in Mexico vary in their abilities to acculturate, and some choose to maintain their ethnic identities, especially as they ascend the Mexican economic and social ladder.[17] As a historian, I rely on this flexibility of identity to examine Arabs in Mexico both as a Mexican American and an Arab American.

Looking for Arabs in Mexico

When I was in graduate school at Georgetown University, feeling somewhat shy, I mentioned after class one day that my great-grandfather was a Lebanese Muslim who migrated to Mexico and married my great-grandmother, a supposed Aztec princess. My advisor mentioned that no one had written about *los turcos* (the Turks) in Mexico, and the topic was ripe for research. I then mulled over the idea. A year later, I talked my mother into going with me to Mexico for a preliminary research visit to see where my grandfather was buried and what kind of information the townspeople could provide. It was Christmas break in 1994 (the time of Mexican peso devaluation, and a time of uncertainty in Mexico). We met in Monterrey, Nuevo León, and took a bus to Saltillo to visit my Aunt Nora—actually my *tía-abuela* (my great aunt)—and her children.

My book began with this trip, and it was subsequently published in 2007. Although my journey to learn about my great-grandfather began in the 1990s, much of my childhood and early adulthood memories were about my mother's aspirations as a second-generation Mexican and Spanish American. No matter what happened in life, I was told "you can do anything you want" because the explicit message was that we are in the United States. This can-do attitude is not uncommon among first- and second-generation immigrant families, but rather well documented in the sociology of U.S. immigration.[18] In my experience, the can-do/anything-is-possible attitude was paired to a sanitized version of our Mexican heritage. That did not make sense to me and piqued my curiosity.

After college, I started to wonder about my Mexican heritage. Being a young adult, the disconnect between my experience and those embodied in family stories became apparent, and I read and researched everything I could find that had to do with Latin America. Slowly, I began to identify as Latina. By the time I arrived at Georgetown and met my advisor, I was eager to learn about Latin America.

According to the family story, my great-grandfather Antonio Itt—whose last name was never clear nor consistently spelled—married Justa Alfaro. They had six children, most of whom were given Muslim names—Said, Mustafa, Jalil, Ali, Amine, Nora, Rosa—and were then to be raised Catholic. My grandfather and my Uncle Mustafa were also given traditional Mexican names that they used outside of the family—Rubén and Román, respectively. The eldest of the six, my grandfather Said (Rubén) Haitt ('Eid) Alfaro, migrated to the United States after a drunken night during which he was rumored to have been killed. This broke Justa's heart, and she apparently died shortly thereafter. Why my grandfather was rumored to be killed and why his mother (Justa Alfaro) did not investigate whether her eldest son had indeed been killed has never been made clear to me. The remaining children were sent to live with Justa's relatives, and my great-grandfather disappears from the story. In Paso Nacional, Durango (approximately 150 miles from Torreón, Coahuila), the tombstone of my great-grandfather Hamud Said 'Eid, aka Antonio Itt Aychur, indicates that he died on April 25, 1942—the same year my grandfather (his son) migrated to the United States.

I never knew my great-grandfather and very little of his eldest son, my grandfather, Said (Rubén) Haitt Alfaro. When my grandfather came to the United States as a bracero worker in the 1940s, U.S. immigration officials changed his name to Ruben H. Alfaro. His brothers and sisters in Mexico retained the Haitt name, but with variations in spelling. Whether my grandfather came as a legal bracero also remains unknown. He married a second-generation Spanish American, Eugenia Garcia, and they had four children—three sons and a daughter (my mother). My mother, Eugenia Alfaro (also known as Chata), grew up in Brooklyn, New York, and her first language was Spanish. Later, she was determined not to raise me speaking Spanish, facing discrimination as she had. It was not until I was in my late twenties that my mother told me that neighbors had sent a petition around in an effort to prevent her family from moving into Mount

Glenn (West Milford), New Jersey, because they were *spics* whose presence would lower property values. This happened in the early 1960s, and, although the family moved to Mount Glenn, my mother and uncles have proudly retained the Brooklyn accents of their early childhood.

Recently, I learned that my mother and uncles went to Mexico when they were children and met their aunts and uncles. However, it was an expedition in 1966 when my grandfather bought a new car and drove to Mexico to visit his family and friends that my mother and uncles still reminisce about the most. My grandparents and their four teenage children drove from New Jersey to Mexico to visit family and friends whom Rubén had not seen in many years. The family spent nearly a month in Mexico visiting places such as Paso Nacional, Torreón, Coahuila, and Mexico City.

When my grandfather was diagnosed with stomach cancer in the summer of 1979, he made clear to his children that he wanted to be buried next to his parents in Paso Nacional, Durango. He passed away on November 18, 1979, and my mother and uncles Tony and Richie drove his body from Chula Vista, Arizona, to Mexico. By living in California, my mother had maintained enough of her Spanish to become the family translator and she connected with several of the people in the community. So when my family went to Paso Nacional in 1981, they remembered "La Chata."

I remember parts of the 1981 journey. We flew from California to Mexico City and stayed with my uncle Mustafa. He was my *tío-abuelo* (great uncle). We visited with various relatives, as my mom spoke for my brother, my father, and me. After several days, we drove from Mexico City to Torreón, Coahuila, ending up in Paso Nacional, Durango, after countless hours on the road. I vaguely remember the drive, but my parents vividly recall my uncle Mustafa's terrible driving. When we arrived on a dirt road into Paso Nacional, hammer and sickle graffiti marked whitewashed walls of the pueblo (small town) and there was no electricity. I quickly learned there was also no hot water, and most toilets were not working. Yet, meals were full of delicious homemade tortillas served with salt and butter. I remember the sense that we were important for traveling to visit my grandfather's grave.

After the brief excursion, we rarely talked about our Mexico trip, but it had a lasting impact on me. When I returned in 1994 with my mother, I was excited to see Mexico with the fresh eyes of a newly trained historian.

During this visit in 1994, we stayed with my mom's cousins in Saltillo for a few days and then we took a bus to Mexico City. There my mom's aunt Amine (*tia-abuela* Amine) picked us up and drive us to her seemingly opulent home, especially when compared to my other relatives. Aunt Amine was tiny and beautiful. She spoke quickly and peppered each sentence with a *grosería* (swear word), which embarrassed and shamed my Uncle Mustafa because he felt women were not supposed to use such language. During this Mexico City stay, we spent time with Uncle Mustafa and his six children (my mom's first cousins) and their children. When I began dissertation research in 1998, I lived with one of Uncle Mustafa's children, Arturo, and his family in Nueva Santa María in Mexico City. All of Uncle Mustafa's children and grandchildren were extremely gracious and generous with me while I conducted research and traveled between Washington, D.C., and Mexico City. It was through many conversations and extensive research on Arturo's part that an elaborate family tree in Mexico has been developed.

Although I interviewed Uncle Mustafa, Aunt Amine, Aunt Nora, and my uncles in the United States, I never learned very much history from them. All agreed that my great-grandfather had a store in Paso Nacional and would meet with his countrymen in his house, and sometimes pray. My great-grandmother was a *curandera* (a local healer), and was well liked—seeming to suggest that no one liked my great-grandfather. Frustrated and confused by the lack of information (and my relatives' seeming lack of interest in knowing about their family history), I had moved to archival research by 1998 as part of my dissertation research.

I learned about boxes of Lebanese immigrant cards at the Mexican Archivo General de la Nación, and began the task of compiling a database of all Middle Eastern immigrants who came to Mexico and registered with the Department of Migration in the 1930s. While in my final stages of examining more than eight thousand immigrant cards, I stumbled upon the *ficha* (card) of Antonio Aychur Itt, my great-grandfather. His picture and description matched what I had been told. Moreover, his picture on the card had an uncanny resemblance to my brother. This is the only tangible piece of my family's immigration history that I have ever collected.

From the immigration card, I learned that my great-grandfather migrated from the southern Lebanese town of Sibline in 1907. The name on the card was Antonio Aychur Itt. No one in Mexico had mentioned the name Aychur, and only one uncle had the Itt spelling of Haitt. The card confirmed that my great-grandfather was Muslim, but that he identified his nationality as *Árabe*, indicating that he probably did not feel like a Turkish subject in the Ottoman Empire, nor part of the emerging Lebanese national identity of the 1920s. The card also indicated that he had no references, which was surprising after nearly twenty-five years of residency in Mexico, corroborating my sense that he was not well liked, or indicating that he was afraid to give Mexican authorities any names.

As I speculate in my book, *So Far from Allah, So Close to Mexico*, Antonio probably traded with revolutionaries and federalists during the Mexican Revolution (which began in 1910 and continued for roughly a decade), given his store's location along the Nazas River in Paso Nacional. I also suggest that several other

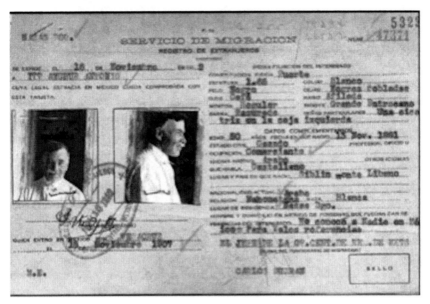

FIGURE 8. Mexican registration card for Antonio Aychur Itt (the author's great-grandfather) in 1932.

Muslims in the area probably met with my great-grandfather, and that they prayed together in the early part of the twentieth century. (To my knowledge, there was no formal mosque that they used; rather, they prayed in individual homes.) As of 1999, the only mosque in Mexico was located in Torreón, Coahuila, in Colonia Los Ángeles.[19]

Journey to Lebanon

In June 2004, I received a travel grant from Sonoma State University and went to Lebanon hoping to find a trace of my great-grandfather. Ottoman historian Elyse Semerdjian,[20] who was a colleague in graduate school at Georgetown University, met me in London, and we took the same flight to Beirut. Once in Beirut, Middle East historian Nadya Sbaiti,[21] also a colleague from graduate school, introduced us to well-known Lebanese singer May Nasr.[22] After hearing about my family story and May's own family connections to Mexico (her mother and aunt had lived in Mexico as children and still spoke Spanish), she offered to drive me to Sibline to search for information about my great-grandfather.

With his arrival in Mexico in 1907, my journey nearly a century later seemed unlikely to succeed. May, Elyse, and I went to the home of the local *mukhtar*, the Muslim administrative leader in the community, explaining that I was looking for information about a family member who had emigrated to Mexico at the turn of the twentieth century. After coffee, long stares, and explanations of my family history, I was told I looked like an 'Eid because of the shape of my face, and I was directed to the 'Eid family in the next village, near Sibline. There, at a distant relative's home, we were treated with caution until an elderly man with piercing blue eyes, cropped white hair, and no teeth arrived and said, "Hamud (Said) rah 'al-Meksik" (Hamud [Said] went to Mexico).[23] This elderly man, Ali Hasan, said that his prayers had been answered because he had been trying to reach Said 'Eid, my grandfather, in Brooklyn, New York, since the 1970s. I explained that my grandfather had passed away at that time, and the family was still in Mexico, with the exception of Said's children. The man then said my great-grandfather's name had been Hamud Said 'Eid. The Arabic 'Eid became the Hispanicized Itt, as Elyse Semerdjian and Christina Civantos had suspected;[24] however, he lost the name Hamud and gave the name Said (meaning "happy" in Arabic) to my grandfather. The Aychur name came from his maternal side, and the name Antonio appears to be an attempt at assimilation into Mexican culture.

After this initial meeting in early June 2004, I was given the address of an English-speaking relative, named Mohamad, in Damascus, Syria. When Elyse and I arrived in Damascus about a week later, we went to lunch at Mohamad's home. Although he was initially somewhat skeptical of my story, his wife Majida nevertheless prepared an extravagant meal of homemade filo dough stuffed with vegetables and rice. Over lunch, Mohamad became more comfortable with me and politely suggested that I cover my bare arms. Whether Mohamad saw me as a family member who had lapsed or as an American whose short sleeves were not respectful of Muslim culture, I do not know; but during our next visit, I covered my arms.[25]

A week later in Beirut I met with Mohamad's brother Ramiz and his family of three daughters. (It turned out that Rana, his middle daughter, would come to live in the San Francisco Bay Area in California in 2007.) During this second stay in Beirut in late June 2004, May drove me to southern Lebanon to see Ali Hasan and the family. I learned that the Lebanese side of the family believed my great-grandmother, Justa, was a second-generation Lebanese Christian from Jbail (Byblos). According to Ali Hasan (as translated by May), Hamud Said was supposed to marry someone in the Chamut family, not Justa Alfaro. By not marrying the Chamut relative, Hamud Said jeopardized his relationship with Zain Chamut, a fellow Muslim Lebanese immigrant living in northern Mexico in the early twentieth century. Ali Hasan said there was land for our family. Shortly into the conversation, a representative from the closest side of my family showed up driving a BMW and invited us to lunch. According to May, they had killed a lamb and prepared a special southern Lebanese dish for us. With a delicate stomach after three weeks in the Middle East, I told May that we should return to Beirut. When I tell this story to Middle Eastern colleagues, they gasp at my bad manners, although Rana claims that she has not heard of this incident. Despite my faux pas, contacts have continued.

Following my 2004 trip, I sent detailed letters and pictures of the Mexican and American family trees to various family members. I also received phone calls from the 'Eids in London and France. In 2005, I returned to Mexico City and shared my discovery with my uncle Mustafa and his children and grandchildren. He seemed proud, but a bit confused as to why the *gringa* relative had made all of these connections. Was Antonio Aychur Itt/Said Hamud 'Eid really worth all of this effort? In that moment, I felt anything but a *gringa*; rather I felt part of a large Mexican family whose circumstances had crossed two borders. I will never know how my uncle Mustafa saw me because he died in his sleep in May 2009 during the H1N1 flu outbreak, and we could not travel to Mexico. He, like my grandfather, wanted to be buried next to his parents in Paso Nacional, Durango. Since Torreón, Coahuila, is the closest major airport and in the heart of much of the present-day drug violence, my mother and I have not been able to visit his grave.

In April 2008, thanks to an offer from the American University of Beirut, I was invited to give a talk on *So Far from Allah, So Close to Mexico*, and I had an opportunity to see Mohamad again. After my talk, Mohamad drove from Damascus to Beirut. He picked up Elyse, who was coincidentally back in Syria on a Fulbright grant, and me at our hotel in Beirut and drove us to Tyre (in southern Lebanon) for lunch. During the drive, we stopped to pick up fresh fish caught in the morning to be prepared in Tyre, and discussed the 2008 U.S. presidential campaign, the Israeli-Lebanese war in 2006, and our family history. As we passed through security checkpoints with white United Nations security tanks and billboard images of Hizbullah martyrs and politicians, I reflected on how far my family research had taken me.

As I left Lebanon in 2008, I realized that I was still unclear about who my great-grandmother Justa was and what could be made of the pictures that I had of her. Could my Aztec princess family myth relate to a Lebanese princess instead? What interests me in this possibility is that Hassan Chamut was the architect for the Suraya Mosque in Torreón, and one of my informants in 1999. His father, Zain Chamut, had migrated to the Laguna region of Mexico.[26] How strange that Hassan had not known about my great-grandfather. Could Justa have been a Lebanese Mexican? Perhaps she could only be an Aztec princess in the context of a Lebanese Mexican identity. After spending time with the Lebanese descendants in Torreón, I realized that what is not said is just as powerful as what is said, and anything was possible. As Ann Twinam has written about colonial Latin American history, "historical silence can be more revealing than historical sound."[27]

As most family historians know, the Mormon genealogical records (now part of Ancestry.com) have an extensive archive of people's birth dates and locations. Through this public information, I learned that Justa Alfaro Esquivel was born in 1898 in Guanajuato, Mexico, but no other information is provided about her parents or her ethnicity. Although I now have this information for Justa and the records indicate that she is Mexican, I wonder whether she may also be of Lebanese background. For now, I am going to let Justa continue to capture the imagination of our family and let her *curandera* story live on.

Conclusion

My background seems typical when I speak with friends and colleagues in the San Francisco Bay Area. We are all multiethnic and live in a diverse context, which is not the case in all places. My story is different in that I chose to make a profession out of exploring the intersections of history and immigration in Mexico.

To finish the story, the week following my lunch with Mohamad in Tyre in 2008 his niece, Rana, called to say she and her new husband (a naturalized U.S. citizen) were living in the East Bay of California, near Berkeley. We quickly organized a family dinner, and soon afterward we celebrated my daughter's birthday, and Rana was introduced as my cousin from Lebanon. No one was surprised, and she blended into our diverse, evolving family. In January 2011, Rana became a U.S. citizen, participating in the monthly naturalization ceremony in Oakland.

The journey began with my great-grandfather migrating from Lebanon to Mexico, and his eldest son coming to the United States, and ends with his great-granddaughter returning to visit Lebanon and now residing in California. I am not sure what future generations will think of these migrations, and how my young children, *habayeb* (beloved) Magdalena and Alec, will see themselves and their identity—as Mexican Lebanese North Americans or as something else. And as my husband reminds me, this story is only one part of theirs.

NOTES

I thank Elyse Semerdjian for introducing me to Lebanon and Syria and for helping me to find my family. Her friendship and scholarship are a source of inspiration. She helped me to remember many aspects of our journeys to Lebanon and Syria and to prepare this article by reading numerous drafts and making insightful comments. It is indeed a privilege to write about my family history, and I thank Alan Kraut and David Gerber for giving me this opportunity to do so. Robert McLaughlin, Angus Wright, Myrna Santiago, Bill Taylor, Laura Nader, Mary Mackey, Ed Berger, Lynn Donk, and Chata Alfaro all provided support and guidance at critical moments in preparing this chapter. All shortcomings and errors are my own.

1. See Theresa Alfaro-Velcamp and Robert H. McLaughlin, "Immigration and Techniques of Governance in Mexico and the United States: Recalibrating National Narratives

through Comparative Immigration Histories," *Law and History Review* 29, no. 2 (May 2011): 573–606.

2. *Beirut Buenos Aires Beirut*, http://www.aljazeera.com/programmes/aljazeeraworld/2012/08/201281212202938973I.html.

3. Kitty Calavita, *Inside the State: The Bracero Program, Immigration and the I.N.S.* (New York: Routledge, 1992), and Manuel Garcia y Griego, "The Importation of Mexican Contract Laborers to the United States, 1942–1964," in *Between Two Worlds: Mexican Immigrants in the United States*, ed. David G. Gutiérrez (Wilmington, Del.: Scholarly Resources, 1996), 45–85.

4. Gustavo Arellano, "¡Ask a Mexican! From Puebla to Palestine," *OC Weekly* (April 23, 2009).

5. James Scott, *Domination and the Arts of Resistance: Hidden Transcripts* (New Haven: Yale University Press, 1990), 4–5 and n8.

6. "How one identifies oneself—and how one is identified by others—may vary greatly from context to context: self- and other-identification are fundamentally situational and contextual." See Rogers Brubaker and Frederick Cooper, "Beyond 'Identity,'" *Theory and Society* (2000): 14.

7. James Sturcke, "Key Events in Lebanon," *Guardian* (February 12, 2007). http://www.guardian.co.uk/world/2007/dec/12/syria.lebanon1.

8. Colum Lynch and Leila Fadel, "U.N. Concludes Probe of Hariri Assassination," *Washington Post* (January 18, 2011). http://www.washingtonpost.com/wp-dyn/content/article/2011/01/17/AR2011011704403.html.

9. William B. Taylor, *Shrines and Miraculous Images: Religious Life in Mexico before the Reforma* (Albuquerque: University of New Mexico Press, 2010), 2.

10. As Jeremy Popkin points out, "autobiography by its very nature is thus something of a scandal for the historian" because it signifies an "alternative approach to narrating the past." The idea that autobiographers will be read as historians can make historians uncomfortable with a sense of responsibility in portraying their own past and memories. Jeremy D. Popkin, *History, Historians, and Autobiography* (Chicago: University of Chicago Press, 2005), 12, 13.

11. Friedrich Katz, "El exilio centroeuropeo: Una Mirada autobiográfica," in *México, País Refugio: La Experiencia de los Exilios en el Siglo XX*, ed. Pablo Yankelevich. (Mexico: Instituto Nacional de Antropología e Historia [INAH], 2002), 44.

12. Friedrich Katz, "Mexico, Gilberto Bosques and the Refugees," *The Americas* 57 (2000).

13. Jürgen Buchenau, *Tools of Progress: A German Merchant Family in Mexico City, 1865–Present* (Albuquerque: University of New Mexico Press, 2004), 9.

14. A few scholars of the ethnic history in Mexico are the following: Liz Hamui de Halabe, coordinator, *Los Judíos de Alepo en México* (Mexico City: Maguén David, 1989); Michael Kenny, Virgina García A, Carmen Icazuriaga M., Clara Elena Suárez A., Gloria Artís E., *Inmigrantes y Refugiados Españoles en México (Siglo XX)* (Mexico City: Ediciones de la casa chata, 1979); Clara E. Lida, in *Inmigración y Exilio: Reflexiones Sobre el Caso Español* (Mexico City: Siglo veintiuno editores, 1997); María Teresa Huerta, "Penetración comercial francesa en México en la primera mitad del siglo XIX," in *Los Inmigrantes en el Mundo de los Negocios*, coordinated by Rosa María Meyer and Delia Salazar (Mexico City: Plaza y cales editores, 2003); Brígida con Mentz, Verena Radkau, Beatriz Scharrer, and Guillermo Turner, *Los Pioneros del Imperialismo Alemán en México* (Mexico City: Ediciones de la casa chata, 1982); and José B. Mánica Zilli, *Italianos en México* (Xalapa, Mexico: Ediciones San José, 1981). For studies on Japanese, Korean, Chinese, Arab, Palestinian, Philippine, and Indian immigrant groups in Mexico, see María Elena Ota

Mishima, ed., *Destino México: Un Estudio de las Migraciones Asiáticas a México, Siglos XIX y XX* (Mexico City: Colegio de México, 1997).

15. Allen Wells, *Tropical Zion: General Trujillo, FDR, and the Jews of Sosúa* (Durham, N.C.: Duke University Press, 2009).

16. See Prasenjit Duara, "Historicizing National Identity, or Who Imagines What and When," in *Becoming National: A Reader*, ed. Geoff Eley and Ronald Grigor Suny (New York: Oxford University Press, 1996), 151–177.

17. Duara examines national communities as relationships based on inclusions and exclusions and how the competing visions intersect with alternative criteria of identity formation. I build on Duara's framework that nationalism is a continually contested and negotiated space for multiple groups to live. *Becoming National*, 162.

18. Although their work looks at a different immigrant profile than my mother's family, they note that "educational and occupation aspirations among all second-generation youth are quite high . . . the majority of children have high hopes for the future." Alejandro Portes and Rubén G. Rumbaut, *Immigrant America: A Portrait*, 2nd ed. (Berkeley: University of California Press, 1996), 264.

19. Theresa Alfaro-Velcamp, "Mexican Muslims in the Twentieth Century: Challenging Stereotypes and Negotiating Space," in *Muslims in the West: Sojourners to Citizens*, ed. Yvonne Haddad (New York: Oxford University Press, 2002), 278–292.

20. Elyse Semerdjian teaches Islamic and Middle Eastern history at Whitman College in Walla Walla, Washington. Her book is titled *"Off the Straight Path": Illicit Sex, Law, and Community in Ottoman Aleppo* (Syracuse, N.Y.: Syracuse University Press, 2008).

21. Nadya Sbaiti is a professor at Smith College.

22. May is a well-known Lebanese singer and microfinancing consultant. http://en .wikipedia.org/wiki/May_Nasr.

23. E-mail correspondence with Elyse Semerdjian, August 1, 2011.

24. Christina Civantos and I had met in Buenos Aires, Argentina, while she was doing fieldwork on the Syrian and Lebanese community there. She is the author of *Between Argentines and Arabs: Argentine Orientalism, Arab Immigrants, and the Writing of Identity* (Albany: State University of New York Press, 2006).

25. I thank Myrna Santiago for bringing this issue to my attention.

26. *So Far from Allah*, 50n31.

27. Ann Twinam, "Purchasing Whiteness: Conversations on the Essence of Pardo-ness and Mulatto-ness at the End of the Empire," in *Imperial Subjects: Race and Identity in Colonial Latin America*, ed. Andrew B. Fischer and Matthew D. O'Hara (Durham, N.C.: Duke University Press, 2009), 142.

Coda

ALAN M. KRAUT

I suspect that very few historians stop to reflect on their personal pasts before calibrating the direction of their scholarship. And yet, as a former graduate student once observed, historians often seem to write their autobiographies with the subjects they address in their books and articles. Perhaps the process is inevitable. As the great jazz saxophonist Charlie Parker observed, "If you don't live it, it won't come out of your horn."

The process is most frequently unselfconscious, the product of imagination and improvisation as much as what we have read and taught. We follow our inclinations, our curiosities, the "hot" historiographical trends of our era, and it is only in retrospect that we are able to see how our work has followed certain patterns. Some historians, including my coeditor David Gerber, have at times written about personal influences upon their professional choices.[1] Others of us have not pondered the connections.

Certainly, when as a young boy I trailed after my late father in walks around lower Manhattan, it never occurred to me or to him that I might be headed for a career as an academic historian. History was fun, but my blue-collar roots made thoughts of becoming a college professor somewhat implausible.

I knew the answer my father wanted to hear on those Saturday mornings when I accompanied him to the factory loft on John Street in lower Manhattan for a half-day's work. He wanted me to say George Washington, not Macy's. The answer was a response to the question, "Where would you like to go after lunch?" George Washington sent us walking a few blocks to Wall Street after we dined on some sandwiches at a local luncheonette. When we reached Federal Hall, I would stand, mesmerized, in front of the statue of George Washington, his hand perpetually extended toward an invisible Bible upon which he was taking the oath of office as the first president of the United States. For the umpteenth time I would ask, "Was he really that tall?" Six- and seven-year-old boys tend to be very concerned about height. Who Washington was and what he did, I already knew. My father had been buying me age-appropriate history books, including ones on George Washington. We read them together at night. Harry Kraut, a high school dropout during the Great Depression, was my first history teacher.

After Federal Hall, we would walk to Fraunces Tavern at 54 Pearl Street, where Washington said farewell to his officers at the conclusion of the Revolutionary War. Because my dad was a poorly paid factory worker, a plater and polisher of metals at the Regal Emblem Company, we could never afford to eat in Fraunces Tavern. But on an upper floor of this, Manhattan's oldest surviving structure, there was a modest exhibit dealing with Washington's speech and his military career. Making eye contact with a sympathetic waiter and nodding toward me, my father got us past the dining room without purchasing a meal. Then it was up the staircase leading to the little museum. "How much better is this than Macy's toy department!" my father would say. At Macy's, we could look, but only look, at the pricey toy soldiers in their colorful uniforms, many of them collectors' items. There, too, history could come alive, as we discussed the wars in which such soldiers had fought, and I would ponder how I might arrange those soldiers in various formations on the linoleum floor of the apartment if we could afford to buy them. But Federal Hall and Fraunces Tavern were better. That's where history actually happened, and no purchase was required.

After visiting with George Washington and touring the Trinity Churchyard, where Alexander Hamilton is buried, father and son would hop the subway home to the South Bronx. Neither George Washington nor my father ever disappointed.

We always got off the subway at the Prospect Avenue station on the IRT White Plains Road line, an elevated stop in the Mott Haven section of the Bronx. From there, it was a three-block walk to our South Bronx tenement owned by a very short Italian immigrant landlady, Virginia, and her very tall Swedish immigrant husband, Charley, who had been rendered deaf by World War I artillery. He drank considerably and shouted a lot, but my mother reassured me that he was not mad at anybody. The building was immaculately clean except for the roaches that far outnumbered the tenants in most Bronx tenements.

We lived with my mother's American-born parents, Julia and William Schendel, in a six-room apartment. It was cramped, especially when we crowded around the nine-inch Admiral television set to watch the *Ed Sullivan Show* or *I Love Lucy*. Entertainment was important in our household. It had been the family business—almost. My grandfather had been a vaudevillian, a song and dance man, albeit briefly. His claim to fame was to have once danced on vaudeville stages on New York's Lower East Side. Once he danced on the same program as the great entertainer Jimmy Durante. One performer went on to stardom, the other did not. My great grandfather, an immigrant from Prussia, thought all entertainers were bums and so now, in the twilight of his life, Bill Schendel was reduced to performing a soft-shoe dance and pratfalls for me, his grandson, so that I would laugh and laugh and finally go to bed without a struggle.

With a father who labored in a factory and a grandfather who concluded his work life as an elevator operator at M. Lowenstein and Sons, a dry goods company in lower Manhattan, my milieu was decidedly blue collar. Class, as much as religion or ethnicity, shaped my worldview. Upward mobility and greater integration into the American mainstream were my parents' goals for me, but the path was unclear. How did one negotiate a place at the American table? And how did one explain those negotiations to the relatives?

My paternal grandparents, Elchanan and Anna, were very Orthodox Polish Jews who arrived in the United States in 1907. My father was the youngest of six sons and two daughters, survivors of my grandmother's many, many pregnancies. Because my parents and maternal grandparents did not keep a kosher home or speak Yiddish in the house, I had to be prepped before going to visit my religious grandparents at their apartment on Charlotte Street, lest the family peace be shattered over matters of ritual observance. "What you ate for lunch?" Grandma Anna would ask lovingly in her broken English. "Boiled chicken, kosher," I always replied, in as angelic a voice as I could muster. That was a good answer. Truth be known, I hated boiled chicken, but only once in all our visits did I accidentally forget the script and reveal my mother's secret. I answered truthfully, "Hot dogs and beans!" The volume of the reprimand for the indiscretion taught me to value confidentiality, a lesson of some worth to historians who rely on the oral testimony of human sources. This mandated "little white lie" taught me to be, in later years, critical of oral history and always to appreciate context. Most of all, the episode taught me never to cross my mother, even accidentally.

In the South Bronx of the early 1950s, immigration and ethnicity were assumed dimensions of life. Before, during, and immediately after World War II, the neighborhood consisted of working-class Eastern European Jews and southern Italians with a smattering of Germans and Irish. The sounds of European languages being spoken and the aromas of European dishes being cooked were everywhere. So, too, was another reminder of Europe: men and women with numbers tattooed on their arms, refugees from Hitler's concentration camps, survivors of the death camps. Their children, my friends, had been born in Europe's Displaced Persons camps. Their sons were the only friends I had who could kick a soccer ball more skillfully than they could throw a baseball.

There were also West Indian Blacks. Colin Powell lived in the neighborhood. His parents were from Jamaica. My closest friend throughout my life has been

Patrick Inniss, whose parents were from Trinidad. We met on the first day of first grade in 1953 in front of P.S. 52 on Kelly Street, the same block on which Yiddish humorist Sholem Aleichem (née Solomon Rabinowitz), had passed away in 1916. In the apartment buildings and shops, ethnic succession was well under way.

If immigration and ethnicity were everywhere in my life growing up in New York, so, too, was history. My father loved to read history when he was young and now he had a willing companion in his search for the past. In addition to Fraunces Tavern, we were regulars at the Museum of the City of New York and the American Museum of Natural History, as well as the Museum of the American Indian. On some Sundays, my mother joined us and the three of us went to Eldridge Street on the Lower East Side, where there were immigrant men with heavy Eastern European accents selling books in English, Yiddish, and Hebrew. In crowded delicatessens we ate thick corned beef sandwiches and drank Dr. Brown's black cherry soda. Many people looked as if they had just arrived in the United States. For me, as for Deborah Dash Moore, Dominic Pacyga, and other contributors to this book, place has been critically important in stirring my fascination with the past.

There were even history lessons at Yankee Stadium, where my father and I cheered for stars of the 1950s and early 1960s, such as Mickey Mantle, Yogi Berra, and Whitey Ford. We, and tens of thousands of others, were occasionally joined by former president Herbert Hoover. In the last years of his life, Hoover was sometimes a guest of the Yankees. On Memorial Day, the Fourth of July, or Labor Day, Hoover might be seen sitting next to the Yankee dugout along side of Claire Ruth, the Babe's widow, and Eleanor Gehrig, widow of great Yankee first baseman Lou Gehrig, who had been a Columbia University student (a fact my father never let me forget). On one of these occasions, the widows were introduced to the thunderous cheers of more than sixty thousand voices. However, there was equally thunderous booing following Hoover's introduction. Turning to my father, I asked, "Dad, who is that man?" My father replied, "The biggest son of a bitch to ever sit in the White House." Harry Kraut, a Henry Wallace liberal with Trotskyite inclinations, remembered all too well the Bonus Army's ouster from Anacostia Flats and the seeming coldness of Hoover toward those suffering during the Great Depression. My father never minced words or feared overstatement. I have taught history in Washington, D.C., since 1974, and I know well that there are other candidates for the title my father bestowed on Hoover. The Hoover presidency was more complex than my father suggested, but the comment and the passion of the utterance could not fail to stir my child's historical imagination.

The highlight of each summer in the 1950s and early 1960s, in addition to Yankee baseball, was our boat ride to the Statue of Liberty. Later, in the late 1970s when Ellis Island was first reopened to visitors and before the renovation, my father and I went to see where Grandpa Elchanan and Grandma Anna had entered the "Golden Door."

By the mid-1950s, the South Bronx was in transition. Once, it had been the destination of upwardly mobile Jews. In the first talkie, *The Jazz Singer,* the cantor's son, played by Al Jolson, expresses his devotion to his mother by promising her an apartment in the Bronx. For European immigrants and their children, the borough was now a place to flee, not a destination. Whenever a family relocated to a house with a white picket fence in Queens, Long Island, or New Jersey, their apartment was rented by new arrivals from Puerto Rico or Cuba. Boarding houses were springing up to accommodate young male workers who hoped to bring their families from the Caribbean, even as young migrants of earlier generations and different ethnic groups had done.

Poverty and dislocation led the South Bronx of my early years to begin a slow decline that would explode onto the front pages in the 1970s when President Jimmy Carter stood near the Charlotte Street tenement where Elchanan and Anna had lived and declared the South Bronx an urban disaster. Carter promised aid, but the help did not arrive in time. The patient died and was cremated. During the second game of the 1977 World Series, sportscaster Howard Cosell commented on the fires consuming Bronx buildings that were visible in camera shots from the Goodyear blimp. It is an urban legend that Cosell said, "There it is, ladies and gentlemen, the Bronx is burning." Those were not his exact words, but millions of viewers saw the blazes on their television screens. Sometimes buildings were torched by landlords fraudulently seeking insurance payments and sometimes by tenants calculating that they would be placed in new and better housing if they were left homeless by fire. My neighborhood was soon being referred to as "Fort Apache." A nearby police precinct house was called "The Little House on the Prairie" because it could be seen for miles around, one of the few structures towering above the rubble, all that was left of the tenements and the immigrant world of my youth. A generation of more recent arrivals and their children would struggle to rebuild the neighborhood, but the process is still far from complete.

As the immigrant world of my childhood was in decline, my love of the past was in ascent. In 1961, I gained admission to the Bronx High School of Science. The instructor in my mechanical drawing class, a required course, glanced around the classroom on the first day and said, "You, ladies and gentlemen, will take us to the moon before the Russians get there." But even as he spoke, I was more interested in the Cold War than in the intricacies of rocketry. My favorite courses were history and literature classes, including one on the History and Development of Science. By the time I entered Hunter College (Bronx campus, now Lehman College) in autumn 1964, I knew I wanted to be a historian. Any doubts were dispelled by the influence of Professor Lorman Ratner, a specialist in American cultural history and an inspiring teacher, who had studied with David Brion Davis at Cornell. My father never met Lorman Ratner, but once he asked me if I trusted the professor's judgment. "Yes!" I said emphatically. "Good," my father said, and then, in a gentle voice, "Do whatever he tells you. I can't help you anymore. You are going somewhere that I have never been." My father did not own a car, but in June 1968 he paid a neighbor to drive us and my boxes of books and a suitcase of wash-and-wear shirts and slacks to Ithaca, where I began work on a PhD at Cornell under the direction of political historian Joel Silbey.

As Deborah Dash Moore explains in her essay, our generation of historians was inspired by the civil rights movement of the 1960s to study slavery in the antebellum South and those who demanded its abolition. Lorman Ratner had written *Powder Keg: Northern Opposition to the Anti-Slavery Movement, 1831–1840* about events that were part of the crescendo leading to the Civil War.[2] I crafted a voting study of the abolitionist third party, the Liberty Party, in the electorally critical state of New York. Inspired by the methodology of Lee Benson's brilliant classic, *The Concept of Jacksonian Democracy,* and Silbey's insistence that every political historian needed to operate with the systematic approach of the social scientist, I wrote about those who cast ballots to end slavery.[3] However, it was the ethnic vote that fascinated me, and within a year of completing my dissertation I realized that I wanted to focus my attention on immigration. My first book, *The Huddled Masses: The Immigrant in American Society, 1880–1921,* was not my dissertation revised but my first venture into immigration history. As I wrote it, I felt as if I were coming home instead of venturing into unchartered waters.[4] My personal past and my training as a historian were meeting on the page.

My father never saw my first book. He collapsed and died of a massive heart attack on Fourteenth Street in Manhattan in October 1981, mere months before *Huddled Masses* was published. Yet, he lived on in its pages. Among other topics, the book described the processing of newcomers on Ellis Island. It told the story of how families such as my own entered this country. Three years later, I was appointed to the History Advisory Committee of the Statue of Liberty–Ellis Island Foundation, a committee I now chair. The committee's responsibility has been to work with the Foundation and the National Park Service to ensure that the restoration of the main building and the exhibits in the museum on Ellis Island reflect state-of-the-art historical understanding. Perhaps the little girls and boys who visit Ellis Island and the Statue of Liberty with their parents feel as I did when I stood next to my father in front of Federal Hall and looked up at George Washington.

In the 1980s, I decided to retrain in the history of medicine. I wanted to study the influence of disease and public health on the lives of immigrants. I also hoped to explore how Americans' fears of disease from abroad became a popular nativist trope. Others had written about the migration of the late nineteenth and early twentieth century before me. My contribution would be to explain how immigrant identity and integration into American society was shaped by matters of health and disease. The stigmatization of the Haitian community for Acquired Immune Deficiency Syndrome (HIV-AIDS) after the Centers for Disease Control mistakenly classified the Haitians as a "high risk group" aroused my curiosity. Had earlier immigrant groups been suspected of bringing disease to the United States? It turned out that they had. When I published *Silent Travelers, Germs, Genes, and the "Immigrant Menace"* in 1994, memories of my history of science class at Bronx High School of Science made the research and writing of that book and subsequent volumes in the history of medicine and migration feel comfortable. My past continues to find its way onto my pages.[5]

Among the books that most influenced my interest in immigration history during my undergraduate years in the late 1960s was Oscar Handlin's 1951 work, *The Uprooted: The Epic Story of the Great Migrations That Made the American People.* Handlin, the son of Eastern European Jewish immigrants, wrote a grand narrative, a stirring and inspirational saga of America's peopling through international migration.[6] Handlin's book offered a fresh perspective. Earlier scholars of immigrant stock, such as Carl Wittke on the Germans, Theodore Blegen on the Norwegians, and George Stephenson on the British, had focused their immigration studies on how the presence of specific groups had benefited the United States.[7] Handlin shifted the scholarly emphasis from what the immigrants did for the development of the United States to what the United States did to its newest arrivals. He wanted to know how the newcomers were altered by what he dubbed their "arduous transplantation."[8]

Handlin may have redefined the discussion, but *The Uprooted* was a flawed work that received withering criticism from the next generation of scholars who objected to his sweeping generalizations and lack of specificity in his portrayal of "The Immigrant." Leading the charge was Rudolph J. Vecoli, the son of Italian immigrants, who taught for many years at the University of Minnesota, founding the Immigration History Research Center there. Relying on the example of the *contadini*, or townsmen of the Mezzogiorno in southern Italy who emigrated to Chicago in the late nineteenth and early twentieth centuries, Vecoli demonstrated the insufficiency of Handlin's broad-brush approach.[9] Vecoli demanded that historians "respect the unique cultural attributes of the many and varied ethnic groups which sent immigrants to the United States."[10] If Handlin considered religion in general an important factor in the lives of immigrants, Vecoli insisted that the specific qualities of Roman Catholicism as practiced in Italy's southern provinces must be appreciated and understood in order to know about the lives of Italian immigrants.

The students of Vecoli's generation of immigration scholars, including myself and many of my cohort, sought to expand on his critique of Handlin. In our respective books, John Bodnar and I followed Handlin's example of focusing on the immigrant experience. However, as had Vecoli, we both maintained that newcomers were active, not passive, in the face of larger social forces. Newcomers assessed their options in the context of what was possible in the capitalist system of which they were now a part. They had a measure of agency and, in consultation with family members before and after their migration, they made choices among options, some more appealing than others; they were not the abject prisoners of their former lives. Taking our cue from Vecoli, we wrote that the specific aspects of each group's experience were instrumental in shaping their identities, options, and opportunities.[11]

As were Handlin and Vecoli, most of the scholars who contributed essays to this book are second- or third-generation Americans. Those who received their PhD degrees prior to 1990 discuss their lives in terms of ethnicity, religion, place, generation, race, class, and gender. Why? Those were the conceptual constructs that appeared to be most important in comprehending assimilation, the process that Oscar Handlin, and those who followed, understood to be the final outcome of the migration process. These variables promoted the degree to which newcomers of various ethnic groups became embedded in American society. This ethnic paradigm, then, was the kaleidoscope through which post-Handlin immigration historians view the past. Many of these scholars also included race and gender in their analyses far more than either Handlin or Vecoli had.

For these scholars, the ethnic paradigm and desirability of assimilation was more than just a historical perspective encountered in the seminar room or graduate library. Before they ever reached graduate school, the post-Handlin generation of historians was taught to pursue behaviors and goals, including graduate education, that might be conducive to assimilation. Integration, even conformity to American society and culture, was considered a positive value, one worth pursuing in one's own life, albeit one often tempered by the equally positive value of retaining one's ethnic identity and customs within the privacy of one's own community.

It is rare that one theme alone inspires the choice of any scholar's interests. As in jazz, themes vary in relation to one another and no two riffs are ever identical. Among the scholars of earlier vintage who are of European heritage and study European immigrant groups, ethnicity and religion play crucial roles and often are intertwined. Whether it is Timothy Meagher's Irish Roman Catholicism or John Bodnar's Slovak Catholicism or Deborah Dash Moore's Eastern European Judaism, there can be little doubt that ethnicity and religion influence the historians of European descent in this collection. Meagher recalls that while his father, a Harvard-educated judge, disliked Irishmen who wore their Irish identity on their sleeves, Catholicism was another matter. Meagher is keenly aware that his Irish Catholic identity influenced his scholarship. He reflects, "If many of my siblings remained vitally interested in 'Irishness,' I made a career of it in researching and writing Irish American history" (108). So, too, his parents', and especially his mother's, devotion to the Irish version of Roman Catholicism influenced him. In Worcester, Massachusetts, Catholicism was the very bedrock of Meagher's community. "Religion, then . . . defined us as Catholics with Protestants as the principal 'others.'"

For John Bodnar, too, ethnicity and religion are tightly bound, shaping his early historical ambitions. It was the stories of his Slovak grandparents and their Catholic identity that moved him. As workers in the coal-mining region of northeastern Pennsylvania, their faith and traditions sustained them. Bodnar recalls his beloved grandfather spending many hours of his leisure time "reading his well-worn book of prayers printed in Old Church Slavonic, a devotional practice he had learned from his father in Klecenov, a small village in eastern Slovakia" (46–47).

Deborah Dash Moore's ethnicity was grounded in modern American Judaism. Her family attended the Society for the Advancement of Judaism for the Jewish holidays and her maternal grandparents were followers of Reconstructionist rabbi Mordecai Kaplan. Moore is clear about what steered her in the direction of Jewish history. She recalls, "Years of Hebrew school at the SAJ, including study for Bat Mitzvah [still rare among other than Reconstructionist Jews in the era when Moore was growing up], followed by four additional years of Hebrew high school, introduced me not only to Jewish religious life but also stimulated intellectual interest in studying Jews" (34).

Religion was ubiquitous in the Chicago world of the young Dominic Pacyga. "Twelve Catholic churches could be reached within a fairly easy walk from my house. Irish, German, Polish, Lithuanian, Czech, Slovak, Ukrainian, French, and Mexican Catholic Churches rang their bells three times a day for the Angelus prayers" (80). Those bells calling the faithful to prayer echo in Pacyga's scholarship on Polish immigrant workers on the South Side of Chicago and the vital role of religion in their lives as a nexus of community in the late nineteenth and early twentieth centuries. Among the influences that shaped Pacyga's "sense of history, justice, and even my approach to teaching" were "the smells and bells of Catholicism" (88). There was no doubt in his mind that "the Catholic parishes . . . with their parochial schools, fraternal organizations, and ability to organize large numbers of immigrants and their children, empowered Polish Chicago. Those Catholic parishes built for worship proved to be engines of upward mobility" (91).

Religion and ethnicity do not intersect in a vacuum. Place counts. For Deborah Dash Moore, as for me, New York City was the place where perceptions of ethnic diversity were sharpened. Her essay's title, "Sidewalk Histories," suggests the importance to her of her urban roots. She recalls that in her neighborhood,

Greenwich Village, there was "a small French church next to the Hebrew Arts School; across Seventh Avenue on Sixteenth Street, working-class six-story tenements housed a Catholic mix of Irish, Puerto Ricans, and Italians." For Dominic Pacyga, Eileen Tamura, and Virginia Yans, place is key. For Pacyga, Chicago's Union Stockyards and the surrounding neighborhood was his small universe, with the past so close at hand. The neighborhood around the yards he describes as filled with "a sense of history." He observes that its streets "literally told the story of American immigration; while the stockyards spoke volumes on industrialization, labor history, and social class" (80).

For Eileen Tamura, the place that stirred her historical imagination was the Hawaiian Islands where she was born and raised. She recalls, "Although I never doubted my identity as an American, my Japanese ancestral background and life in Hawai'i made me very interested in understanding what an American was and how American the islands were" (134–135).

Mamaroneck, New York, was the place where Virginia Yans found special inspiration to write about immigration and ethnicity. The juxtaposition of the Mamaroneck of boats and big houses and the flats, where the poorest Italians and Blacks rented ramshackle homes and rooms, captured the imagination of the young Italian American girl. Recalling her youth, Yans remembers, "I heard Italian and English spoken in the flats. I saw the junkman and the ragman pushing their carts through the streets, heard the singsong shouts and the banging pots and pans announcing their arrival" (18). The other place that inspired her was one that she heard about but had not seen in her youth, Italy, where a clandestine love affair led to her grandmother's birth. Studying Italian immigrants and family relationships, as she did, was a nod to her own history and her grandmother's romantic secret.

The contrasts in lifestyle she saw in Mamaroneck sharpened Yans's awareness of the role of class in society. There were rich and poor in the town and even though Yans's family did not live in the impoverished flats, she grew up knowing who had more or was suspected of having more: "My father worked for wealthy Jews who, he considered, were better than we were. People who worked with their hands, my people, were not as good as well-educated people" (25).

Class might be wealth or education or some combination. However defined, class mattered a great deal to many of the historians descended from the Euroethnic groups who arrived in the early twentieth century. Driven to migrate by poverty and persecution, their parents or grandparents found no clear road to affluence on this side of the Atlantic. Historians of this era were usually the children of blue-collar parents. But not always.

Migrants who are refugees often arrive in the United States in a higher socioeconomic class position than those who arrive as immigrants. The politics of the Cuban revolution of 1959, not grinding poverty, drove María Cristina

García's parents to bring their family to the United States. Although her parents "arrived in Miami essentially penniless, without any idea of where to go or what to do next," her father was a lawyer in Cuba and soon "found employment as legal counsel for a well-known U.S. corporation" (146). Although the family initially lived in several countries around the Caribbean, the United States became home. García was drawn to immigration and ethnic history by the memory of her childhood need to "become American," entering a society only ninety miles from her home country. Was George Washington the father of her country or José Martí, as her grandmother insisted? García embraced the notion of becoming American. So, too, did her cosmopolitan, well-educated parents. Even gender distinctions were put aside. García recalls, "To my parents' credit (especially my mother, who was my strongest advocate), they ignored the considerable resistance they encountered from Cuban family and friends, and permitted me to be the first of my female cousins to attend college away from home" (150). It was García's own migration experience, then, that resulted in her interest in Latino studies.

Just as being a first-generation refugee led María Cristina García to want to write about refugees, generation as well as race and gender found ample expression in the memories of Eileen Tamura and Judy Yung as they pondered the origins of their scholarship. Tamura, a Japanese American in Hawai'i, identifies as a Sansei, a third-generation Japanese American. Considering which group on the island she found most interesting and worthy of pursuing in her research, Tamura decided on the Nikkei, ethnic Japanese living on the islands. She initially dismissed the Nisei, her parents' generation, because "by the 1890s [they] had become part of the state's political and economic establishment . . . too politically conservative to be of any interest to me. Furthermore, I recalled being disturbed at racist remarks I heard as a youth, made by my Nisei relatives about other minority groups" (136). However, as she learned more about the oppressive conditions the Nisei faced in Hawai'i when they first arrived, Tamura was drawn to write about their struggles.

Yung identifies as "the fifth daughter" of Chinese immigrants. Even as a child, Yung was told that being the fifth daughter was especially lucky because she had the privilege of leading her brother (the first son) into the world. However, as she notes, her father thought her generational placement lucky for another reason as well. Her father thought her lucky "to be born after World War II, when increased educational and economic opportunities for Chinese Americans allowed me to make more of my life than he or my mother ever could." Yung also recognizes that boys were so valued over girls that she "would not have been born at all if my brother had preceded me" (112).

Both Tamura and Yung were educated when ethnicity, not race, was the prevailing paradigm for the study of the migration experience, but both are aware that, as non-Whites and women, they were trailblazers as scholars. As Yung recalls, "I could not identify with being an American for the longest time, as we were taught a very Eurocentric version of U.S. history in American school. Our history textbooks did not include people of color, or women for that matter." She recalls that Chinese women were often depicted in popular media in a demeaning role or else as a kind of Suzie Wong, the seductive prostitute in the 1960 Hollywood film *The World of Suzie Wong*. Her parents "expected their daughters to finish high school, get an office job, and help support the family until it was time for us to marry a rich Chinese man and start our own family" (114).

Barbara Posadas had the additional complexity of being the female child of a mixed-race couple. Her father was an immigrant from the Philippines who was working on the railroad as a Pullman club car attendant when she was born. Her mother was the child of Polish immigrants. It was her father, an engineering student who had never completed his degree, who wanted a college education for Posadas, but "higher education had no place in the lives of my female cousins on the Polish side who thought of work after high school only as a prelude to marriage" (68). Posadas's mother was the third of seven children born to Polish immigrants, who, like many others, thought of life in the United States as a temporary way station to earn money toward a better life when they returned to their homeland. Her Polish grandfather even sent his wife and three children back to Europe in 1912 to await his return a year later. Only rumors of war altered family plans and Posadas's grandmother returned, with children in tow, to Chicago.

As a child of a mixed race couple, Posadas only gradually came to realize the degree to which fear shaped her parents' lives: "In the 1950s and 1960s, apart from our attendance at Catholic mass or a rare dinner excursion to Chinatown with other interracial couples, my parents avoided being seen together in public. I knew they feared verbal abuse, and that my mother feared worse for my father. I regularly went out with my mother *or* my father, shopping at Marshall Fields, eating hamburgers at Wimpy's, going to the local park, but never with *both* of my parents" (73).

While the few women in her Northwestern University graduate classes made Posadas aware of gender barriers, it was being of mixed race that she recalls as the link between her past and the page. Posadas's self-definition was more grounded in a biracial identity than class, as well: "Several others made clear their Euro-American working-class backgrounds, [and] I would have defined myself similarly as part Polish and part Filipino" (69). Posadas began her scholarship in ethnic history by interviewing "Filipino immigrants of my father's generation" lest they die without anyone having recorded their experiences. Posadas's desire to preserve her father's place in the past drove her initial research on Filipinos in the United States, research that has since expanded in scope as she follows the migration of Filipinos back and forth across the globe.

Although scholars such as Yung, Tamura, and Posadas focused primarily on race and gender in their work, their arguments generally echo the ethnic paradigm in which they were trained prior to 1990. Scholars whose doctoral degrees are of more recent vintage, however, were raised in an America that championed diversity and difference in life and on the page. The possibility and even the desirability of assimilation seemed problematic. This new generation of scholars describes their lives in terms that reflect the newer conceptualizations of the migration history in which they were trained, including the centrality of race, transnationalism, and diasporic patterns of movement.

Although most of her work reflects the older paradigm, Barbara Posadas's more recent work on Filipinos reflects the newer perspective. Her discussion here of that work suggests a diasporic consciousness. Observing that although she still considers herself an American historian, she explains a transformation that has led her "in recent years" to recognize "the global context of Philippine migration." In a diasporic pattern reminiscent of the Irish in the mid-nineteenth century, impoverished Filipinos emigrated to various countries in search of work. Their government urged migration, tempted by the prospect of remittances. Posadas observes that "[a]s its postwar economy faltered, the Philippine government systematically encouraged Filipinos to work overseas so that the remittances they send home to their relatives will help sustain the nation" (78).

María Cristina García also looks at her own past through the lens of the new paradigm. Just as her own life has led her to transcend many borders, she does not view her work as narrowly confined by national boundaries. She explains that "the study of immigrants and ethnics . . . has forced me to look outward, beyond the nation, to consider interdependencies, and overlapping histories and cultural geographies. Localities are always connected to the broader world . . . and immigrants are characters on international as well as local and national stages." Reflecting on her own personal experience during a recent trip to Cuba, García muses, "It's a very long hundred miles between Cuba and the United States. I've tried to shorten that distance through my teaching and scholarship" (156).

More than any of the other authors in this book, the work of Violet Showers Johnson and Theresa Alfaro-Velcamp reflects the new paradigm. As is García, Johnson is a first-generation arrival, whose odyssey in Africa and the United States echoes diasporic and transnational themes. Born in the city of Lagos, Johnson was raised in Kaduna, Nigeria, which she describes as a "postcolonial society . . . defined by glaring ethnic and religious diversity and challenged by the Hausa-Igbo conflict" (157). A member of a diasporic group, the Saros, Sierra Leoneans in Nigeria, she was ethnically a Krio, and as she explains, crisscrossed linguistic, religious, and other cultural boundaries between the larger Nigerian society and her parents' Saro community. Long before she ever arrived in the United States, then, Johnson experienced the blurring of boundaries because her family fostered ties to its homeland from another West African country, a transnational consciousness that was quite palpable. She recalls, "My parents and others in their generation always paid attention to unfolding political developments (the rise and fall of political parties, elections, riots, and military coups) in Sierra Leone and Nigeria" (170).

Arriving in the United States in 1985, Johnson had already studied American history in Africa and Canada and was convinced of "the magnitude of race and ethnicity in American history." In the United States as a young adult, she was "confronted by an extremely powerful all-pervasive force—race, or more specifically, my blackness" (165). In the United States, race was a much more significant dimension of her identity than it had ever been before. The ethnic neighborhoods in Boston, where she studied for her PhD, confirmed her understanding of the importance of race and ethnicity in the United States. Struck by how little attention had been given in an older historiography to Black immigrants such as herself, Johnson found inspiration for studying Afro-Caribbean migrants in the United States. She focused on Boston's neighborhoods and on migrants from the Caribbean who by virtue of the color of their skin experienced a far different reception than had European groups that settled in the city. The diaspora of Africans across oceans and continents, whether as slaves or free people, captured Johnson's attention because she saw her own experience in the context of such patterns. Johnson describes herself as a "child of the African Diaspora" (171).

Diasporic patterns characterized migration out of the Middle East, as well. Theresa Alfaro-Velcamp, a historian of Mexico, born and raised in the United States, found her research interests stimulated by awareness that she is the great-granddaughter of a Lebanese Shi'a Muslim who migrated to Mexico and whose son came to the United States as a Mexican *bracero* worker in the early 1940s and married a second-generation Mexican. Many Americans can claim Mexican heritage, as does Alfaro-Velcamp, but what captured her imagination was being descended from a Lebanese Muslim. Interviews with relatives during a trip to Mexico in 1994 heightened her curiosity and led her to undertake doctoral research about Middle Easterners who had migrated to the Americas and especially to Mexico. Even as historian Marcus Lee Hansen had postulated that "what the son wishes to forget the grandson wishes to remember," Alfaro-Velcamp, a young American-born doctoral student, pursued her desire to "remember" the migration of an ancestor as the key to a much larger study of a largely neglected migration.[12] Her quest took her to Mexico and Lebanon. Place was important and religion, too, as the title of Alfaro-Velcamp's book suggests: *So Far from Allah, So Close to Mexico: Middle Eastern Immigrants to Modern Mexico.*

Alfaro-Velcamp concludes her essay by reminding us that historians of migration write of the past but for the present and future. Explaining how her research caused her to ponder how her efforts might affect the identity of future generations in her family, Alfaro-Velcamp mused, "I am not sure what future generations will think of these migrations and how my preschool aged children . . . will see themselves and their identity—as Mexican Lebanese North Americans or as something else" (186).

In the nineteenth century, Walt Whitman proclaimed that history's hero is the common man. In their books and articles, our contributors have reminded us that so often, the common women and men who built the United States began life in other countries and on other continents. A child of immigrants, Oscar Handlin reminded his readers that American history is the history of immigration.[13] And who chooses to write that history? So often it emerges from the pens of those whose personal pasts rubbed up against the immigrant experience and inspired their imaginations. Why do they write? Because the influx of strangers, the encounter between native and newcomer, the collision of customs and beliefs, is the great constant in human history. To paraphrase Charlie Parker, because they lived it, they can help others hear its rhythms and beats.

Notes

1. David A. Gerber, "Visiting Bubbe and Zayde: How I Learned about American Pluralism before Writing about It," in *People of the Book, Thirty Scholars Reflect on Their Jewish Identity*, ed. Jeffrey Rubin-Dorsky and Shelley Fisher Fishkin (Madison: University of Wisconsin Press, 1966), 117–134.

2. Lorman Ratner, *Powder Keg: Northern Opposition to the Antislavery Movement, 1831–1840* (New York, Basic Books, 1968).

3. Lee Benson, *The Concept of Jacksonian Democracy: New York as a Test Case* (Princeton: Princeton University Press, 1969).

4. Alan M. Kraut, *The Huddled Masses: The Immigrant in American Society, 1880–1921*, 2nd ed. (Wheeling, Ill.: Harlan Davidson, 2001).

5. Alan M. Kraut, *Silent Travelers, Germs, Genes, and the "Immigrant Menace"* (New York: Basic Books, 1994).

6. Oscar Handlin, *The Uprooted, The Epic Story of the Great Migrations That Made the American People* (Boston: Little, Brown and Company, 1952).

7. Carl F. Wittke, *We Who Built America: The Saga of the Immigrant* (New York: Prentice-Hall, 1939); Theodore Blegen, *Norwegian Migration to America, 1825–1860* (Northfield, Minn.: Norwegian-American Historical Association, 1931); George M. Stephenson, *History of American Immigration, 1820–1924* (Boston: Ginn and Company, 1926); and *The Religious Aspects of Swedish Immigration: A Study of Immigrant Churches* (Minneapolis: University of Minnesota Press, 1932).

8. Handlin, *Uprooted*, 4.

9. Rudolph J. Vecoli, "*Contadini* in Chicago: A Critique of *The Uprooted*," *Journal of American History* 51 (December 1964): 404–417.

10. Ibid., 404.

11. John Bodnar, *The Transplanted: A History of Immigrants in Urban America* (Bloomington: Indiana University Press, 1985); Kraut, *Huddled Masses*.

12. Marcus Lee Hansen, "The Problem of the Third Generation Immigrant," republication of the 1937 address with introductions by Peter Kivisto and Oscar Handlin by the Swenson Swedish Immigration Research Center and Augustana College (Rock Island, Ill., 1987), 15.

13. Oscar Handlin's *The Uprooted* begins with one of the most lyrical and memorable sentences ever penned by an American writer: "Once I thought to write a history of the immigrants in America. Then I discovered that the immigrants *were* American history." Handlin, *Uprooted*, 3.

NOTES ON CONTRIBUTORS

THERESA ALFARO-VELCAMP is an associate professor of history at Sonoma State University in California. She is also a research associate at the Centre for Social Science Research at the University of Cape Town in South Africa. Her book, *So Far From Allah, So Close to Mexico: Middle Eastern Immigrants in Modern Mexico*, was published in 2007 by the University of Texas Press. Her work in immigration has appeared in *Law and History Review, Hispanic American Historical Review, The Americas,* and *Comparative Studies of South Asia and the Middle East.* She has also contributed to *Cancer Epidemiology, Biomarkers & Prevention* regarding cancer incidence among Latinos/Hispanics. Professor Alfaro-Velcamp holds a PhD in history (2001) and an MA in Latin American studies from Georgetown University, and an MSc in comparative politics from the London School of Economics and Political Science in England.

JOHN BODNAR is Chancellor's Professor, History, at Indiana University in Bloomington. He earned his PhD in 1975 from the University of Connecticut. His publications include *Immigration and Industrialization: Ethnicity in an American Mill Town* (1977), *Worker's World: Kinship, Community, and Protest in an Industrial Society, 1900–1940* (1982), and *The Transplanted: A History of Immigrants in Urban America* (1985).

MARÍA CRISTINA GARCÍA is the Howard A. Newman Professor of American Studies in the Department of History at Cornell University. She is the author of *Havana USA: Cuban Exiles and Cuban Americans in South Florida, 1959–1994* and *Seeking Refuge: Central American Migration to Mexico, the United States, and Canada,* both published by the University of California Press, and numerous articles and book chapters on migration from Latin America. She is completing a book project on refugee and asylum policy in the post–Cold War era.

DAVID A. GERBER is University at Buffalo Distinguished Professor of History Emeritus. He continues to do teaching and administrative work at the university, both in the History Department and at the Center for Disability Studies. He is the author recently of *American Immigration: A Very Short Introduction* (2011) and, as editor, *Disabled Veterans in History* (second, expanded edition, 2012). His present research interests concern mid-twentieth-century historians of the American experience of Jewish immigrant and ethnic backgrounds.

VIOLET M. SHOWERS JOHNSON is a professor of history and the director of Africana Studies at Texas A&M University. A scholar of the history of race, ethnicity, and immigration in the United States, she studies the experiences of immigrants of African descent. Her publications include *The Other Black Bostonians: West Indians in Boston, 1900–1950* (2006), her coedited volume (with Isabel Soto Garcia) *Western Fictions, Black Realities: Meanings of Blackness and Modernities* (2011), and "'What, Then, Is the African American?' African and Afro-Caribbean Identities in Black America," in *Journal of American Ethnic History* (Fall 2008). With Marilyn Halter of Boston University, she is completing a book under contract with NYU Press titled *African and American: Post-Colonial West Africans in Post–Civil Rights America*. She is also working on a monograph titled *When Blackness Stings*, on the high-profile late twentieth-century tragic assaults on Ethiopian immigrant Mulegeta Seraw, Haitian American Abner Louima, and Guinean immigrant Amadou Diallo.

ALAN M. KRAUT is University Professor of History at American University. He specializes in immigration and ethnic history and the history of medicine in the United States. He is the prize-winning author or editor of nine books and many scholarly articles including *Silent Travelers: Germs, Genes, and the "Immigrant Menace"* (1994) and *Goldberger's War: The Life and Work of a Public Health Crusader* (2003), a study of U.S. Public Health Service physician Dr. Joseph Goldberger and his investigation of pellagra in the early twentieth-century South. In 2007 he coauthored *Covenant of Care: Newark Beth Israel and the Jewish Hospital in America*. His research has been supported by the Rockefeller Foundation, National Endowment for the Humanities, the Smithsonian Institution, and the National Institutes of Health. He chairs the Statue of Liberty–Ellis Island History Advisory Committee and regularly serves as an historical consultant on PBS and History Channel documentaries. He is the past president of the Immigration and Ethnic History Society and a fellow of the Society of American Historians. In 2013 he was elected president of the Organization of American Historians.

TIMOTHY J. MEAGHER is an associate professor of history and curator of American Catholic History Collections at Catholic University. Before taking up his appointment at Catholic University, he worked as a program officer at the National Endowment for the Humanities, where he directed the National Conversation on American Pluralism and Identity. Professor Meagher received

his doctorate in American history from Brown University in 1982. His publications include *Inventing Irish America: Generation, Class, and Ethnic Identity in a New
England City, 1880–1928* (2001) and the *Columbia Guide to Irish American History*
(2005). In addition, he edited two collections of essays including, with Ronald
Bayor of Georgia Tech, *The New York Irish* (1996).

DEBORAH DASH MOORE is Frederick G. L. Huetwell Professor of History at
the University of Michigan and the director of the Jean and Samuel Frankel Center for Judaic Studies. She received her PhD in history from Columbia University
in 1975. She focuses on twentieth-century American Jewish history, including *At
Home in America: Second Generation New York Jews* (1981), *GI Jews: How World War II
Changed a Generation* (2004), and *To the Golden Cities: Pursuing the American Jewish
Dream in Miami and L.A.* (1994). She has also edited a number of books, including
the award-winning two-volume *Jewish Women in America: An Historical Encyclopedia* (1997), with Paula Hyman, and *American Jewish Identity Politics* (2008). Her
most recent work includes *City of Promises: A History of Jews in New York* (2012),
for which she served as general editor.

DOMINIC A. PACYGA received his PhD from the University of Illinois at Chicago in 1981. He has been a member of the Humanities, History, and Social Science Department at Columbia College Chicago since 1984. His various books
include *Polish Immigrants and Industrial Chicago: Workers on the South Side, 1880 to
1922* (1991, 2003) and most recently *Chicago: A Biography* (2009).

BARBARA M. POSADAS is College of Liberal Arts and Sciences Distinguished
Professor of History at Northern Illinois University. She holds a BA from DePaul
University and an MA and a PhD in United States history from Northwestern
University. She is the author of *The Filipino Americans* (1999) and numerous
articles on Filipino American history, particularly in the Midwest. In 2008, she
received the Distinguished Lifetime Achievement Award of the Association for
Asian American Studies. Her most recent publications focus on Filipino natu-
ralizations in Chicago in 1946, and on gender, family, and post-1965 Filipino
immigrants in Springfield, Illinois. Her book-length study of *Filipino Chicagoans:
1900–1965* is under advance contract with the University of Illinois Press.

EILEEN H. TAMURA is a professor and chair of the Department of Educational
Foundations, College of Education, University of Hawai'i. She received her PhD
in history in 1990 from the University of Hawai'i. Her publications include *Americanization, Acculturation, and Ethnic Identity: The Nisei Generation in Hawai'i* (1994);
The History of Discrimination in U.S. Education: Marginality, Agency, and Power, as
editor (2008); "Value Messages Collide with Reality: Joseph Kurihara and the

Power of Informal Education," *History of Education Quarterly* 5, no. 1 (2010); "African American Vernacular English & Hawai'i Creole English: A Comparison of Two School Board Controversies," *Journal of Negro Education* 71, no .1 (2002); and "Using the Past to Inform the Future: An Historiography of Hawaii's Asian and Pacific Islander Americans," *Amerasia Journal* 26, no. 1 (2000).

VIRGINIA YANS is Board of Governors Distinguished Professor at Rutgers University. She received her PhD in history from State University of New York at Buffalo in 1970. Her publications include *Ellis Island and the Peopling of America: The Official Guide* (1999) and *Family and Community: Italian Immigrants in Buffalo, 1880–1930* (1971). In addition, she authored and produced a PBS television special, *Margaret Mead: An Observer Observed*, in 1996 and edited *Immigration Reconsidered: History, Sociology, Politics* (1990).

JUDY YUNG is a professor emerita of American studies at the University of California, Santa Cruz. She received her PhD in ethnic studies from the University of California, Berkeley, in 1990. Her publications include *Island: Poetry and History of Chinese Immigrants on Angel Island, Unbound Feet: A Social History of Chinese Women in San Francisco*, and most recently, *Angel Island: Immigrant Gateway to America*.

CPSIA information can be obtained at www.ICGtesting.com
Printed in the USA
BVOW06s0429081013

333150BV00002B/3/P